PRENTICE HALL
LITERATURE

PENGUIN EDITION

Adapted
Reader's Notebook

World Masterpieces

PEARSON

Prentice
Hall

Upper Saddle River, New Jersey
Boston, Massachusetts

ISBN: 0-13-165327-X

2 3 4 5 6 7 8 9 10   09 08 07 06

ACKNOWLEDGMENTS

Grateful acknowledgment is made to the following for copyrighted material:

Ruth Harwood Cline and The University of Georgia Press
From *Perceval:* The Grail, by Chretien de Troyes from *Perceval* or *The Story of the Grail,* translated by Ruth Harwood Cline. Copyright © 1983 by Ruth Harwood Cline. Reprinted by permission of The University of Georgia Press.

Toby Cole, Actors & Authors Agency
"War" from *The Medals and Other Stories* by Luigi Pirandello. © E.P. Dutton, NY, 1932, 1967. Reprinted by permission of Toby Cole, Agent for the Pirandello Estate. All rights reserved. For performance rights in all media apply to Toby Cole, Agent for the Pirandello Estate, 295 Derby Street, #225, Berkeley, CA 94705.

Dorling Kindersley Ltd.
"India" by Debra Clapson, Project Editor from *Ultimate Pocket Book of the World Factfile.* Copyright © 1996, 1998, 1999 Dorling Kindersley Limited, London.

Doubleday, a division of Random House, Inc.
"Half a Day," from The Time and the Place and Other Stories by Naguib Mahfouz, translated by Denys Johnson-Davies. Copyright © 1991 by the American University in Cairo Press. Used by permission of Doubleday, a division of Random House, Inc.

Duke University
"The Holocaust Haggadah," from Duke Magazine, May-June 2004. Copyright © 2004 by Duke Magazine. Reprinted by permission.

Farrar, Straus & Giroux, Inc.
"The Bracelet" from *The Collected Stories of Colette* by Colette. Translation copyright © 1957, 1966, 1983 by Farrar, Straus & Giroux, Inc.

The Jewish Publication Society
"The Book of Ruth," (originally titled "Ruth: 1-4") reprinted from *Tanakh: A New Translation of the Holy Scriptures According to the Hebrew Text.* Copyright date © 1985, by the Jewish Publication Society. Reprinted by permission.

Museum of Science, Boston
From "The Quest for Immortality" brochure. Materials courtesy of the Museum of Science, Boston.

New York Times Co.
"Leonardo: The Eye, the Hand, the Mind" by Holland Cotter from *The New York Times,* January 24, 2003. Copyright © 2003 by the New York Times Co. Reprinted by permission.

Oxford University Press, Inc. and David Higham Associates Ltd.
From *Faust:* Prologue in Heaven, (originally titled "from *Faust, Part 1 & 2*"), by Johann Wolfgang von Goethe, translated by Louis MacNeice, copyright © 1951, 1954 by Federick Louis MacNeice; renewed 1979 by Hedi MacNeice. Used by permission of Oxford University Press, Inc.

Oxford University Press, UK and Columbia University Press
From *The Pillow Book of Sei Shonagon:* "In Spring It Is the Dawn," "The Cat Who Lived in the Palace," "Things That Arouse a Fond Memory of the Past," "I Remember a Clear Morning," from *The Pillow Book of Sei Shonagon* by Sei Shonagon, translated and edited by Ivan Morris. Copyright (c) Ivan Morris 1967.

Pearson Education, Inc. publishing as Pearson Prentice Hall
"What is an Insect?" from *Prentice Hall Biology* by Kenneth R. Miller, Ph.D., and Joseph Levine, Ph.D. © 2002 Pearson Education, Inc. publishing as Pearson Prentice Hall. Used by permission.

(Acknowledgments continue on page V39)

Contents

PART 1

UNIT 1 Origins and Traditions: Ancient Worlds (3000 B.C. – A.D. 1400)

Build Skills: *from* The Epic of Gilgamesh translated by N.K. Sanders 2
Prologue • The Battle of Humbaba
Preview 3
The Death of Enkidu
Preview 4
Selection 5
The Story of the Flood • The Return
Preview 6
Apply the Skills 7
Build Skills: *from the* Bible: Genesis 1-3 • Genesis 6-9,
translated by the Jewish Publication Society 9
Preview 10
Apply the Skills 11
Build Skills: *from the* Bible: Book of Ruth • Psalms 8, 19, 23, 137
translated by the Jewish Publication Society 13
The Book of Ruth
Preview 14
Selection 15
Psalms 8, 19, 23, 137
Preview 20
Apply the Skills 21
Build Skills: *from the* Qur'an: The Exordium • Night • Daylight • Comfort
translated by N.J. Dawood 23
Preview 24
Apply the Skills 25
Build Skills: *from* The Thousand and One Nights translated by N.J. Dawood 27
The Fisherman and The Jinnee
Preview 28
Apply the Skills 29
Build Skills: *from* The Rubáiyát • *from the* Gulistan
from The Manners of Kings 31
from The Rubáiyát by Omar Khayyám
Preview 32

from the Gulistan: *from* The Manners of Kings by Sa'di

   Preview 33

   Apply the Skills 34

Build Skills: **Elephant in the Dark • Two Kinds of Intelligence • The Guest House • Which Is Worth More?** by Rumi, translated by Coleman Barks 36

   Preview 37

   Apply the Skills 38

Build Skills: **African Proverbs •** *from* **Sundiata: An Epic of Mali** translated by D.T. Niane 40

   Preview 41

   Apply the Skills 42

READING INFORMATIONAL MATERIALS

Brochures 44

UNIT 2 Sacred Texts and Epic Tales: Indian Literature
         (c. 1400 B.C. – A.D. 500)

Build Skills: *from the* Rig Veda: **Creation Hymn • Night** 51

   Preview 52

   Selection 53

   Apply the Skills 55

Build Skills: *from the* **Mahabharata: Sibi •** *from the* **Bhagavad-Gita: The Yoga of Knowledge •** *from the* **Ramayana: Rama and Ravana in Battle** 57

   Preview 58

   Apply the Skills 59

Build Skills: *from the* **Panchatantra: Numskull and the Rabbit,** translated by Arthur W. Ryder 61

   Preview 62

   Selection 63

   Apply the Skills 66

READING INFORMATIONAL MATERIALS

Atlases and Maps 68

UNIT 3 Wisdom and Insight: Chinese and Japanese Literature
         (1000 B.C. – A.D. 1890)

Build Skills: *from the* Tao Te Ching • *from the* Analects 73

from the Tao Te Ching, by Lao Tzu

   Preview 74

from the **Analects, by Confucius**

    Preview 75

    Selection 76

    Apply the Skills 78

Build Skills: **Chinese Poetry:** *from* **The Book of Songs** 80

    Preview 81

    Apply the Skills 82

Build Skills: **Tanka • Haiku** 84

    Preview 85

    Apply the Skills 86

Build Skills: *from* **the Pillow Book by Sei Shōnagon** 88

    Preview 89

    Selection 90

    Apply the Skills 94

Build Skills: **Zen Parables compiled by Paul Reps** 96

    Preview 97

    Apply the Skills 98

READING INFORMATIONAL MATERIALS
Reference Materials 100

UNIT 4 Classical Civilizations: Ancient Greece and Rome (c. 800 B.C. – A.D. 500)

Build Skills: *from the* **Iliad:** *from* **Book 1: The Rage of Achilles** • *from* **Book 6:**
Hector Returns to Troy by Homer 111

    Preview 112

    Apply the Skills 113

Build Skills: *from the* **Iliad:** *from* **Book 22: The Death of Hector** • *from* **Book 24:**
Achilles and Priam by Homer 115

    Preview 116

    Apply the Skills 117

Build Skills: **Classical Poetry by Sappho and Pindar** 119

    Preview 120

    Apply the Skills 121

Build Skills: **Pericles' Funeral Oration** *from* **History of the Peloponnesian War:**
by Thucydides 123

    Preview 124

    Selection 125

    Apply the Skills 131

Build Skills: *from the* Apology by Plato 133

Preview 134

Apply the Skills 135

Build Skills: Oedipus the King, Part I, by Sophocles 137

Preview 138

Apply the Skills 139

Build Skills: Oedipus the King, Part II, by Sophocles 141

Preview 142

Apply the Skills 143

READING INFORMATIONAL MATERIALS

Web Research Sources 145

Build Skills: *from* the Aeneid, Book II: How They Took
the City by Virgil 149

Preview 150

Selection 151

Apply Skills 157

Build Skills: *from the* Metamorphoses, The Story of Daedalus
and Icarus by Ovid 159

Preview 160

Apply Skills 161

Build Skills: *from the* Annals: The Burning of Rome by Tacitus 163

Preview 164

Apply the Skills 165

UNIT 5 From Decay to Rebirth: The Middle Ages (A.D. 450 – 1300)

Build Skills: *from* the Song of Roland • *from* The Nibelungenlied:
How Siegfried Was Slain 167

Preview 168

Apply Skills 169

READING INFORMATIONAL MATERIALS

Interviews 171

Build Skills: *from* Perceval: The Grail • The Lay of the Werewolf 177

from **Perceval: The Grail** by Chrétien de Troyes

Preview 178

Selection 179

The Lay of the Werewolf by Marie de France

    Preview 185

    Apply the Skills 186

Build Skills: *from the* **Divine Comedy: Inferno** by Dante Alighieri:
Canto I: The Dark Wood of Error • Canto III: The Vestibule of Hell 188

Canto I: The Dark Wood of Error

    Preview 189

    Selection 190

Canto III: The Vestibule of Hell

    Preview 193

    Apply the Skills 194

Build Skills: *from the* **Divine Comedy: Inferno** by Dante Alighieri:
Canto V: Circle Two • Canto XXXIV: Ninth Circle .196

    Preview 197

    Apply the Skills 198

UNIT 6 Rebirth and Exploration: The Renaissance and Rationalism (1300 – 1800)

Build Skills: *from* **Canzoniere: Laura • The White Doe • Spring**
by Francesco Petrarch • **To Hélène • Roses,** by Pierre de Ronsard 201

    Preview 202

    Apply the Skills 203

Build Skills: *from the* **Decameron, Federigo's Falcon** by Boccaccio 205

    Preview 206

    Selection 207

    Apply the Skills 214

Build Skills: *from* **Starry Messenger •** *from* **The Assayer** by Galileo Galilei . .216

    Preview 217

    Apply the Skills 218

Build Skills: *from* **Don Quixote** by Miguel de Cervantes 220

    Preview 221

    Selection 222

    Apply the Skills 227

Build Skills: **The Fox and the Crow • The Oak and the Reed**
by Jean de La Fontaine 229

    Preview 230

    Apply the Skills 231

Build Skills: *from* **Candide** by Voltaire 233

    Preview 234

    Apply Skills 235

Feature Articles 237

Unit 7: Revolution and Reaction: Romanticism and Realism (1800 – 1890)

Build Skills: *from* Faust: Prologue in Heaven • The First Part of the Tragedy
Prologue in Heaven by Johann Wolfgang von Goethe 247
    Preview 248
    Selection 249
The First Part of the Tragedy by Johann Wolfgang von Goethe
    Preview 252
    Apply the Skills 253
Build Skills: I Have Visited Again by Alexander Pushkin •
The Lorelei • The Lotus Flower by Heinrich Heine 255
    Preview 256
    Apply the Skills 257
Build Skills: Invitation to the Voyage • The Albatross by Charles Baudelaire •
The Sleeper in the Valley • Ophelia by Arthur Rimbaud • Autumn Song
by Paul Verlaine 259
    Preview 260
    Apply the Skills 261
Build Skills: Two Friends • How Much Land Does a Man Need? •
A Problem 263
Two Friends by Guy de Maupassant
    Preview 264
    Selection 265
How Much Land Does a Man Need? by Leo Tolstoy
    Preview 269
A Problem by Anton Chekhov
    Preview 270
    Apply the Skills 271
Build Skills: A Doll House: Act I, by Henrik Ibsen .273
    Preview 274
    Apply the Skills 275
Build Skills: A Doll House: Act II, by Henrik Ibsen .277
    Preview 278
    Apply the Skills 279
Build Skills: A Doll House: Act III, by Henrik Ibsen .281
    Preview 282
    Apply the Skills 283

READING INFORMATIONAL MATERIALS
Critical Reviews 285

Unit 8: From Conflict to Renewal: The Modern World (1890 – 1945)

Build Skills: The Metamorphosis by Franz Kafka 295
    Preview 296
    Apply the Skills 297

READING INFORMATIONAL MATERIALS
Scientific Texts 299

Build Skills: The Bracelet by Colette 304
    Preview 305
    Selection 306
    Apply the Skills 309
Build Skills: War by Luigi Pirandello 311
    Preview 312
    Selection 313
    Apply the Skills 317
Build Skills: The Guitar by Federico García Lorca • Ithaka by Constantine
Cavafy • Fear • The Prayer by Gabriela Mistral • Green by Juan Ramón
Jiménez 319
    Preview 320
    Apply Skills 321
Build Skills: The Artist by Rabindranath Tagore 323
    Preview 324
    Apply the Skills 325

Unit 9: Voices of Change: The Contemporary World (1946 – Present)

Build Skills: The Handsomest Drowned Man in the World
by Gabriel García Márquez 327
    Preview 328
    Apply the Skills 329
Build Skills: *from* Annie John: A Walk on the Jetty by Jamaica Kincaid 331
    Preview 332
    Apply the Skills 333

Build Skills: The Guest by Albert Camus 335

    Preview 336

    Apply the Skills 337

Build Skills: *from* Survival in Auschwitz • *from* Night

• When in early summer 339

from Survival in Auschwitz by Primo Levi

    Preview 340

    Selection 341

from Night by Elie Wiesel • When in early summer . . . by Nelly Sachs

    Preview 346

    Apply the Skills 347

READING INFORMATIONAL MATERIALS

Magazine Articles 350

Build Skills: A Song on the End of the World by Czesław Milosz

• The End and the Beginning by Wisława Szymborska 354

    Preview 355

    Apply the Skills 356

Build Skills: Freedom to Breathe • *from* Nobel Lecture • Visit 358

Freedom to Breathe by Alexander Solzhenitsyn • **Visit** by Yevgeny Yevtushenko

    Preview 359

from Nobel Lecture by Alexander Solzhenitsyn

    Preview 360

    Apply Skills 361

Build Skills: Half a Day by Naguib Mahfouz 363

    Preview 364

    Selection 365

    Apply the Skills 368

Build Skills: Pride by Dahlia Ravikovitch • The Diameter of the Bomb

• From the Book of Esther I Filtered the Sediment by Yehuda Amichai 370

    Preview 371

    Apply the Skills 372

Build Skills: Comrades • Marriage is a Private Affair 374

Comrades by Nadine Gordimer

    Preview 375

Marriage is a Private Affair by Chinua Achebe

    Preview 376

    Apply the Skills 377

Build Skills: Thoughts of Hanoi by Nguyen Thi Vinh • All by Bei Dao • Also All • Assembly Line by Shu Ting 379

    Preview 380

    Apply the Skills 381

PART 2 Turbo Vocabulary

Prefixes V2

Suffixes V4

Word Roots V6

Etymology V8

How to Use a Dictionary V12

Academic Words V14

Word Attack Skills: Phonics and Word Patterns V16

Denotation and Connotation V18

Vocabulary and the SAT® V20

Communication Guide: Diction and Etiquette V24

Words in Other Subjects V28

Build Vocabulary: Flash Cards V29

Build Vocabulary: Fold-a-List V33

Commonly Misspelled Words V37

As you read your hardcover student edition of *Prentice Hall Literature,* use the ***Reader's Notebook,*** Adapted Version, to guide you in learning and practicing the skills presented. In addition, many selections in your student edition are presented here in an interactive format. The notes and instruction will guide you in applying reading and literary skills and in thinking about the selection. The examples on these pages show you how to use the notes as a companion when you read.

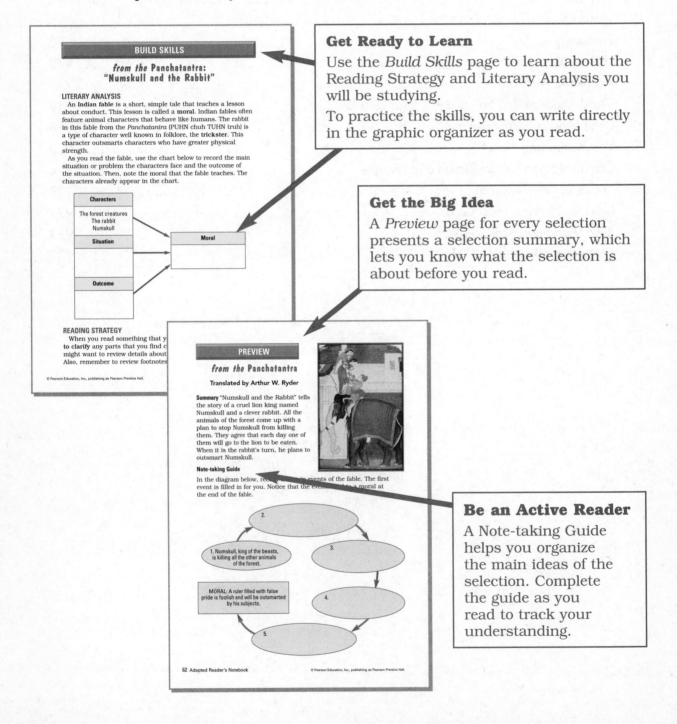

Get Ready to Learn

Use the *Build Skills* page to learn about the Reading Strategy and Literary Analysis you will be studying.

To practice the skills, you can write directly in the graphic organizer as you read.

Get the Big Idea

A *Preview* page for every selection presents a selection summary, which lets you know what the selection is about before you read.

Be an Active Reader

A Note-taking Guide helps you organize the main ideas of the selection. Complete the guide as you read to track your understanding.

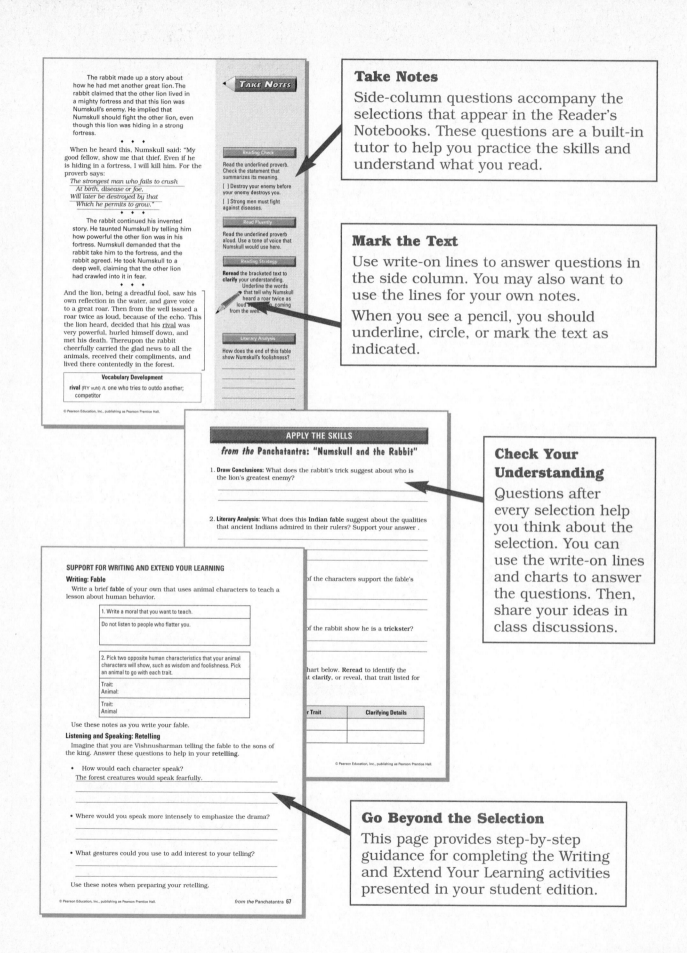

The rabbit made up a story about how he had met another great lion. The rabbit claimed that the other lion lived in a mighty fortress and that this lion was Numskull's enemy. He implied that Numskull should fight the other lion, even though this lion was hiding in a strong fortress.

• • •

When he heard this, Numskull said: "My good fellow, show me that thief. Even if he is hiding in a fortress, I will kill him. For the proverb says:

The strongest man who fails to crush
At birth, disease or foe,
Will later be destroyed by that
Which he permits to grow."

• • •

The rabbit continued his invented story. He taunted Numskull by telling him how powerful the other lion was in his fortress. Numskull demanded that the rabbit take him to the fortress, and the rabbit agreed. He took Numskull to a deep well, claiming that the other lion had crawled into it in fear.

• • •

And the lion, being a dreadful fool, saw his own reflection in the water, and gave voice to a great roar. Then from the well issued a roar twice as loud, because of the echo. This the lion heard, decided that his *rival* was very powerful, hurled himself down, and met his death. Thereupon the rabbit cheerfully carried the glad news to all the animals, received their compliments, and lived there contentedly in the forest.

Vocabulary Development

rival (RY vuhl) *n.* one who tries to outdo another; competitor

© Pearson Education, Inc., publishing as Pearson Prentice Hall.

TAKE NOTES

Reading Check

Read the underlined proverb. Check the statement that summarizes its meaning.

[ ] Destroy your enemy before your enemy destroys you.

[ ] Strong men must fight against diseases.

Read Fluently

Read the underlined proverb aloud. Use a tone of voice that Numskull would use here.

Reading Strategy

Reread the bracketed text to **clarify** your understanding. Underline the words that tell why Numskull heard a roar twice as loud as his own, coming from the well.

Literary Analysis

How does the end of this fable show Numskull's foolishness?

_____

_____

_____

Take Notes

Side-column questions accompany the selections that appear in the Reader's Notebooks. These questions are a built-in tutor to help you practice the skills and understand what you read.

Mark the Text

Use write-on lines to answer questions in the side column. You may also want to use the lines for your own notes.

When you see a pencil, you should underline, circle, or mark the text as indicated.

APPLY THE SKILLS

***from the* Panchatantra: "Numskull and the Rabbit"**

1. **Draw Conclusions:** What does the rabbit's trick suggest about who is the lion's greatest enemy?

_____

2. **Literary Analysis:** What does this **Indian fable** suggest about the qualities that ancient Indians admired in their rulers? Support your answer.

_____

Check Your Understanding

Questions after every selection help you think about the selection. You can use the write-on lines and charts to answer the questions. Then, share your ideas in class discussions.

SUPPORT FOR WRITING AND EXTEND YOUR LEARNING

Writing: Fable

Write a brief **fable** of your own that uses animal characters to teach a lesson about human behavior.

1. Write a moral that you want to teach.
Do not listen to people who flatter you.

2. Pick two opposite human characteristics that your animal characters will show, such as wisdom and foolishness. Pick an animal to go with each trait.
Trait: Animal:
Trait: Animal:

Use these notes as you write your fable.

Listening and Speaking: Retelling

Imagine that you are Vishnusharman telling the fable to the sons of the king. Answer these questions to help in your **retelling**.

• How would each character speak?
The forest creatures would speak fearfully.

_____

• Where would you speak more intensely to emphasize the drama?

_____

• What gestures could you use to add interest to your telling?

_____

Use these notes when preparing your retelling.

© Pearson Education, Inc., publishing as Pearson Prentice Hall.   *from the* Panchatantra **67**

of the characters support the fable's

_____

of the rabbit show he is a **trickster**?

_____

hart below. **Reread** to identify the
at **clarify**, or reveal, that trait listed for

r Trait	Clarifying Details

© Pearson Education, Inc., publishing as Pearson Prentice Hall.

Go Beyond the Selection

This page provides step-by-step guidance for completing the Writing and Extend Your Learning activities presented in your student edition.

from The Epic of Gilgamesh

LITERARY ANALYSIS

An **archetype** is a basic plot, character, symbol, or idea that appears in the literature of many cultures. One archetype is the **hero's quest,** a plot in which an extraordinary person goes on a difficult journey or mission. The hero may search for:

- a person, place, or object of value
- the answer to a problem or puzzling question
- some other kind of special knowledge

Part of telling a quest story involves the description of the person at the center of the action. **Characterization** is the means by which characters are created and developed. Authors reveal characters' traits

- through direct statements, as when the narrator describes a character
- through the actions, speech, and thoughts of the character
- through descriptive details

READING STRATEGY

Gilgamesh was a real Sumerian king. You will better appreciate the story of Gilgamesh if you learn about the culture in which he lived. To **understand the cultural context,** or cultural setting, of the story, look for details about how people lived and worked. Find clues that reveal their beliefs and values. Read the passages from *Gilgamesh.* As you read, use the chart shown to record at least two details that give information about ancient Sumerian culture.

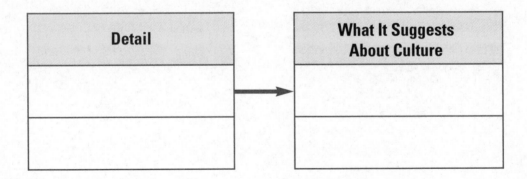

Detail	What It Suggests About Culture

from The Epic of Gilgamesh: Prologue • The Battle with Humbaba

Translated by N.K. Sandars

Summary The Prologue describes the greatness and perfection of King Gilgamesh. It tells how he carves the stories of his adventures into stone. It also describes the great wall he built to protect Uruk. In "The Battle with Humbaba," Gilgamesh and Enkidu fight with Humbaba, the giant who guards the cedar forest.

Note-taking Guide

Use this diagram to record information about Gilgamesh from the "Prologue" and "The Battle with Humbaba." The section "What character thinks" has been filled in for you.

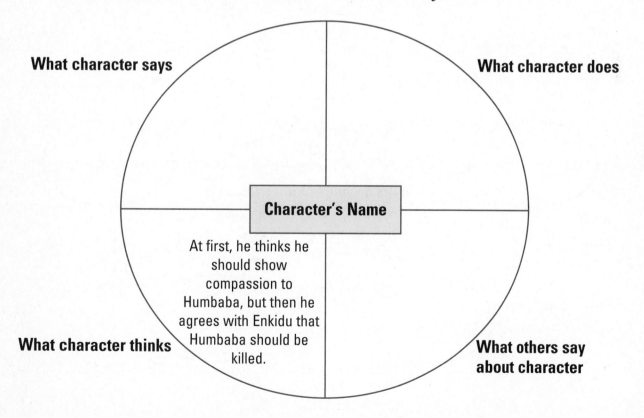

What character says

What character does

Character's Name

At first, he thinks he should show compassion to Humbaba, but then he agrees with Enkidu that Humbaba should be killed.

What character thinks

What others say about character

from The Epic of Gilgamesh: The Death of Enkidu

Translated by N.K. Sandars

Summary Enkidu is a loyal friend of Gilgamesh, a great Sumerian king. Gilgamesh and Enkidu have killed a wild bull. Enkidu is worried that he will be punished by the gods for slaying the bull. He has a dream in which he dies and travels to the underworld. There he meets a vicious man-bird. He sees dead kings and princes who are now servants. Enkidu meets the Queen of the Underworld and the keeper of the book of death. When the keeper speaks to Enkidu, Enkidu wakes up, terrified.

Note-taking Guide

Use the chart below to record the images that Enkidu sees in his dream.

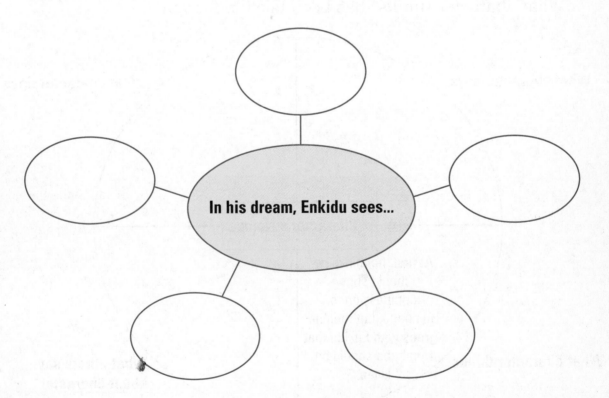

In his dream, Enkidu sees...

from The Epic of Gilgamesh
The Death of Enkidu

Translated by N. K. Sandars

Enkidu has a dream about death. As the dream begins, heaven and earth roar. Enkidu stands before a terrifying creature described as part man and part bird.

◆　◆　◆

"His was a vampire face, his foot was a lion's foot, his hand was an eagle's <u>talon.</u> He fell on me and his claws were in my hair, he held me fast and I <u>smothered</u>; then he <u>transformed</u> me so that my arms became wings covered with feathers. <u>He turned his stare towards me, and he led me away to the palace of Irkalla, the Queen of Darkness, to the house from which none who enters ever returns, down the road from which there is no coming back.</u>

"There is the house whose people sit in darkness; dust is their food and clay their meat."

◆　◆　◆

Enkidu repeats that the people sit in complete darkness. He notices that former kings are now poor servants. They carry food and water in the underworld. Enkidu sees priests, their faithful followers, and the god of cattle. Then he meets Ereshkigal, the Queen of the Underworld and Belit-Sheri, the keeper of the book of death. Belit-Sheri speaks to Enkidu. She wants to know who brought him to the palace. When Belit-Sheri speaks, Enkidu wakes up. He is terrified by his horrible dream.

Vocabulary Development

talon (TAL in) *n.* claw of a bird
smothered (SMUTH erd) *v.* unable to breathe
transformed (tranz FORMD) *v.* changed in appearance

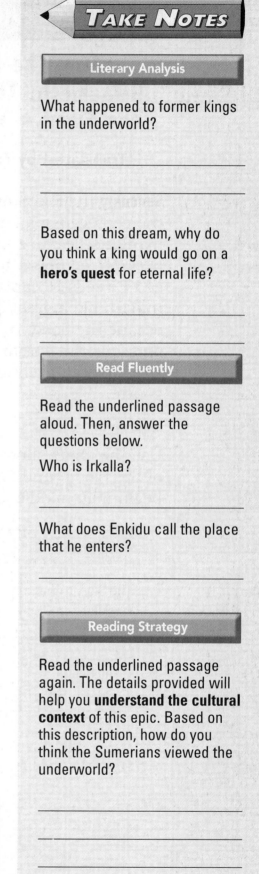

TAKE NOTES

Literary Analysis

What happened to former kings in the underworld?

_____

_____

Based on this dream, why do you think a king would go on a **hero's quest** for eternal life?

_____

_____

Read Fluently

Read the underlined passage aloud. Then, answer the questions below.

Who is Irkalla?

_____

What does Enkidu call the place that he enters?

_____

Reading Strategy

Read the underlined passage again. The details provided will help you **understand the cultural context** of this epic. Based on this description, how do you think the Sumerians viewed the underworld?

_____

_____

from The Epic of Gilgamesh: The Story of the Flood • The Return

Translated by N.K. Sandars

Summary In "The Story of the Flood," the gods cause a flood to destroy mankind because the people have become too noisy. In a dream, the god Ea tells Utnapishtim that he must build a great boat in order to escape the flood. In "The Return," Gilgamesh visits Utnapishtim and fails the test to gain immortality, or everlasting life. Utnapishtim then tells him where to find the flower of eternal youth.

Note-taking Guide

Use the chart shown to summarize the main events of "The Story of the Flood" and "The Return." Write notes that describe the beginning, middle, and end of each story.

Story	Beginning	Middle	End
"The Story of the Flood"			
"The Return"			

from The Epic of Gilgamesh

1. **Deduce:** Enkidu and Gilgamesh are enemies at first. After a while, they become good friends. Give three reasons why this happens.

_____

_____

2. **Literary Analysis:** Do you think Enkidu supports Gilgamesh's **quest** for eternal life? List three details from the dream that support your answer.

_____

_____

3. **Literary Analysis: Characterization** is the way that an author creates believable characters. List three examples of actions, speech, or thoughts that contribute to the characterization of Gilgamesh as a hero. Use the chart shown to explain what each example shows about Gilgamesh's personality, values, or talents.

Example of Characterization	What It Shows about Gilgamesh

4. **Reading Strategy:** The **cultural context** of a work of literature includes where people live, what jobs they hold, and what beliefs they share. Identify three qualities or beliefs that the Sumerians and the Babylonians in _Gilgamesh_ seem to value.

_____

_____

5. **Reading Strategy:** Identify three details that show that Sumerian or Babylonian society was highly organized.

_____

_____

SUPPORT FOR WRITING AND EXTEND YOUR LEARNING

Writing: Comparison-and-Contrast Essay

Gilgamesh goes on a quest to find everlasting life. Think of a modern-day hero who is also on a quest. Then, write a **comparison-and-contrast essay** about the two heroes.

Prewriting: Think about how Gilgamesh and a modern-day hero are similar or different. Answer each question below in a complete sentence.

• How are the heroes' goals similar or different?

_____

• How are the heroes' strengths similar or different?

_____

• Do the heroes succeed in their quests?

_____

Use your notes to draft your **comparison-and-contrast essay**.

Research and Technology: Research Report

Archaeologists rediscovered a version of *The Epic of Gilgamesh* in the nineteenth century. Consult the Internet to find out more about this rediscovery. Present your research in a short **research report**.

Use the chart below to record your findings.

The Rediscovery of *Gilgamesh*	
Details of the rediscovery: **Where:** _____ **When:** _____ **Who:** _____	**Web site:** _____ **Web site:** _____ **Web site:** _____

Use your notes to write a brief research report.

Genesis 1-3: The Creation and the Fall •
Genesis 6-9: The Story of the Flood

LITERARY ANALYSIS

An **archetypal setting** is a time, place, or landscape that connects to powerful, universal human experiences. One example is a paradise like the Bible's Garden of Eden. Archetypal settings may include

- a series of opposites
- a landscape that starts with water or chaos
- a circle that is a symbol of completion
- a tree that connects heaven and earth

The Bible contains **dialogue,** or conversation between characters. Dialogue can reveal information about characters, present events, add variety to narratives, and create interest.

READING STRATEGY

Chronological order is the order in which events happen. *First, later, on the next day*, and *after that* are called transitional words. Transitional words can be used to make chronological order clear. Use this chart to track the sequence of events for the first six days of creation in Genesis 1-3.

Chronological Order of the Creation

Day 1	Day 2	Day 3
Day 4	Day 5	Day 6

Genesis 1-3: The Creation and the Fall • Genesis 6-9: The Story of the Flood

Summary Genesis 1-3 tells how God created heaven and earth and how man fell from grace. After He creates earth and heaven, God plants the Garden of Eden. He puts man and woman within this garden. God tells man not to eat the fruit from the tree of knowledge. The serpent persuades woman to eat this tree's fruit. Woman then convinces man to eat it. God punishes man, woman, and serpent for their disobedience. He drives them out of the Garden of Eden.

In Genesis 6-9, God decides to punish man for his wickedness by causing a great flood to destroy all living creatures. However, God spares Noah and his family. He tells Noah to build an ark and place two of every animal inside with him. After the flood, Noah and his family leave the ark. Noah's sons resettle the land.

Note-taking Guide

Use this organizer to follow the major events in "The Creation and the Fall." Begin with creation and end with Adam and Eve being sent out of the Garden of Eden.

Starting Event

Final Event

Genesis 1-3: The Creation and the Fall • Genesis 6-9: The Story of the Flood

1. **Interpret:** The first thing that God creates is light. What do light and darkness seem to stand for in the first chapter of Genesis?

_____

2. **Literary Analysis:** An **archetypal setting** is a time, place, or landscape feature that has similar meaning for many different cultures. Which details in the first three chapters of Genesis reveal the archetypal setting of a universe made up of opposites?

_____

_____

_____

3. **Literary Analysis:** In **dialogue** with Himself, God speaks about several sets of opposites in Genesis 8:22. Use the chart below to record the opposites that are mentioned.

Opposites in Genesis 8:22	

4. **Reading Strategy: Chronological order** is the order in which events happen in time. In chronological order, summarize the reasons that God decides to destroy the earth with a flood.

_____

_____

Writing: Definition of Paradise

The Garden of Eden is a famous **archetypal setting.** Imagine that you had to define the meaning of paradise for someone who had never heard the word. Use the descriptions in Genesis 2-3 to write an extended definition of paradise. To do this, reread Genesis 2-3. Then, write down three quotations that explain the idea of paradise. Include the numbers of the lines. Then, write down three ways that paradise is different from our world today. Use your notes to write your definition.

Quotation:	**Line:**
Quotation:	**Line:**
Quotation:	**Line:**
How paradise is different from our world today: _____

Listening and Speaking: Choral Reading

A **choral reading** is an activity in which a group of people read out loud together. Choose ten lines from Genesis and prepare a choral reading that you can perform with others.

- Read through the passage aloud. Which words are hard to pronounce? Write them down here._____

  _____

- Look in a dictionary to find out how to pronounce the difficult words. Rewrite the words in a way that shows how to say them aloud.

  _____

- Choose three words or phrases from the passage. Write notes on how they should be said. For example, you can make your voice louder or softer when you say them aloud.

  _____

  _____

Use your notes to perform a **choral reading.**

from the Bible: from The Book of Ruth • Psalm 8 • Psalm 19 • Psalm 23 • Psalm 137

LITERARY ANALYSIS

Parallelism is a biblical style of writing. When parallelism is used in biblical writing, an idea is stated in the first part of a biblical verse. Then, in the second part of the verse, the idea is either

- repeated
- completed
- elaborated upon (expanded)
- negated (denied or canceled out)

The example below from "Book of Ruth," shows repetitive parallelism.

Don't go to glean in another field. Don't go elsewhere, but stay here close to my girls.

READING STRATEGY

Readers **use context clues** to figure out the meanings of unfamiliar words. Context clues are hints in the text that surround the unfamiliar word. These hints may be similar words, opposites, or examples that make a word's meaning clear. Use the chart below to find the meaning of an unfamiliar word using context clues.

Passage	Unfamiliar Word	Context Clues	Type of Hint	Conclusion

from the Book of Ruth

Translated by The Jewish Publication Society

Summary The "Book of Ruth" is a brief but powerful Bible story. A great famine forces Naomi, her husband, and their two sons to leave Bethlehem and settle in Moab. The sons marry Ruth and Orpah. After the death of her husband and sons, Naomi decides to return to her home. Her daughter-in-law Orpah remains in Moab, but Ruth insists on returning to Bethlehem with Naomi. During the harvest, Ruth works in the fields owned by Boaz, a wealthy relative of Naomi. Boaz grows to care for Ruth. When another family member decides not to buy Naomi's and Ruth's family property, Boaz is able to buy the land. Then he and Ruth marry and have a son. Their son, Obed, becomes an ancestor of David.

Note-taking Guide

As you read the "Book of Ruth," write a summary sentence for each chapter in the chart below.

Chapter 1	Chapter 2
Chapter 3	**Chapter 4**

from the Book of Ruth

Translated by The Jewish Publication Society

Chapter 1

At the beginning of the "Book of Ruth," the people of Bethlehem in Judah have no food to eat. As a result, a family leaves Bethlehem to settle in another country, called Moab. The husband's name is Elimelech. His wife is called Naomi. They have two sons.

Elimelech dies and Naomi's sons marry women from Moab. About ten years later, Naomi's two sons die. She decides to return to her homeland with her daughter-in-laws, Orpah and Ruth.

On the way back to Judah, Naomi tells Orpah and Ruth to return to Moab. She wants them to find husbands there. Naomi knows that she will never have more sons of her own.

◆ ◆ ◆

They broke into weeping again, and Orpah kissed her mother-in-law farewell. But Ruth clung to her.

So she said, "See, your sister-in-law has returned to her people and her gods. Go follow your sister-in-law."

But Ruth replied, "Do not urge me to leave you, to turn back and not follow you. For wherever you go, I will go; wherever you lodge, I will lodge; your people shall be my people, and your God my God.

Where you die, I will die, and there I will be buried. Thus and more may the LORD do to me[1] if anything but death parts me from you."

---

1. **do to me** Punish me.

TAKE NOTES

Stop to Reflect

What feelings do you think people have when they leave their homeland?

_____

_____

Reading Check

How do Ruth and Orpah react when Naomi tells them to return home?

Ruth

_____

_____

Orpah

_____

_____

Literary Analysis

Underline the examples of **parallelism** in the first bracketed passage. Then circle the type of parallelism used.

Repetition
Completion
Elaboration
Negation

Stop to Reflect

Read Ruth's words in the second bracketed text. What do Ruth's words reveal about her character?

_____

_____

Notice that the word *kinsman* is underlined in the bracketed passage. Circle the **context clues** you used to figure out the word's meaning. Write the meaning of *kinsman* on the lines below.

_____

_____

Read aloud the second bracketed passage. Why do you think Ruth wants to work in the fields with someone who will treat her kindly?

_____

_____

Read the third bracketed passage aloud.

What four things does Boaz tell Ruth to do?

1._____

2._____

3._____

4._____

Think about Boaz's words to Ruth. What kind of person do you think he is?

_____

When [Naomi] saw how determined she was to go with her, she ceased to argue with her;

♦   ♦   ♦

So Ruth and Naomi continue to Bethlehem. The people there are pleased to see Naomi after so many years. Naomi and Ruth arrive in Bethlehem at the start of the barley harvest.

Chapter 2

Now Naomi had a <u>kinsman</u> on her husband's side, a man of substance, of the family of Elimelech, whose name was Boaz.

Ruth the Moabite said to Naomi, "I would like to go to the fields and <u>glean</u> among the ears of grain, behind someone who may show me kindness." "Yes, daughter, go," she replied.

♦   ♦   ♦

By chance, Ruth finds work in a field owned by Boaz. He greets the workers. Then he notices Ruth. Another worker explains to Boaz who Ruth is. She tells him that Ruth has had little rest all morning.

♦   ♦   ♦

Boaz said to Ruth, "Listen to me, daughter. Don't go to glean in another field. Don't go elsewhere, but stay here close to my girls.

Keep your eyes on the field they are reaping, and follow them. I have ordered the men not to <u>molest</u> you. And when you are thirsty, go to the jars and drink some of [the water] that the men have drawn."

Vocabulary Development

glean (GLEEN) *v.* to collect grain left in the field after harvesting

molest (muh LEST) *v.* to annoy, disturb, or bother

She <u>prostrated</u> herself with her face to the ground, and said to him, "Why are you so kind as to single me out, when I am a foreigner?"

♦   ♦   ♦

Boaz had heard about Ruth's loyalty to Naomi, and he is very kind and generous to Ruth. In the evening Ruth returns home to Naomi. The women eat. Then Ruth tells her mother-in-law where she worked that day. Naomi is happy because Boaz is related to them. He is a relative who is responsible for helping to care for them. She tells Ruth to keep working in his field. Ruth works there until the harvest is over.

Chapter 3

Naomi, her mother-in-law, said to her, "Daughter, I must seek a home for you, where you may be happy.

Now there is our kinsman[2] Boaz, whose girls you were close to. He will be <u>winnowing</u> barley on the threshing floor tonight.

So bathe, anoint[3] yourself, dress up, and go down to the <u>threshing floor</u>. But do not <u>disclose</u> yourself to the man until he has finished eating and drinking."

♦   ♦   ♦

Vocabulary Development

winnowing (WIN oh ing) *v.* exposing grain to wind and air to blow away the outer layer

threshing floor (THRESH ing flor) *n.* a place where grain is separated from a cereal plant, such as wheat

disclose (dis CLOHZ) *v.* reveal

---

2. **kinsman** According to Jewish law, the closest unmarried male relative of Ruth's deceased husband was obligated to marry her.
3. **anoint** (uh NOYNT) *v.* rub oil or ointment on.

TAKE NOTES

Reading Strategy

Reread the sentence with the word *prostrated.* Circle the **context clues** that help you figure out the word's meaning.

Check the correct meaning of *prostrated* from the choices below:

[ ] laid down with the face downward

[ ] stood up straight

[ ] raised the head

Stop to Reflect

Underline the words in the bracketed passage that show how Naomi intends to help Ruth. What does Naomi want Ruth to do?

_____

_____

Reading Check

What four things does Naomi tell Ruth to do to get Boaz's attention?

1. _____

2. _____

3. _____

4. _____

Ruth follows Naomi's instructions. That night she finds Boaz asleep beside a pile of grain. Then she lies down at his feet. He is surprised to find her there. Ruth knows that Boaz is a relative who can marry her. Boaz tells Ruth that another, even closer relative can marry her too. If that relative does not want to accept that responsibility, then Boaz will do it.

The next morning Boaz gives Ruth some barley to take home with her. Ruth returns to Naomi. Naomi is certain that Boaz will settle the matter that day.

Chapter 4

At the town gate, Boaz sees his relative. He asks the man if he wants to buy land that is owned by Naomi and Ruth. If he does, he must also marry the wife of the dead man. The relative cannot marry Ruth. He gives up his right to buy the property. He tells Boaz to buy the land instead.

◆ ◆ ◆

And Boaz said to the elders and to the rest of the people, "You are witnesses today that I am acquiring from Naomi all that belonged to Elimelech and all that belonged to Chilion and Mahlon.

I am also acquiring Ruth the Moabite, the wife of Mahlon, as my wife, so as to <u>perpetuate</u> the name of the deceased upon his estate, that the name of the deceased may not disappear from among his kinsmen and from the gate of his home town. You are witnesses today."

◆ ◆ ◆

Reading Strategy

Circle the **context clues** you used to figure out the meaning of the underlined word *perpetuate*. Then, write the meaning of *perpetuate* on the lines below.

_____

_____

Reading Check

To whom is Boaz speaking when he says he is acquiring Ruth.

_____

What is he asking these people to do?

_____

_____

Everyone at the town gate gives their blessings to the marriage. They are hopeful that Ruth will have a child. Later Boaz and Ruth marry, and they have a son. The women of the town are very happy for Naomi.

◆ ◆ ◆

"<u>He will renew your life and sustain your old age; for he is born of your daughter-in-law, who loves you and is better to you than seven sons.</u>"

Naomi took the child and held it to her bosom. She became its foster mother,
and the women neighbors gave him a name, saying, "A son is born to Naomi!" They named him Obed; he was the father of Jesse, father of David.

This is the line of Perez: Perez begot Hezron,
Hezron begot Ram, Ram begot Amminadab,
Amminadab begot Nahshon, Nahshon begot Salmon,
Salmon begot Boaz, Boaz begot Obed,
Obed begot Jesse, and Jesse begot David.

Psalm 8, Psalm 19, Psalm 23, and Psalm 137

Translated by The Jewish Publication Society

Summary Psalm 8 praises God for creating the earth and making man its master. Psalm 19 tells how God created day and night. It also describes how God guides the speaker, keeping him free of sin. Psalm 23 describes God as a shepherd. He guides the speaker through the course of his life. Psalm 137 tells about the sadness of the people after they were forced to leave Jerusalem.

Note-taking Guide

For each Psalm, place an "X" in the column or columns which best describe the theme or emotion of the Psalm.

	Praise	Sadness	Security
Psalm 8			
Psalm 19			
Psalm 23			
Psalm 137			

from the Bible: from the Book of Ruth, Psalm 8, Psalm 19, Psalm 23, and Psalm 137

1. **Interpret:** In what way is God present throughout the "Book of Ruth" and the Psalms, even when He does not appear directly in the story?

_____

_____

2. **Literary Analysis:** Give one example of each type of **parallelism** in a chart like the one shown. Your examples can be from the "Book of Ruth" or the Book of Psalms. Then, explain what makes your choice parallelism.

Type of Parallelism	Example	Explanation
repetition with variation		
completion of an idea		
elaboration of an idea		

3. **Literary Analysis:** Review the parallelism in Ruth 4:9-12. In what ways does this parallelism emphasize the **theme** of making an outsider part of the community?

_____

_____

4. **Reading Strategy: Context clues** are hints in the surrounding passage about the meanings of unfamiliar words. Using the context clues in Ruth 1:11-13, define the words *lot* and *debar*.

lot _____

debar _____

5. **Reading Strategy:** Choose one word from the Psalms that was unfamiliar to you. Explain how context clues helped you figure out its meaning.

_____

_____

Writing: Response to a Biblical Narrative

Write a response to the "Book of Ruth."

Which element of the "Book of Ruth" affected you the most: characters, events, or ideas? Write it on the line.

_____

Use the chart shown to summarize your reaction to the element that you identified.

My response to this element:
Details in the "Book of Ruth" that help explain my response:

Use your notes to help you draft a response.

Research and Technology: Multimedia Report

Prepare a **multimedia report** on musical versions of the Psalms.

- Do research.
  - Check library or other music collections for nonfiction about religious music.
  - Go to local churches and talk to choir members.
  - Look at Web sites.
- List the sources you find and use.

_____

_____

- Decide what media to use to present your findings. You might use live or recorded music, written or oral explanations, and sheet music.

_____

_____

Use your notes to organize and present your multimedia report.

from the Qur'an: "The Exordium" • "Night" • "Daylight" • "Comfort"

LITERARY ANALYSIS

Imagery is language used to create word pictures. Imagery appeals to the reader's sense of sight, hearing, taste, smell, and touch. An **image** is a single instance of imagery. "Hot, dry, wind" and "cold, wet, rain" are images.

One form of imagery makes differences stand out by putting together images that contrast, or are opposite. **Antithesis** is the use of strongly contrasting language, images, or ideas. For example, the phrase "By the light of day, and by the dark of night" pairs two opposite images (the "light of day" and "the dark of night").

Use the chart to note images as you read the selections from the *Qur'an*. Write down the sense or senses to which each image appeals.

Image	Selection	Sense(s)

READING STRATEGY

Before you start to read, **set a purpose for reading**. Follow these steps:

1. Decide why you are reading.
2. Choose something to focus on as you read.

The chart shows an example purpose for reading the *Qur'an*.

Selection	Why You Are Reading	What You Will Focus On
the *Qur'an*	to learn more about Islamic culture	guidelines for how people should act

from the Qur'an:
"The Exordium," "Night,"
"Daylight," and "Comfort"

Translated N.J. Dawood

Summary The speaker in "The Exordium" praises God and asks for guidance. "Night" is about the difference between living a good life and living a sinful life. The passage says that a sinner will be punished and a good person will be rewarded. In "Daylight," God promises to take care of Mohammed, the prophet. Mohammed is reminded that he will receive his reward in the afterlife. God also advises Mohammed to take care of others in the same way that God cares for him. The passage "Comfort" reassures the people of Mecca. Repeated phrases explain that comfort can be found even in hard times.

Note-taking Guide

Each selection from the *Qur'an* contains a different message. Use this chart to restate each message.

	Message
"The Exordium"	
"Night"	
"Daylight"	
"Comfort"	

from the Qur'an: "The Exordium" • "Night" • "Daylight" • "Comfort"

1. **Interpret:** Think about the passage "Daylight." In what ways should human behavior reflect the Lord's behavior?

_____

_____

2. **Literary Analysis:** Does the **imagery** in "Night" appeal to the senses of sight, hearing, taste, smell, or touch? Give examples of images to support your answer.

_____

_____

3. **Literary Analysis:** Identify three examples of contrasting language, images, or ideas from the *Qur'an*. Choose examples that make the language, imagery, or ideas clearer.

_____

_____

4. **Reading Strategy:** Imagine that your **purpose for reading** is to learn about the Islamic view of Allah, or God. Reread each selection. Then, write down the main characteristic of Allah that it expresses. Record your examples in this chart.

Selection	Characteristic of Allah
"The Exordium"	
"Night"	
"Daylight"	
"Comfort"	

5. **Reading Strategy:** If your purpose for reading is to learn about Islamic views of the afterlife, what do you find out by reading these selections?

_____

_____

SUPPORT FOR WRITING AND EXTEND YOUR LEARNING

Writing: Guidelines for Personal Behavior

The Five Pillars of Wisdom provide guidelines for living a good life. Think about the Five Pillars of Wisdom and the selections from the *Qur'an*. Then, write your own **guidelines for personal behavior**.

To prepare, think about a person that you admire. Write the name of the person on the left side of the chart shown. On the right side of the chart, under the heading *Traits*, list five traits that you admire in this person. Use your list to help you write guidelines for personal behavior.

Person	Traits

Listening and Speaking: Speech

Prepare a short **speech** on what compassion and mercy mean to you. Follow these steps for help in preparing your speech.

- Define *compassion* and *mercy* in your own words on the lines below.

Now, write each definition on a note card.

- Reread the selections from the *Qur'an*. Write down one example of compassion and one example of mercy that appear in the selections.

Now, write each example on a note card.

- Think about examples of compassion and mercy that might occur today. Write down one act of compassion and one act of mercy that you could imagine happening today.

Now, write each example on a note card.
Use these notes as a guide when you give your speech.

from The Thousand and One Nights: The Fisherman and the Jinnee

LITERARY ANALYSIS

Folk tales are part of oral tradition. The oral tradition includes stories, poems, and songs that are passed down by people who tell or recite them aloud. Most folktales have:
- a lesson about life
- magical elements
- characters who are simple and easy to understand
- a clear separation between good and evil

The way in which a story is told is called its **narrative structure**. *The Thousand and One Nights* contains framed stories. Characters in one story tell other stories. As you read, use this chart to map the narrative structure of "The Fisherman and the Jinnee."

First Story
Narrator: Scheherazade **Story:**

Second Story
Narrator: **Story:**

Third Story
Narrator: **Story:**

READING STRATEGY

A summary is a brief statement that includes the most important details of a story. To **summarize**, write down the most important events or details. Then, organize that information into a short, clear statement.

from The Thousand and One Nights: The Fisherman and the Jinnee

Translated by N.J. Dawood

Summary "The Fisherman and the Jinnee" discusses the importance of appreciating people for their kindness. This message is shown in three inter-locking stories. In the main story, a fisherman frees a jinnee that is trapped in a bottle. In return, the jinnee plans to kill him. The jinnee is angry that he has been trapped in the bottle for two hundred years.

The fisherman returns the jinnee to the bottle. He tells two stories to the jinnee. In the first story, a king kills a doctor who cured him of leprosy. His advisers convince him that this doctor will destroy him. However, the king is punished for killing the doctor. This king tells his advisers the story of King Sindbad. King Sindbad kills his pet falcon. He regrets his act because the falcon prevented him from drinking poison. After the fisherman tells these stories, he throws the bottle into the sea.

Note-taking Guide

Use this chart to summarize the action in the main story of "The Fisherman and the Jinnee." Begin with the fisherman finding the bottle and setting the jinnee free. End with the fisherman throwing the bottle back into the sea.

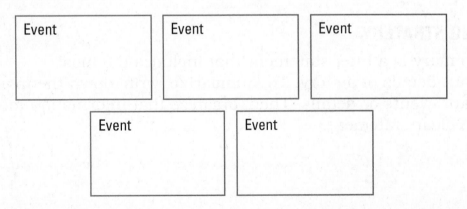

Event

Event

Event

Event

Event

from The Thousand and One Nights: The Fisherman and the Jinnee

1. **Analyze:** Which detail of the jinnee's personality allows the fisherman to defeat him? Explain.

   _____

   _____

2. **Literary Analysis:** A supernatural element is an action or an event in a story that cannot be explained. Identify the magical or supernatural element in each of the three **folk tales**.

   _____

   _____

3. **Literary Analysis:** Use this chart to identify the main personality traits, or elements, of the jinnee, King Yunan, and the Vizier. Include details from the story to support your answers.

Character	Personality Trait	Supporting Detail
The jinnee		
King Yunan		
Vizier		

4. **Reading Strategy:** List the main events and key details you would include in a summary of the main story about the fisherman.

   _____

   _____

5. **Reading Strategy:** In what way would a summary help a reader who is having trouble understanding the **narrative structure** of these interlocking stories?

   _____

   _____

Writing: Essay

Think about why these stories have been popular in different places and time periods. Then, write a brief **essay** explaining your thoughts.

- What are five details from "The Fisherman and the Jinnee" that would make it appealing to readers from different places and times?

_____

_____

_____

- From your list of details, choose three that you think give the story universal appeal.

_____

_____

_____

Use these details to help you write your essay.

Research and Technology: Research Report

Write a **research report** about jinnees and their role in Persian and Middle Eastern stories. Use a variety of sources.

- First, use the word *jinni* or *genie* to perform a keyword search online. Write down three facts about genies and list the sources where you found the information.

Facts: _____	Sources: _____
_____	_____

- Then, find two Persian or Middle Eastern stories about a jinnee. List your sources.

Story title: _____	Sources: _____
_____	_____

Use your notes to write a research report.

from The Rubáiyát • from the Gulistan

LITERARY ANALYSIS

Didactic literature teaches **morals**, or general lessons about right and wrong behavior. Didactic literature uses the following literary tools:

- **Aphorisms**—short, pointed statements about life, such as "The early bird catches the worm."
- **Personification**—describing nonhuman things as having human characteristics, such as "The <u>old chair groaned</u> as the man sat down." (Chairs do not "groan.")
- **Metaphor**—a figure of speech that compares two different things without using the words "like" or "as." For example, "The <u>full moon was a bright coin</u> in the sky." (In this sentence, the full moon is compared to a bright coin.)

READING STRATEGY

Break down long sentences to help you understand their meaning. Consider one section at a time. Separate a sentence's key parts (the *who* and the *what*) from the difficult language. Then, restate the sentence in your own words. Use the chart below to break down the sentence shown.

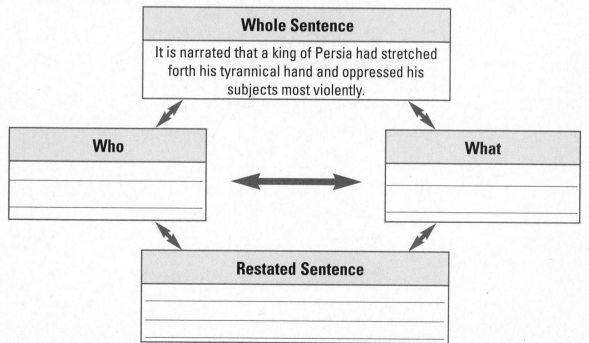

Whole Sentence

It is narrated that a king of Persia had stretched forth his tyrannical hand and oppressed his subjects most violently.

Who

What

Restated Sentence

from The Rubáiyát

by Omar Khayyám
Translated by Edward FitzGerald

Summary The Rubáiyát is a collection of short poems. These poems stress the importance of enjoying life now because the future is uncertain. Many of these poems use images from nature to express this message.

Note-taking Guide

Use this diagram to record information about images in *The Rubáiyát.*

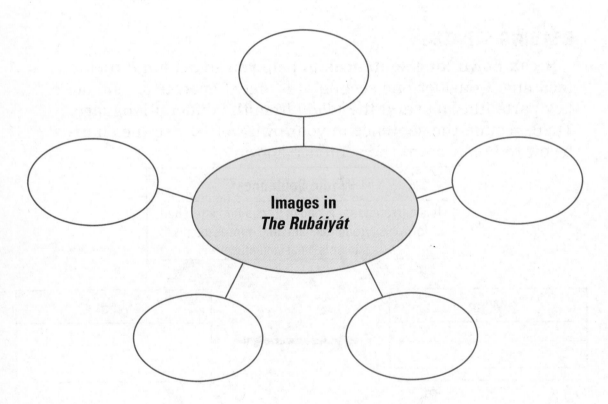

Images in
The Rubáiyát

from the Gulistan: from The Manners of Kings

by Sa'di
Translated by Edward Rehatsek

Summary In the "Manners of Kings," Sa'di gives advice to rulers. The advice is given in the form of stories. These stories explain when to show mercy, how to win the loyalty of subjects, and why it is important to understand human behavior.

Note-taking Guide

Use this chart to record information about the morals of the stories from "The Manners of Kings."

Story	Moral
1	
6	
7	
35	

from The Rubáiyát • from the Gulistan

1. **Analyze Cause and Effect:** In story 1 from "The Manners of Kings," a vizier tells the king that a prisoner is praising him. In reality, the prisoner is insulting the king. Why does the vizier lie on the prisoner's behalf?

   _____

   _____

2. **Literary Analysis: Didactic literature** teaches lessons about right and wrong behavior. Write down two lessons that *The Rubáiyát* teaches.

   _____

   _____

3. **Literary Analysis:** In the chart, list one **aphorism** from *The Rubáiyát* and one from the *Gulistan*. Then, in the circle on the left, list the qualities that the aphorisms share. In the circle on the right, list the ways that the aphorisms are different.

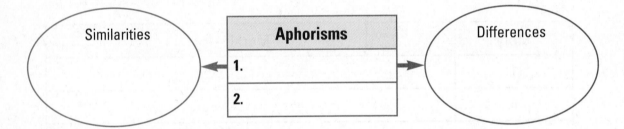

4. **Reading Strategy: Break down the long sentence** in poem I of *The Rubáiyát:* "Wake! For the Sun, who scatter'd into flight / The Stars before him from the Field of Night, / Drives Night along with them from Heav'n, and strikes / The Sultan's Turret with a Shaft of Light." Who performs the main action?

   _____

5. **Reading Strategy:** In the long sentence in poem I of *Rubáiyát*, what action is performed?

   _____

   _____

SUPPORT FOR WRITING AND EXTEND YOUR LEARNING

Writing: Fable

"The Manners of Kings" is a **fable**. Each character in a fable usually has just one flaw or one virtue. The characters are often animals that act like people. Write a fable that offers a lesson for modern-day leaders. Follow these steps to get started:

1. Think about issues that modern-day leaders face. Write down three.

____

____

2. Choose one issue to write about.

____

3. Ask yourself, what lesson would help a leader make a wise decision about this issue? Write the lesson here.

____

____

Use your notes to help you write a fable.

Research and Technology: Annotated Anthology

The Rubáiyát expresses the philosophy of life known as *carpe diem.* The phrase is Latin for "seize the day." Make an **annotated anthology** of poems that express the *carpe diem* philosophy.

1. Look in library resources or on the Internet for poems.
   - Pair the phrase *carpe diem* with the word "poem" or "poetry" to search the Internet or an electronic card catalogue.
   - Look at essays on the theme of *carpe diem* in poetry. These essays will likely include examples of poems.
2. List the poems, authors, and sources in the chart below.

Poem	Author	Source

Use your notes when preparing your anthology.

Elephant in the Dark • Two Kinds of Intelligence • The Guest House • Which is Worth More?

LITERARY ANALYSIS

An **analogy** is an explanation of how two things are alike. Analogies usually make comparisons using a familiar object or idea. They frequently use figurative language such as similes and metaphors.

A **metaphor** compares two unlike things without using the words *like* or *as*. **Direct metaphors** connect the two terms directly. **Implied metaphors** suggest a comparison without stating it outright. Look for examples of metaphors as you read Rumi's poems.

READING STRATEGY

A **generalization** is a broad statement that applies to many situations. As you read, use the details in Rumi's poems to make generalizations about the author's beliefs, philosophy, and main ideas or messages. Use the diagram shown to record a generalization from the poems.

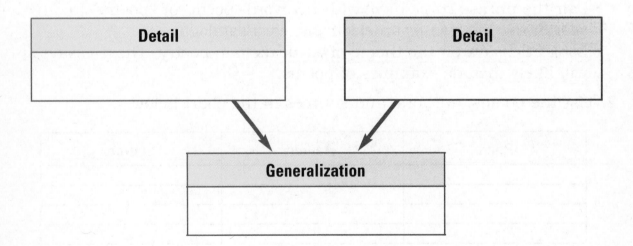

Elephant in the Dark •
Two Kinds of Intelligence •
The Guest House •
Which Is Worth More?

by Rumi
Translated by Coleman Barks

Summaries In "Elephant in the Dark,"
five people go into a dark room.
There is an elephant in the room and
they have never before seen one. Because the elephant is big, each
person can touch only one part of it. Everyone describes the whole
elephant based on the one part they touch. In each of the other
short poems, Rumi asks his readers to look at life from a different
view. **"Two Kinds of Intelligence"** is about the nature of knowledge. **"The Guest House"** is about negative emotions. **"Which Is
Worth More?"** is about the importance of the self.

Note-taking Guide

Use this chart to record the main idea and author's purpose in
each poem.

Poem	Main Idea	Author's Purpose
"Elephant in the Dark"		
"Two Kinds of Intelligence"		
"The Guest House"		
"Which Is Worth More?"		

Elephant in the Dark • Two Kinds of Intelligence • The Guest House • Which is Worth More?

1. **Interpret:** In "Two Kinds of Intelligence," the speaker describes a schoolchild who memorizes facts and learns information only in school. What kind of person does this schoolchild grow up to be?

_____

_____

2. **Literary Analysis:** An **analogy** explains how two things are similar. In "Elephant in the Dark," Rumi uses an analogy of knowing only part of an elephant to define ignorance. Reread the last two lines. What do they suggest about working together?

_____

_____

3. **Literary Analysis:** Use the chart shown to summarize the analogy in "Two Kinds of Intelligence."

First Kind of Intelligence	Second Kind of Intelligence
Key Theme:_____	

4. **Reading Strategy:** When you **make a generalization,** you develop a broad statement that applies to many situations. What generalizations can you draw from "Elephant in the Dark" about a human being's ability to figure out the truth?

_____

_____

5. **Reading Strategy:** "The Guest House" is about welcoming and learning from all emotions. Based on this poem, what **generalization** can you make about Rumi's philosophy of life?

_____

_____

SUPPORT FOR WRITING AND EXTEND YOUR LEARNING

Writing: Poem

Write a **poem** modeled after the style and content of Rumi's works. The subject of your poem should be a message about life.

- Choose a message or life lesson that you will write about in your poem.

____

- Write an analogy that will help express the main idea of your poem.

____

____

- In your poem, either give advice, ask a question, or tell a story. Choose an approach, and explain why you chose it.

____

____

Use your answers to write a poem in the style of Rumi's poems.

Research and Technology: Research Report

Rumi became a teacher of Sufism. Sufism is a part of the Islamic religion. He founded a group known as "Whirling Dervishes." Write a brief **research report** on Sufism and whirling dervishes. Use the chart below to record facts and the sources where you find information. Use your notes to write your report.

Definition of Sufism:	**Source:**
Main Belief of Sufism:	**Source:**
Definition of Whirling Dervishes:	**Source:**
Description of the Dance:	**Source:**

African Proverbs • *from* Sundiata: An Epic of Old Mali

LITERARY ANALYSIS

An **epic** is a story or poem about a hero. In an **epic conflict**, a hero faces one or more challenges and is usually successful. The challenges may appear in the form of enemies, natural dangers, difficult decisions, or fate. Notice which challenges appear as you read *Sundiata: An Epic of Old Mali.*

Proverbs are short sayings that offer advice about life. As you read the African proverbs, consider how they deal with human experiences. When you read *Sundiata: An Epic of Old Mali,* notice how the proverbs affect the characters.

READING STRATEGY

When a passage of writing is difficult, **rereading** the passage can often help you understand it. Also, earlier passages may provide a key to understanding information.

Use this chart to record difficult passages. Write the confusing text in the first column. Then, look for an earlier passage that contains helpful information. Write it in the second column. Finally, write what you learn in the third column.

Difficult Passage	Earlier Passage	Understanding

African Proverbs •
from Sundiata: An Epic of Old Mali

by D.T. Niane

Summaries These African proverbs, or "wise sayings," come from various African tribes. Some of the proverbs explain the importance of friendship, the necessity of planning, and the danger of acting without thinking first. Other proverbs use colorful images from nature to explain human behavior.

Sundiata: An Epic of Old Mali is about the slow growth of a great African ruler named Mari Djata. Mari Djata is destined to be a great ruler. However, this prophecy is forgotten because he does not begin to walk until the age of seven. One day, the queen mother insults Mari Djata's mother because he still cannot walk to pick the leaves of the baobab tree. Mari Djata makes up for the insult by standing and pulling an entire baobab tree from the ground.

Note-taking Guide

Use this chart to record details about the characters in *Sundiata: An Epic of Old Mali.*

Mari Djata	Naré Maghan	Sogolon	Balla Fasséké

African Proverbs • *from* Sundiata: An Epic of Old Mali

1. **Infer:** One **proverb** says that "The one who has not made the journey calls it an easy one." Does this mean that all journeys are easy? Explain.

_____

_____

_____

2. **Literary Analysis:** An **epic conflict** is a challenge that a hero faces. In what sense is Mari Djata's epic conflict a conflict with society?

_____

_____

3. **Literary Analysis:** Using the chart, explain two **proverbs** that appear in *Sundiata: An Epic of Old Mali.* Explain how they apply to Mari Djata.

Proverb	General Meaning	How it Applies

4. **Reading Strategy: Reread** the first two paragraphs of "The Lion's Awakening" in Sundiata. Which details explain why the king left Mari Djata the throne?

_____

_____

_____

_____

Writing: Retelling a Story

The storytellers of Old Mali told stories from memory. However, a storyteller today might want to use notes. Create notes for a retelling of a story that you know. Choose a story that you know besides *Sundiata: An Epic of Old Mali.* Use the chart to record information you will need to retell the story.

Character Name	Character Description
Setting:	
Plot Summary:	
Lesson or Main Idea:	

Research and Technology: Booklet of Proverbs

A proverb is a short saying that gives advice about life. Do some research to find common proverbs from around the world. Then, collect the proverbs in a booklet.

• Write down three sources of proverbs from around the world.

_____

_____

• Write down two different ways to organize the proverbs in a booklet.

_____

_____

• Choose one proverb. Write it down. Explain what it means to you.

_____

_____

_____

Collect the proverbs you find in a booklet. Find or draw a picture to go with each proverb. List the sources where you found the proverbs in the back of your booklet.

BROCHURES

About Brochures

A **brochure** is a pamphlet that combines information and advertising to draw attention to a place of interest. Brochures usually contain some of the following elements:

- Historical background
- Details about the attraction
- A map to guide visitors
- Hours of operation
- Ticket and contact information

Reading Strategy

Brochures often include more information than you want or need. To find the information you want quickly, **adjust your reading rate.** The techniques of skimming and **scanning** will help you to locate information quickly. The chart below gives instruction for skimming and scanning.

Obtaining Information Quickly	
To Skim	• Read quickly across a page, without reading word for word. • Stop at headlines, italics, and other text features if the words are related to what you want to know.
To Scan	• Run your eyes across and down the page. • Scan headlines, bold type, italics, and other text features to locate information quickly

As you read this brochure, adjust your reading rate by skimming and scanning the material.

BUILD UNDERSTANDING

Knowing these terms will help you understand this brochure.

archaeologists (ar kee AHL uh jists) *n.* people who study how people lived in the past

immortality (im mor TAL i tee) *n.* the state of living or lasting forever

THE QUEST for IMMORTALITY

Treasures of Ancient Egypt

EXHIBIT GUIDE

THE QUEST FOR IMMORTALITY
Treasures of Ancient Egypt

ON EXHIBIT
November 20, 2002 –
March 30, 2003

Museum of Science, Boston

Confronting the mystery of death is a fundamental human endeavor[1]. The ancient Egyptians believed they could ensure[2] their continued existence after death, and they devoted tremendous energy and resources to achieving this goal. The pursuit of immortality was the central feature of a complex, evolving set of beliefs that characterized Egyptian civilization[3] throughout its first 3,000 years of history.

For modern archaeologists, Egyptian tombs are treasure houses—not of objects, but of evidence. It is through examination and excavation[4] of tombs and their furnishings that archaeologists have begun to understand the remarkably complex religion of ancient Egypt. This exhibition explores Egyptians' quest for immortality from the Old Kingdom (2686–2125 BCE*) through the Late Period (664–332 BCE). It also tells the story of archaeologists' 200-year quest to understand the thought and practices of an accomplished and intricate culture.

*Before Common Era

---

1. **endeavor** (en DEV er) *n.* a serious attempt or effort.
2. **ensure** (en SHORE) *v.* to make sure of.
3. **civilization** (siv uh luh ZAY shuhn) *n.* the way of life of a particular people.
4. **excavation** (eks kuh VAY shuhn) *n.* the act of uncovering by digging.

TAKE NOTES

Reading Brochures

A **brochure** includes images to highlight the attraction. Why was the image of the ancient sphinx probably selected for the cover of this brochure?

_____

_____

_____

Stop to Reflect

Read the first paragraph. Why would the information in this section of the brochure be helpful to visitors?

_____

_____

_____

Read Fluently

Read the underlined sentences aloud. Why are Egyptian tombs important to modern archaeologists?

_____

_____

Reading Informational Materials **45**

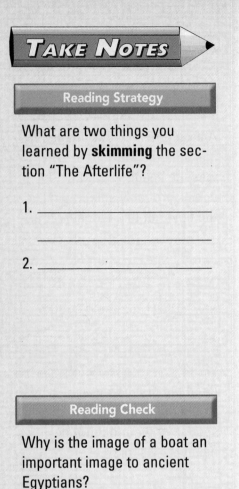

TAKE NOTES

Reading Strategy

What are two things you learned by **skimming** the section "The Afterlife"?

1. _____

_____

2. _____

Reading Check

Why is the image of a boat an important image to ancient Egyptians?

_____

_____

_____

The Afterlife

The boat is a recurring image in Egyptian funerary[5] art. It is a reminder of Egypt's reliance on the Nile River, the country's life giver and major artery. For the Egyptians, the Nile was the center of the world. It was also a metaphor for the soul's journey through the netherworld[6]: sailing in a solar boat, the sun god Re travels through the hours of night to be reborn with each dawn. In imitation of the gods, pharaohs[7] hoped to secure their own immortality. While some rituals seemed to have been reserved exclusively for the pharaohs, the quest was shared by all Egyptians. Scribes and maids, mayors and generals all sought to deny the impermanence of the body. Through the material remains of their endeavors, their names and histories live again—immortality of a sort.

---

5. **funerary** (FYOO nuhr eh ree) *adj.* having to do with a funeral or burial.
6. **netherworld** *n.* the world of the dead.
7. **pharaohs** (FAR ohz) *n.* the title of the kings of ancient Egypt.

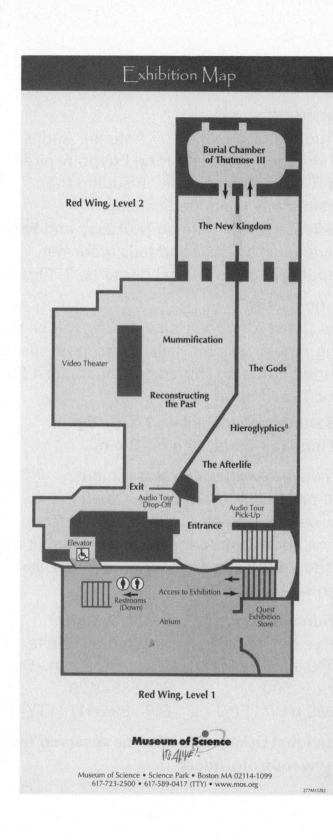

Exhibition Map

Burial Chamber of Thutmose III

Red Wing, Level 2

The New Kingdom

Mummification

Video Theater

The Gods

Reconstructing the Past

Hieroglyphics[8]

The Afterlife

Exit
Audio Tour Drop-Off

Audio Tour Pick-Up

Entrance

Elevator

Restrooms (Down)

Access to Exhibition

Atrium

Quest Exhibition Store

Red Wing, Level 1

Museum of Science
It's Alive!

Museum of Science • Science Park • Boston MA 02114-1099
617-723-2500 • 617-589-0417 (TTY) • www.mos.org

277M11/02

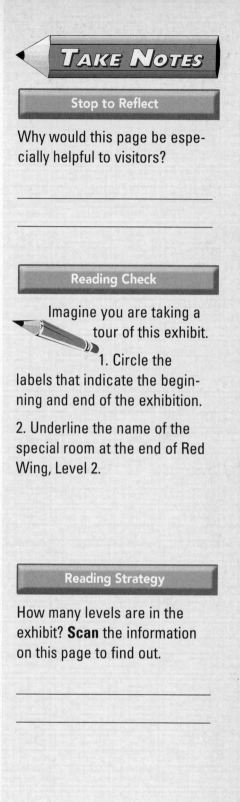

TAKE NOTES

Stop to Reflect

Why would this page be especially helpful to visitors?

_____

_____

Reading Check

Imagine you are taking a tour of this exhibit.

1. Circle the labels that indicate the beginning and end of the exhibition.

2. Underline the name of the special room at the end of Red Wing, Level 2.

Reading Strategy

How many levels are in the exhibit? **Scan** the information on this page to find out.

_____

_____

---

8. hieroglyphics (HY ur oh GLIF iks) *n.* pictures or symbols representing objects, words, or sounds used in writing by ancient Egyptians.

1. By **skimming** this page, what are two facts you can learn about ticketing information and reservations?

1. _____

   _____

2. _____

   _____

2. As you **scan** this page, which heading would you use to find information about the Science Street Café?

_____

EXHIBITION INFORMATION

EXHIBITION AMENITIES[9]

- Audio tour provided by Antenna Audio.
- Exhibition store featuring Egypt-inspired gifts and merchandise, including the beautifully illustrated catalog.
- Science Street Café on Thursday and Friday evenings, offering cocktails, gourmet appetizers, and special desserts, 6–10 p.m.

EXHIBITION HOURS

The Quest for Immortality gallery will be open during regular Exhibit Halls hours, plus special extended hours on Thursday evening, just for adults. Timed ticket entry.

- **Saturday–Wednesday: 9 a.m.–5 p.m.**
- **Thursday–Friday: 9 a.m.–9 p.m.**

TICKETING INFORMATION AND RESERVATIONS

Full-price admission to *The Quest for Immortality* includes a separate ticket for general admission to the Exhibit Halls that may be used on the same day or on another day within six months.

Individual & Group	**Event Options**
Reserve by Phone *(daily 9 a.m.–5 p.m.)* 617-723-2500 617-589-0417 (TTY)	Reserve by Phone *(Mon.–Fri. 9 a.m.–5 p.m.)* 617-589-0125 617-589-0417 (TTY)

Individual tickets may also be reserved online at www.mos.org/quest

---

9. **amenities** (uh MEN uh tees) *n.* agreeable or pleasant features.

WWW.MOS.ORG/QUEST

Find out more about ancient Egypt, explore a 3-D mummy, or learn how to play the ancient game of senet. This site also offers the latest information about *The Quest for Immortality* exhibition and related Museum attractions, tickets, events, lectures, hotel packages, special offers, shopping, visiting tips, and directions.

MUSEUM MEMBERSHIP

Becoming a member is the best way to receive priority treatment for *The Quest for Immortality* and enjoy the Museum all year long. Hold on to your Exhibit Halls ticket vouchers— we will apply a portion of your ticket price toward the cost of any membership level.

For details, visit the Membership Booth or contact us at 617-589-0180, membership@mos.org.

UNITED EXHIBITS GROUP

The Quest for Immortality is organized by the United Exhibits Group™, Denmark, and the National Gallery of Art, Washington, in association with the Supreme Council of Antiquities, Cairo.

Reading Informational Materials

Brochures contain information about hours of operation.

1. At what time does this exhibition open on Tuesdays?

_____

2. At what time does the exhibition close on Fridays?

_____

THINKING ABOUT THE BROCHURE

1. In what ways was the Nile River important to the ancient Egyptians?

   _____

2. Look at the Exhibition Information page. What reason might someone have to visit the Museum of Science Web site?

   _____

   _____

READING STRATEGY

3. What four heads are used in the Exhibition Information section that help you locate information when you **skim**?

   _____

   _____

4. **Scan** the first page of the brochure. What are the dates of the period covered by the exhibition?

   _____

   _____

TIMED WRITING: PERSUASION (20 minutes)

Write a persuasive letter that encourages people to visit *The Quest for Immortality* exhibit.

- Think about how you felt when you read the brochure. Did the brochure spark your interest in certain parts of the exhibit? Explain.

   _____

   _____

- Write a sentence describing the part of the exhibit that sounded the most interesting to you. Use at least two adjectives to make your description more exciting.

   _____

   _____

Use these notes to write your persuasive letter.

from the Rig Veda: Creation Hymn • Night

LITERARY ANALYSIS

A hymn is a poem or song of praise. Hymns from the sacred text of India, the Rig Veda (RIG VAY duh), are called **Vedic** (VAY dik) **hymns.** In Vedic hymns, poets
- focus on the importance of gods in Hindu life.
- wonder about the mysteries of nature.
- ponder timeless questions.

At first Vedic hymns were said aloud. The repetition of words and phrases helped people memorize and recite them. Later the hymns were written. As you read, look for the repetition of words in each hymn.

READING STRATEGY

When you **paraphrase**, you restate information in your own words. Paraphrasing a poem can help you better understand the poem's meaning. Here is an example:

Poet's Words
". . . there was neither the realm of space nor the sky which is beyond. . . ."

Paraphrase
There was no space and no sky.

As you read these two Vedic hymns, use the chart below to restate in your own words what the poets are saying.

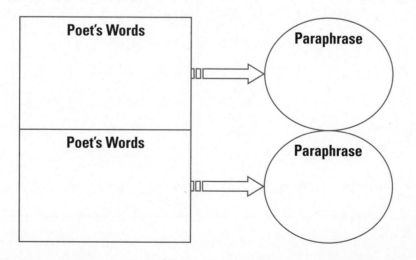

from the Rig Veda
Creation Hymn and Night

Translated by Wendy Doniger

Summary The Rig Veda is the oldest and most important text of the Indian religion of Hinduism. The Rig Veda is made up of 1,028 hymns, or poems, about the forces of nature. The **"Creation Hymn"** explores the mystery of how the universe began. The speaker says that only darkness existed at first. Everything was covered with water. Then, the forces of heat and desire powered life. The gods came with the creation of the universe. The speaker wonders if the universe formed itself or if a higher power created it. The poet of **"Night"** refers to Night as a goddess. Night is strong and deserves praise. In darkness, people and animals return to their homes. The speaker asks Night to protect these living creatures from the dangers of the darkness.

Note-taking Guide

Use the chart below to record information about the two hymns. A beginning note appears for each poem.

Rig Veda: Hymns About the Mysteries of Creation and About the Night	
"Creation Hymn": What the Speaker Says	**"Night": What Happens in the Poem**
Nothing existed then.	The goddess Night approaches and looks around.

from the Rig Veda

Translated by Wendy Doniger

"Creation Hymn"

There was neither non-existence nor existence then; there was neither the realm of space nor the sky which is beyond. What stirred? Where? In whose protection? Was there water, bottomlessly deep?

◆ ◆ ◆

The speaker says that there was no death, and there was no endless life. There was no difference between night and day. One force of life breathed on its own. But other than that, there was nothing.

◆ ◆ ◆

Darkness was hidden by darkness in the beginning, with no <u>distinguishing</u> sign, all this was water. The life force that was covered with emptiness, that one arose through the power of heat.

◆ ◆ ◆

The speaker suggests that the life force was also powered by desire. Poets look for connections between existence and nonexistence when searching for answers about the life force. They look for signs in the sky above and the earth below. The speaker wonders if anyone really knows what the life force was and when it first arose.

◆ ◆ ◆

<u>Whence</u> this creation has arisen—perhaps it formed itself, or perhaps it did not—the one who looks down on it, in the highest heaven, only he knows—or perhaps he does not know.

Vocabulary Development

distinguishing (di STIN gwish ing) *adj.* marking or pointing out as different

whence (WENS) *adv., conj.* from what place or source

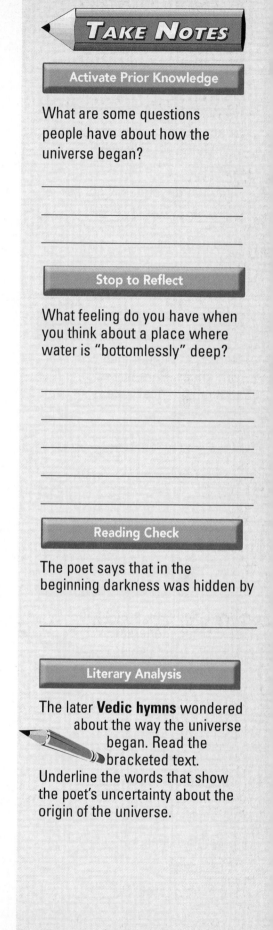

TAKE NOTES

Activate Prior Knowledge

What are some questions people have about how the universe began?

_____

_____

_____

Stop to Reflect

What feeling do you have when you think about a place where water is "bottomlessly" deep?

_____

_____

_____

_____

Reading Check

The poet says that in the beginning darkness was hidden by

_____

Literary Analysis

The later **Vedic hymns** wondered about the way the universe began. Read the bracketed text. Underline the words that show the poet's uncertainty about the origin of the universe.

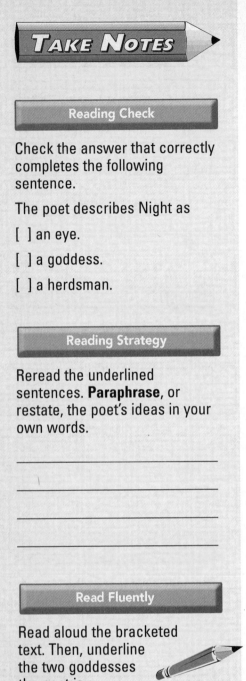

Reading Check

Check the answer that correctly completes the following sentence.

The poet describes Night as

[ ] an eye.

[ ] a goddess.

[ ] a herdsman.

Reading Strategy

Reread the underlined sentences. **Paraphrase**, or restate, the poet's ideas in your own words.

_____

_____

_____

_____

Read Fluently

Read aloud the bracketed text. Then, underline the two goddesses the poet is addressing.

Reading Check

Check the answer that completes the sentence. In the last verse, Night is compared to

[ ] a herdsman.

[ ] a song.

[ ] a conqueror.

"Night"

The goddess Night has drawn near, looking about on many sides with her eyes. She has put on all her glories.

◆ ◆ ◆

The poet describes how Night fills all space with darkness. She pushes aside her sister, the twilight. When darkness comes, all the people and animals go home to rest. The poet asks Night to protect these living creatures from the dangers that hide in the darkness.

◆ ◆ ◆

Darkness—palpable[1] black, and painted— has come upon me. O Dawn, <u>banish</u> it like a <u>debt</u>.
I have driven this hymn to you as the herdsman drives cows. Choose and accept it, O Night, daughter of the sky, like a song of praise to a conqueror.

Vocabulary Development

banish (BA nish) _v._ to drive away; get rid of

debt (DET) _n._ something owed by one person to another

---

1. **palpable** (PAL puh BUHL) _adj._ easily felt; touchable.

from the Rig Veda: Creation Hymn • Night

1. **Interpret:** "Creation Hymn" explores how the universe began. What conclusion, if any, does the hymn reach with regard to this question?

_____

_____

2. **Literary Analysis:** A **Vedic hymn** is an ancient Indian poem originally recited aloud. That is why such a hymn has repetitions. In "Creation Hymn," find one example of a repeated word and one example of a repeated group of words. Write your answers in the chart below.

Device	Example
Repeated Word	
Repeated Group of Words	

3. **Reading Strategy:** Reread the seventh verse of "Creation Hymn." Then, paraphrase the verse.

_____

_____

_____

4. **Reading Strategy:** Paraphrase the eighth verse of "Night."

_____

_____

_____

Writing: Comparison-and-Contrast Essay

Write a **comparison-and-contrast** essay explaining what is similar and different in the ways these two hymns approach nature.

Review the hymns. Focus on the way each one approaches nature. Record what you find on the lines below.

"Creation Hymn"

_____

_____

"Night"

_____

_____

Use your notes as you draft your essay.

Listening and Speaking: Oral Interpretation

With a small group, give an **oral interpretation** of one of the hymns—a recitation that emphasizes the hymn's meaning and emotions. Begin by answering these questions:

- What ideas are expressed in the hymn?

_____

_____

- Which words or phrases would you emphasize to capture the ideas and mood?

_____

_____

Identify words that are hard to pronounce, look them up in a dictionary, and write them in a way that helps you say them correctly.

_____

_____

Have each member of the group use his or her notes to practice reading a verse aloud. Then, perform your reading for the class.

from the Mahabharata • from the Bhagavad-Gita • from the Ramayana

LITERARY ANALYSIS

An **Indian epic** is a long story, often told as a poem, about the actions and adventures of an Indian hero. An **epic hero** is the central figure of an epic. The hero is
- brave
- loyal
- unusually strong

This larger-than-life hero usually faces a challenge. He must do something of great value for his society. Use this chart to compare the epic heroes in these readings.

Epic Hero	Heroic Traits
Sibi	
Arjuna	
Rama	

READING STRATEGY

Pay close attention to the ideas in these selections. These ideas will help you to **infer beliefs of the period** in which these selections were created. For example, Sri Krishna discusses the Atman in the *Bhagavad-Gita* (BUHG uh vehd GEE tah). This discussion shows that Hindus believed that the Atman was an eternal, unchanging, and universal soul. Look for words and actions as you read that tell about the values and beliefs of ancient India.

from the Mahabharata •
from the Bhagavad-Gita •
from the Ramayana

Retold by R.K. Narayan
Translated by
Swami Prabhavananda and
Christopher Isherwood

Summaries In the story "**Sibi**" from the *Mahabharata* (muh HAH BAH ruh tuh), Sibi is a king who protects a dove from a hawk. The hawk wants the dove as food for his family, but the king refuses to hand over an animal that seeks his protection. Instead, Sibi offers his own flesh to the hawk. The large amount of flesh needed to satisfy the hawk endangers Sibi's life.

In "**The Yoga of Knowledge**" from the *Bhagavad-Gita*, Arjuna, a soldier, does not want to fight in a battle. He does not want to kill his cousins and uncles, who are fighting on the other side. Sri Krishna tells Arjuna that it is his duty to fight.

In "**Rama and Ravana in Battle**" from the *Ramayana* (rah MAH yuh nuh), Prince Rama fights the evil giant Ravana in order to free his wife. The gods help Rama by giving him special gifts.

Note-taking Guide

Each of these stories contains a message about living an honorable life. Record the message of each story in the chart below.

	"Sibi"	"The Yoga of Knowledge"	"Rama and Ravana in Battle"
Message			

from the Mahabharata • from the Bhagavad-Gita • from the Ramayana

1. **Apply:** In the *Bhagavad-Gita*, Krishna advises Arjuna. What advice might Krishna give to people in modern society who believe that wealth is the measure of success?

_____

_____

2. **Literary Analysis:** In each of these **Indian epics**, the gods assist the hero. What message do you think this fact conveys?

_____

_____

_____

3. **Literary Analysis:** In what ways does each selection demonstrate the traits of an **epic hero**?

_____

_____

_____

4. **Reading Strategy:** Use the chart below to **infer beliefs** of ancient Indian culture. Give a detail from each epic. Describe the ancient Indian belief that the detail suggests. One detail is provided for you.

Epic	Detail	Belief Suggested
Mahabharata	Sibi protects the dove.	

Writing: Editorial

Write an **editorial** that applies an ancient Indian idea, like *dharma*, to a modern issue. *Dharma* means performing one's obligations to keep harmony in the universe. An example of *dharma* is a politician who tells the truth, even though it may cause him to lose the next election. Persuasively argue your point of view.

Write down other modern situations to which this Indian concept might apply.

_____

_____

Choose a situation to write about. Then, jot down ideas about how the Indian concept applies to the situation.

_____

_____

_____

Draft and revise your editorial.

Research and Technology: Oral Presentation

Use the Internet and library resources to prepare an **oral presentation** about the influence of Indian ideas on Dr. Martin Luther King Jr., and the civil rights movement in the United States. Focus your research by answering these questions:

- In what ways did the writings and actions of the Indian leader Mohandas K. Gandhi reflect Indian ideas?

_____

_____

- How was Dr. King influenced by Gandhi?

_____

_____

BUILD SKILLS

from the Panchatantra: "Numskull and the Rabbit"

LITERARY ANALYSIS

An **Indian fable** is a short, simple tale that teaches a lesson about conduct. This lesson is called a **moral**. Indian fables often feature animal characters that behave like humans. The rabbit in this fable from the *Panchatantra* (PUHN chuh TUHN truh) is a type of character well known in folklore, the **trickster**. This character outsmarts characters who have greater physical strength.

As you read the fable, use the chart below to record the main situation or problem the characters face and the outcome of the situation. Then, note the moral that the fable teaches. The characters already appear in the chart.

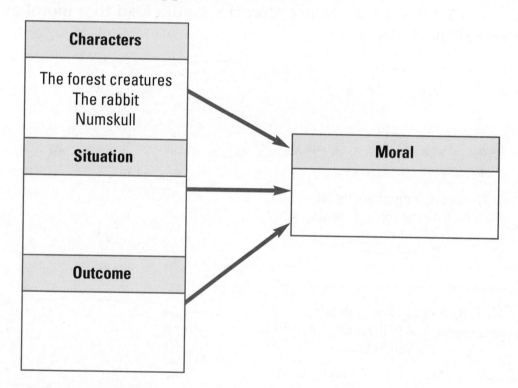

Characters

The forest creatures
The rabbit
Numskull

Situation

Outcome

Moral

READING STRATEGY

When you read something that you do not understand, **reread to clarify** any parts that you find confusing. For example, you might want to review details about the setting or a key event. Also, remember to review footnotes for important information.

from the Panchatantra

Translated by Arthur W. Ryder

Summary "Numskull and the Rabbit" tells the story of a cruel lion king named Numskull and a clever rabbit. All the animals of the forest come up with a plan to stop Numskull from killing them. They agree that each day one of them will go to the lion to be eaten. When it is the rabbit's turn, he plans to outsmart Numskull.

Note-taking Guide

In the diagram below, record the main events of the fable. The first event is filled in for you. Notice that the events lead to a moral at the end of the fable.

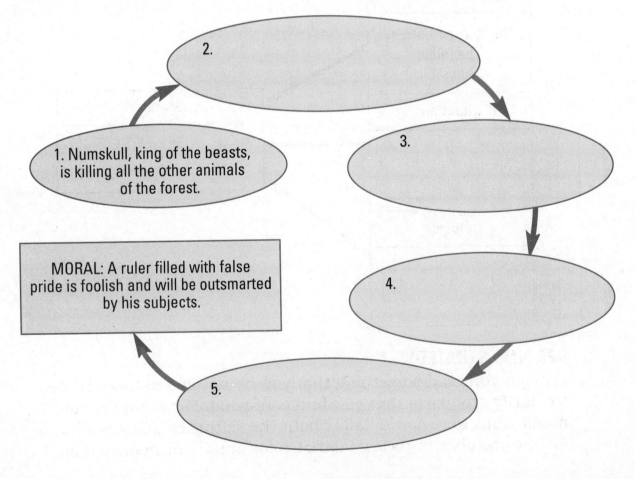

2.

1. Numskull, king of the beasts, is killing all the other animals of the forest.

3.

MORAL: A ruler filled with false pride is foolish and will be outsmarted by his subjects.

4.

5.

from the Panchatantra
"Numskull and the Rabbit"
Translated by Arthur W. Ryder

A lion king named Numskull lived in a forest. He was filled with foolish pride. Numskull constantly killed the other animals. One day all the other animals— deer, boars, buffaloes, wild oxen, rabbits, and others—got together, and begged the lion king to stop the killing. They suggested a deal. If Numskull will stop the slaughter, they will send him one animal each day to be eaten. They quoted a proverb that says:

◆　◆　◆

The king who tastes his kingdom like Elixir,
*　bit by bit,*
Who does not overtax its life,
*　Will fully relish it.*

The king who madly butchers men,
*　Their lives as little reckoned*
As lives of goats, has one square meal,
*　But never has a second.*

◆　◆　◆

After listening to them, Numskull agreed to the deal. However, he threatened to eat them all if one animal did not come each day to be eaten.

◆　◆　◆

One day a rabbit's turn came, it being rabbit-day. And when all the thronging animals had given him directions, he reflected: "How is it possible to kill this lion—curse him! Yet after all,

---

Vocabulary Development

elixir (ee LIKS ir) *n.* a magical potion that cures all illnesses

---

Reading Strategy

When you **reread for clarification**, you improve your understanding. Reread the bracketed text. What do the animals warn the lion not to do to them?

_____

_____

Literary Analysis

In an **Indian fable**, the characters are often animals that act like humans. In this part of the fable, what animal is introduced?

_____

What human characteristics does this animal have?

_____

_____

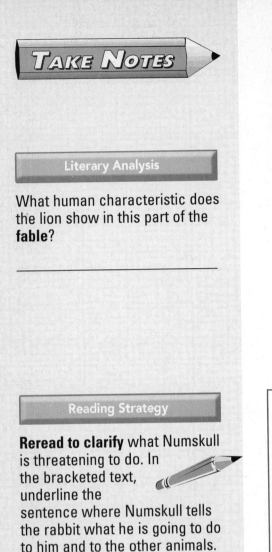

Literary Analysis

What human characteristic does the lion show in this part of the **fable**?

_____

Reading Strategy

Reread to clarify what Numskull is threatening to do. In the bracketed text, underline the sentence where Numskull tells the rabbit what he is going to do to him and to the other animals.

Stop to Reflect

Think about the deal Numskull and the animals made. Why do you think Numskull agreed to the deal?

_____

_____

_____

In what can widsom not <u>prevail</u>?
In what can resolution fail?
What cannot flattery subdue?
What cannot enterprise put through?
    I can kill even a lion."
So he went very slowly, planning to arrive <u>tardily</u>, and meditating with troubled spirit on a means of killing him.

◆ ◆ ◆

Finally the rabbit reached the place where Numskull was waiting. Numskull was thinking about how hungry he was. He was also angry that the rabbit was late and decided he would kill all the animals the next morning

◆ ◆ ◆

While he was thinking, the rabbit slowly drew near, bowed low, and stood before him. But when the lion saw that he was tardy and too small at that for a meal, his soul flamed with wrath, and he <u>taunted</u> the rabbit, saying: "You <u>reprobate</u>! First, you are too small for a meal. Second, you are tardy. Because of this wickedness I am going to kill you, and tomorrow morning I shall extirpate[1] every species of animal."

◆ ◆ ◆

Vocabulary Development

prevail (pree VAYL) _v._ win out; gain control
tardily (TAR dih lee) _adv._ late
taunted (TAWN ted) _v._ made fun of
reprobate (REP ruh BAYT) _n._ a wicked or dishonest person; scoundrel

---

1. extirpate (EX tur payt) _v._ root out, destroy.

The rabbit made up a story about how he had met another great lion. The rabbit claimed that the other lion lived in a mighty fortress and that this lion was Numskull's enemy. He implied that Numskull should fight the other lion, even though this lion was hiding in a strong fortress.

◆　◆　◆

When he heard this, Numskull said: "My good fellow, show me that thief. Even if he is hiding in a fortress, I will kill him. For the proverb says:

<u>The strongest man who fails to crush
　At birth, disease or foe,
Will later be destroyed by that
　Which he permits to grow.</u>"

◆　◆　◆

The rabbit continued his invented story. He taunted Numskull by telling him how powerful the other lion was in his fortress. Numskull demanded that the rabbit take him to the fortress, and the rabbit agreed. He took Numskull to a deep well, claiming that the other lion had crawled into it in fear.

◆　◆　◆

And the lion, being a dreadful fool, saw his own reflection in the water, and gave voice to a great roar. Then from the well issued a roar twice as loud, because of the echo. This the lion heard, decided that his <u>rival</u> was very powerful, hurled himself down, and met his death. Thereupon the rabbit cheerfully carried the glad news to all the animals, received their compliments, and lived there contentedly in the forest.

Vocabulary Development

rival (RY vuhl) *n.* one who tries to outdo another; competitor

Take Notes

Reading Check

Read the underlined proverb. Check the statement that summarizes its meaning.

[ ] Destroy your enemy before your enemy destroys you.

[ ] Strong men must fight against diseases.

Read Fluently

Read the underlined proverb aloud. Use a tone of voice that Numskull would use here.

Reading Strategy

Reread the bracketed text **to clarify** your understanding. Underline the words that tell why Numskull heard a roar twice as loud as his own, coming from the well.

Literary Analysis

How does the end of this **fable** show Numskull's foolishness?

_____

_____

_____

_____

from the Panchatantra: "Numskull and the Rabbit"

1. **Draw Conclusions:** What does the rabbit's trick suggest about who is the lion's greatest enemy?

_____

_____

2. **Literary Analysis:** What does this **Indian fable** suggest about the qualities that ancient Indians admired in their rulers? Support your answer.

_____

_____

_____

3. **Literary Analysis:** Which actions of the characters support the fable's **moral(s)?**

_____

_____

4. **Literary Analysis:** Which actions of the rabbit show he is a **trickster**?

_____

_____

5. **Reading Strategy:** Complete the chart below. **Reread** to identify the earliest details in the story that **clarify**, or reveal, that trait listed for each character.

Character	Character Trait	Clarifying Details
Numskull	cruelty	
Rabbit	cleverness	

SUPPORT FOR WRITING AND EXTEND YOUR LEARNING

Writing: Animal Fable

Write a brief **fable** of your own that uses animal characters to teach a lesson about human behavior.

1. Write a moral that you want to teach.
Example: Do not listen to people who flatter you.

2. Pick two opposite human characteristics that your animal characters will show, such as wisdom and foolishness. Pick an animal to go with each trait.
Trait: Animal:
Trait: Animal

Use these notes as you write your fable.

Listening and Speaking: Retelling

Imagine that you are Vishnusharman telling the fable to the sons of the king. Answer these questions to help in your **retelling**.

• How would each character speak?

_____

_____

_____

• Where would you speak more intensely to emphasize the drama?

_____

_____

_____

• What gestures could you use to add interest to your telling?

_____

_____

_____

Use these notes when preparing your retelling.

ATLASES AND MAPS

About Atlases and Maps

An **atlas** is a book of maps that show physical information about the world. Some atlases also include facts and statistics about the places depicted. For example, the following atlas pages give additional information about the climate, geography, economy, and people of India.

The general purpose of a **map** is to present geographical information in a graphic form. Most maps include these features:

- *legend* or *key*: explains the symbols on a map
- *scale*: shows the ratio between distances on the map and actual distances on Earth
- *compass rose*: shows directions (north, south, east, west)

Reading Strategy

Atlases and maps use visuals and text to provide information. To **locate the information** you need, follow these steps:

1. Decide what category of information you need. Keep in mind that an atlas or a map provides basic facts, not a detailed background.
2. Use the heads on the atlas pages, the titles of the maps, and the map legend or scale to locate the information.

As you look at the atlas page about India, use this graphic organizer to record the information that you find.

Kind of Information	Location	Information Given
Population	Fact File box	953 million

INDIA

Separated from the rest of Asia by the Himalayan mountain range, India forms a subcontinent. It is the world's second most populous country.

GEOGRAPHY

Three main regions: Himalayan Mountains; northern plain between Himalayas and Vindhya Mountains; southern Deccan plateau. The Ghats are smaller mountain ranges on the east and west coasts.

CLIMATE

Varies greatly according to latitude, altitude, and season. Most of India has three seasons: hot, wet, and cool. In summer, the north is usually hotter than the south, with temperatures often over 104°F (40°C).

PEOPLE AND SOCIETY

Cultural and religious pressures encourage large families. Today, nationwide awareness campaigns aim to promote the idea of smaller families. Most Indians are Hindu. Each Hindu is born into one of thousands of castes and subcasts, which determine their future status and occupation. Middle class enjoys a very comfortable lifestyle, but at least 30% of Indians live in extreme poverty. In Bombay alone, over 100,000 people live on the streets.

THE ECONOMY

Undergoing radical changes from protectionist mixed economy to free market. Increasing foreign investment. New high-tech industries. Principal exports are clothing, jewelry, gems, and engineering products.

◆ INSIGHT *India's national animal, the tiger, was chosen by the Mohenjo-Daro civilization as its emblem, 4,000 years ago*

FACT FILE
OFFICIAL NAME: Republic of India
DATE OF FORMATION: 1947 / 1961
CAPITAL: New Delhi
POPULATION: 953 million
TOTAL AREA: 1,269,338 sq miles
(3,287,590 sq km)
DENSITY: 751 people per sq mile

LANGUAGES: Hindi, English, other
RELIGIONS: Hindu 83%, Muslim 11%, Christian 2%, Sikh 2%, other 2%
ETHNIC MIX: Indo-Aryan 72%, Dravidian 25%, Mongoloid and other 3%
GOVERNMENT: Multiparty republic
CURRENCY: Rupee = 100 paisa

Clearly marked sections of the atlas entry provide important information.

Essential information about India is set off in a separate box.

TAKE NOTES

Reading Strategy

Use the small locator map on the atlas page below the title to **locate information**. Name one country that borders India.

_____

Reading Check

What are the three seasons in most of India?

1. _____

2. _____

3. _____

Read Fluently

Read the sentences next to the map on page 70. What three details do you learn about India?

_____

_____

_____

Stop to Reflect

What is one problem India faces due to its large population?

_____

_____

_____

Reading Strategy

Use the map in this atlas to **locate information**. With what symbol are airports in India shown?

_____

Circle each airport on the map.

Reading Strategy

Using the *scale* on the **map**, what is the distance between Chennai (Madras) and Mumbai (Bombay)?

_____

What is the distance between New Delhi and Kota?

_____

Reading Strategy

Atlases and maps use text and visuals to provide information. Which types of information would you expect to locate by using the maps in an atlas?

[ ] information about the geography of each country

[ ] information about the political leader of each country

[ ] information about the history of each country

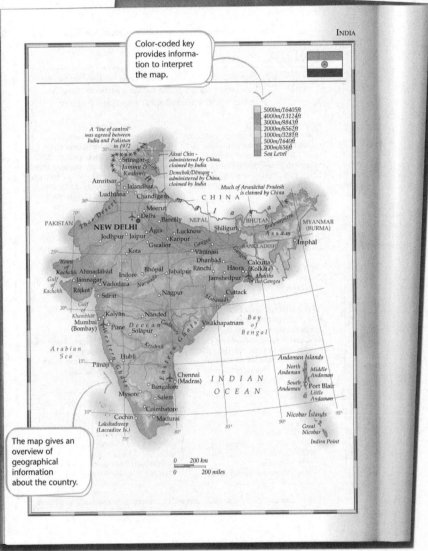

Color-coded key provides information to interpret the map.

The map gives an overview of geographical information about the country.

THINKING ABOUT ATLASES AND MAPS

1. Which part of the atlas and map pages shows you the location of India's capital?

_____

_____

2. Which part of the atlas and map pages provides the most accurate way to determine the total area of India?

_____

_____

Reading Strategy: Locating Information Using Atlases and Maps

3. Approximately how far is New Delhi from Bombay?

_____

_____

4. Reread the "Economy" section of the atlas page. Name two ways in which India's economy is changing.

_____

_____

_____

TIMED WRITING: EXPLANATION

Use the information in the atlas and the map to write a letter to a friend. Explain why you have decided to visit India.

• What features and regions of India interest you?

_____

_____

• When do you want to visit India? Why?

_____

_____

_____

_____

• What topics would you like to explore during your visit?

_____

_____

Use your notes to write your letter.

from the Tao Te Ching • *from* The Analects

LITERARY ANALYSIS

Aphorisms are short sayings that offer general truths. Here are two famous aphorisms:

- "A penny saved is a penny earned." (Benjamin Franklin)
- "Look before you leap." (John Heywood)

The *Tao Te Ching* and *The Analects* are collections of aphorisms that offer truths about how to live life. They do not offer complete explanations. Instead, these aphorisms give hints of truth that allow readers to draw conclusions based on their own experiences.

READING STRATEGY

These selections teach lessons by showing causes and effects. For example, Lao Tzu tells rulers, "Do that which consists in taking no action, and order will prevail." However, Lao Tzu does not fully explain why this statement is true. When you **question causes and effects,** you look at the author's message more fully.

In the chart below, Lao Tzu's aphorism is separated into cause and effect and put into plain words. In the final column is an explanation of why the statement is true. Use a chart like this one to understand the aphorisms in the two selections.

Aphorism	Cause	Effect	Why is this true?
"Do that which consists in taking no action, and order will prevail."	Doing nothing ➡	keeps things in order.	A ruler should keep people from turning against the government. To do this he does not have to do anything except keep them happy.
"To demand much from oneself and little from others is the way (for a ruler) to banish discontent."		➡ gets rid of unhappiness.	

from the Tao Te Ching

Lao Tzu

Translated by D.C. Lau

Summary "Part I" describes the need to understand and balance opposing ideas. To do this, a person must have desires and get rid of desires at the same time. In this way, the person will understand the forces that control the universe. "Part III" tells rulers to take no action in certain matters in order to keep their people at peace. These matters include not calling attention to certain people and not showing off rare and valuable things. By taking no action, and by feeding his people, the ruler prevents fighting and theft. "Part IX" discusses the importance of knowing when to stop. It uses images, such as filling a container with water and sharpening a knife point, to explain this advice. "Part XLIII" explains that doing nothing can help weak people overcome a difficult situation. However, few people understand this idea.

Note-taking Guide

Use the chart below to record the main ideas presented in each section of the *Tao Te Ching*.

Part I	Part III	Part IX	Part XLIII

from The Analects

Confucius

Translated by Arthur Waley

Summary Confucius was a Chinese philosopher who lived in the fifth century B.C. In all his writings, Confucius stresses the importance of living a moral life. He urges ordinary citizens to respect authority figures, such as parents and political leaders. In a time of trouble in China, he teaches leaders that they must rule kindly and wisely in order to gain the respect of their people. Confucius says rulers should demand much from themselves and little from others. This will help keep their people peaceful and happy.

Note-taking Guide

Use the graphic organizer below to record the main ideas of Confucius' teachings.

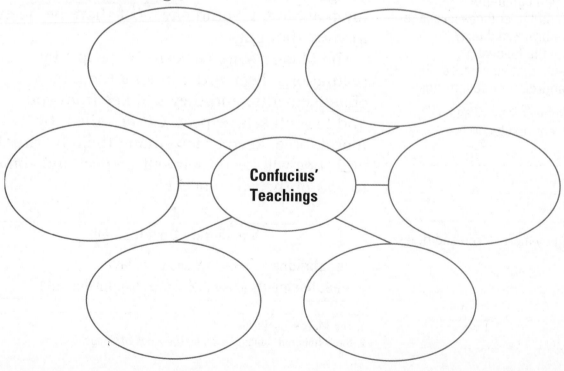

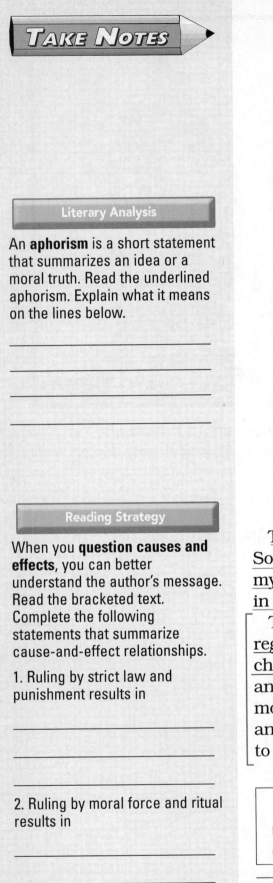

TAKE NOTES

Literary Analysis

An **aphorism** is a short statement that summarizes an idea or a moral truth. Read the underlined aphorism. Explain what it means on the lines below.

_____

_____

_____

_____

Reading Strategy

When you **question causes and effects**, you can better understand the author's message. Read the bracketed text. Complete the following statements that summarize cause-and-effect relationships.

1. Ruling by strict law and punishment results in

_____

_____

_____

2. Ruling by moral force and ritual results in

_____

_____

_____

from The Analects

Confucius
Translated by Arthur Waley

Confucius begins with the following advice: Take pleasure in learning. Stay in touch with distant friends. Do not look for compliments.

He then directs these words of wisdom to young people: Obey your parents and elders. Do not make too many promises, and be sure to keep all the promises you do make. Think good thoughts about everyone. Study good manners.

Confucius points out that good people do not become unhappy if their good deeds go unnoticed. Rather, unhappiness comes from not noticing the good deeds of others. He urges leaders to show good moral values in order to gain the respect of their subjects.

◆ ◆ ◆

The Master[1] said, If out of three hundred Songs[2] I had to take one phrase to cover all my teaching, I would say, "Let there be no evil in your thoughts."

The Master said, Govern the people by regulations, keep order among them by chastisements, and they will flee from you, and lose all self-respect. Govern them by moral force, keep order among them by ritual, and they will keep their self-respect and come to you of their own accord.

◆ ◆ ◆

Vocabulary Development

regulations (reg yoo LAY shuns) *n.* laws
chastisements (chas TYZ mentz) *n.* punishments

---

1. **The Master** Confucius.
2. **three hundred Songs** poems in *The Book of Songs*.

Confucius goes on to say that young people should behave with virtue so that their parents do not need to worry about them. He points out that good people consider all aspects of a question, not just the aspect that directly affects them. Finally, he defines knowledge as recognizing what you don't know as well as what you do know.

Confucius states that the most painful things to see are narrow-minded rulers, insincerity, and fake tears. He urges everyone to behave like the good people that they know and to ignore the bad behaviors of others. He advises us to avoid saying things that we do not mean and to be true to our word. Confucius says to study in order to learn something, not to impress other people.

◆　◆　◆

The Master said, A gentleman is ashamed to let his words outrun his deeds.

The Master said, He who will not worry about what is far off will soon find something worse than worry close at hand.

The Master said, To demand much from oneself and little from others is the way (for a ruler) to banish discontent.

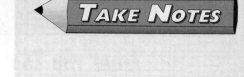
Read Fluently

Read aloud the underlined text. On the lines below, explain this aphorism in your own words.

_____

_____

_____

Reading Strategy

Reread the bracketed text. Circle the **cause** and underline the **effect**.

Why do you think Confucius believes that not worrying about the future will lead to something worse than worry?

_____

_____

_____

Reading Check

According to Confucius, why should a person want to study?

_____

_____

_____

from the Tao Te Ching • *from* The Analects

1. **Compare and Contrast:** Both Lao Tzu and Confucius tell rulers what they should do. Use the Venn diagram below to compare and contrast their advice. When you are pointing out how Lao Tzu and Confucius are different, write their points in each circle. In the area in the middle, write the points on which they agree.

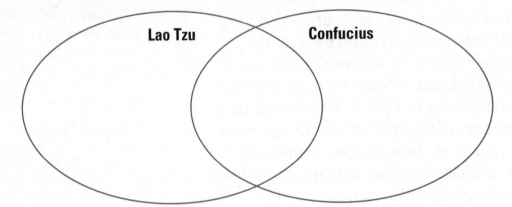

Lao Tzu   Confucius

2. **Literary Analysis:** The last **aphorism** of the *Tao Te Ching* says that a ruler makes people happy by demanding a lot from himself and not much from others. Is this statement true for people other than rulers? Why or why not?

_____

_____

3. **Reading Strategy:** According to Confucius, a person who does not worry about far off things will soon find something "worse than worry close at hand." Is this **cause-and-effect relationship** true? Explain.

_____

_____

4. **Reading Strategy:** In one aphorism, Confucius asks leaders to rule by "moral force." What does he believe will be the effect of a ruler living life by a high moral standard?

_____

_____

SUPPORT FOR WRITING AND EXTEND YOUR LEARNING

Writing: Critical Comparison

Before writing, use the following tips to help you compare and contrast the major ideas of the *Tao Te Ching and The Analects*:

- Reread section III and section XLIII from the *Tao Te Ching*. What does Taoism say is the best way to achieve peace and order?

  _____

  _____

- Skim *The Analects* for suggestions about how to live. What does Confucianism say is the best way to achieve peace and order?

  _____

  _____

- Think about things that are common to both Taoism and Confucianism. Write down two ideas that both philosophies share.

  _____

  _____

Research and Technology: Research Presentation

Use these tips to help find information for your **presentation.**

- Search for the words "Chinese government" or "Chinese dynasties" in a library database or card catalog. List two books that you find.

  _____

  _____

- Look in the indexes of the books for the word "Confucianism." Write down the titles of chapters with information about Confucianism.

  _____

- Search for the words "Chinese government" and "Confucianism" on the Internet. Write down two Web sites you find.

  _____

Take notes on the resources that you find. Use your notes to organize a research presentation explaining the influence of Confucianism.

from The Book of Songs

LITERARY ANALYSIS

Like western literature, Chinese literature has **poetic forms**.

- *Shih* (SHEE) **poems** are poems that have an even number of lines. Each line has the same number of words. Old style *shih* poems can be of any length. The new style has strict rules about length and form.

- **Songs** are poems that were originally set to music and have strong, regular rhythms. Songs may also include **refrains**. These are words or phrases repeated at regular periods. If one or two words within a refrain are different in two stanzas in a row, this is called **incremental variation**.

- **Ballads** are songs that tell stories.

Each speaker in these poems has a unique **tone**, or attitude, toward his or her subject. Tone comes through in the speaker's **diction**, or word choice. Copy the chart shown and use it to record examples of diction from each of the poems. Then, describe the speaker's tone in the poem.

Poem	Diction	Speaker's Tone
"Addressed Humorously to Tu Fu"	"You must have been suffering from poetry again."	playful, ironic
"Jade Flower Palace"		

READING STRATEGY

When you **respond** to a poem, you think about the poet's message and how that message relates to your own life. As you read these poems, take time to respond to them. Think about the emotions you feel and the pictures each work creates in your imagination

from The Book of Songs
Translated by Arthur Waley

Summaries The speaker in **"I Beg of You, Chung Tzu"** (CHUNG DZOO) worries about how others will feel about her love. The speaker in **"Thick Grow the Rush Leaves"** must overcome obstacles for her loved one. The speaker in **"Form, Shadow, Spirit"** thinks about the meaning of death. The speaker of **"I Built My House Near Where Others Dwell"** sees the beauty of nature. A wife describes her love for her husband in **"The River-Merchant's Wife: A Letter."** In **"Addressed Humorously to Tu Fu"** the speaker blames Tu Fu's thinness on poetry. **"Jade Flower Palace"** shares the speaker's feelings about power. In **"Sent to Li Po as a Gift,"** Tu Fu questions Li Po's wild lifestyle.

Note-taking Guide

Record the subject and the speaker's feelings in each poem.

Poem	Subject	Speaker's Feelings
"I Beg of You, Chung Tzu"		
"Thick Grow the Rush Leaves"		
"Form, Shadow, Spirit"		
"I Built My House Near Where Others Dwell"		
"The River-Merchant's Wife: A Letter"		
"Addressed Humorously to Tu Fu"		
"Jade Flower Palace"		
"Sent to Li Po as a Gift"		

from The Book of Songs

1. **Connect:** In "I Built My House Near Where Others Dwell" the speaker shows a deep love for nature. What lines from "Form, Shadow, Spirit" show similar feelings?

   _____

   _____

2. **Literary Analysis:** Identify a **refrain** in the **song** "I Beg You, Chung Tzu."

   _____

3. **Literary Analysis:** Identify a refrain with **incremental variation** in "Thick Grow the Rush Leaves."

   _____

   _____

4. **Literary Analysis:** The speaker's **tone** in "Thick Grow the Rush Leaves" is one of love and celebration. Which words and phrases express this tone?

   _____

   _____

   _____

5. **Reading Strategy:** Use the chart below to write down your **response** to each stanza of "The River-Merchant's Wife: A Letter," as well as to the poem as a whole. Jot down words and phrases that describe how each stanza makes you feel.

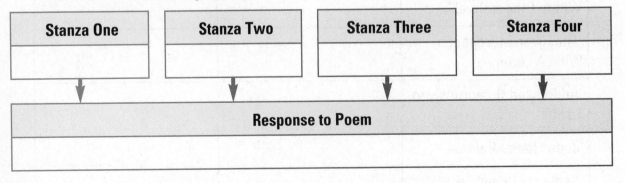

Stanza One	Stanza Two	Stanza Three	Stanza Four

Response to Poem

SUPPORT FOR WRITING AND EXTEND YOUR LEARNING

Writing: Response to Criticism

Use the chart to list details from the poems. The details you list will help you decide whether or not you agree with Giles's comment about what poems say and what they suggest. For each poem, note passages that "say" something directly. Then, note passages in which an idea is only suggested. Use these notes in your essay.

Poem	Passage that states something	Passage that suggests something
"I Beg of You, Chung Tzu"		
"Thick Grow the Rush Leaves"		
"Form, Shadow, Spirit"		
"I Built My House Near Where Others Dwell"		
"The River Merchant's Wife: A Letter"		
"Addressed Humorously to Tu Fu"		
"Jade Flower Palace"		
"Sent to Li Po"		

Listening and Speaking: Oral Report

Choose a poet to research for an **oral report.** As you do your research, write down information about the following:

1. the time and place in which the poet lived

_____

2. the poet's childhood

_____

3. the poet's family

_____

Tanka • Haiku

LITERARY ANALYSIS

The **tanka** is the most popular form of Japanese poetry. Each tanka has only five lines. The lines have five, seven, five, seven, and seven syllables. Most tanka also have a pause called a **caesura** (si ZHYOOR uh). Some tanka tell very short stories. Others tell of a single idea, often about love or nature.

A **haiku** (hy KOO) is a type of poem that is even shorter than a tanka. Haiku have three lines of five, seven, and five syllables. Most haiku tell about nature. They often include a word that lets readers know the time of year the poem describes. This word is called a *kigo*.

Imagery is words and phrases that relate to the senses of sight, touch, hearing, taste, and smell. Most tanka and haiku present two images that are very different. In this haiku by Bashō [bah SHOH], "summer grasses" differ from "soldiers' visions":

Summer grasses—
All that remains
Of soldiers' visions.

READING STRATEGY

You can understand tanka and haiku better if you **picture the imagery**. Try to see, feel, hear, smell, or taste what the poet describes. For example, the image of "summer grasses" makes readers see a green field, feel warm air, and smell grass. Use the chart below to list images from each poem. Write down the feelings and thoughts each image gives you. Notice differences in these feelings and thoughts. Write the differences in the last column.

Image	Feelings	Differences

Tanka • Haiku

Summaries These three tanka are about love, dreams, and feelings. "When I Went to Visit" is about the speaker's visit to his love on a winter night. "Was It That I Went to Sleep" describes a dream the speaker has about a loved one. The speaker of "One Cannot Ask Loneliness" thinks about where loneliness comes from.

The haiku are about connections between people and nature.

Note-taking Guide

Use this chart to write down the main action in each poem.

Poem	Main Action/Event
"When I went to visit…"	
"Was it that I went to sleep…"	
"One cannot ask loneliness…"	
"The sun's way…"	
"Clouds come from time to time…"	
"The cuckoo—"	
"Seven sights were veiled…"	
"Summer grasses…"	
"Spring rain…"	
"Beautiful, seen through holes…"	
"Far-off mountain peaks…"	
"A world of dew…"	
"With bland serenity…"	

Tanka • Haiku

1. **Infer:** The place described in "When I Went to Visit" is very cold. The speaker travels through the winter night anyway. What does this say about the speaker's love for the girl? Explain.

   _____

   _____

2. **Literary Analysis:** What story is told in the **tanka** "When I Went to Visit"?

   _____

   _____

3. **Literary Analysis:** Write down the _kigo_ that appear in two of the **haiku**.

   _____

4. **Literary Analysis:** Use the chart below to write down **images** from the tanka "When I Went to Visit" and the haiku "The Sun's Way." Write images from the tanka in the left circle. Write images from the haiku in the right circle. Write down elements that both poems share in the middle section.

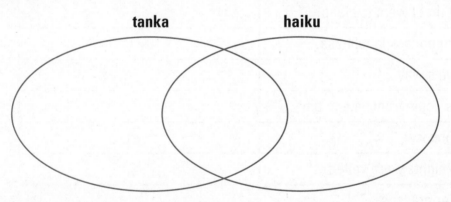

5. **Reading Strategy:** Which words help you to **picture the imagery** in the four haiku by Yosa Buson? Explain.

   _____

   _____

SUPPORT FOR WRITING AND EXTEND YOUR LEARNING

Writing: Short Story

Use your imagination to add details to the world of one tanka or haiku from this collection. Then, use those details to write a **short story** based on the poem. Use these tips to get started:

- Choose a poem you like from this collection.

_____

- Choose a setting (place and time) for your story.

_____

- What characters appear in the poem you chose? If your poem has few or no characters, describe one or two people you think would fit in the poem's setting.

_____

_____

- What problem does the poem make you think about? Write down ideas about how your characters might handle that problem.

_____

_____

Listening and Speaking: Poetry Reading

Hold a **poetry reading** of haiku with a small group of classmates. Follow these steps to get started:

- Search in a library card catalog for poetry books. Write the name of one book that includes haiku.

_____

- Choose two haiku to share. Write their titles and authors here.

_____

- Choose a piece of music that matches each haiku's mood. Select one haiku and explain which piece of music you chose and why.

_____

_____

from The Pillow Book

LITERARY ANALYSIS

A **journal** is a personal record of daily thoughts and experiences. Journals from the past help us understand a particular time period and culture. Journals can also reveal an author's personality. For example, we learn from journals that Sei Shōnagon (SAY SHOH NAH GOHN), the author of *Pillow Book* was emotionally sensitive. The passage below from "The Cat Who Lived in the Palace" shows a sensitive part of her personality.

> ". . . it strikes me as a strange and moving scene; when people talk to me about it, I start crying myself."

As you read the selections from *The Pillow Book*, think about how the details reveal Japanese culture in the 10th century and the author's personality.

The Pillow Book contains many **anecdotes.** Anecdotes are short accounts of funny or interesting events. Anecdotes are used to entertain readers and to explain something the writer learned. In the chart, note insights you learn from Shōnagon's anecdotes.

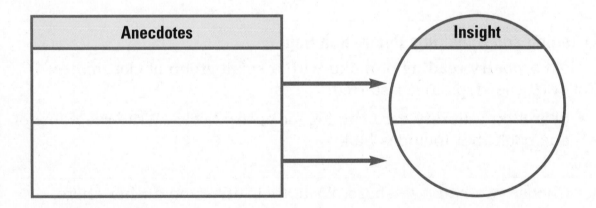

Anecdotes	Insight

READING STRATEGY

Although Shōnagon wrote many centuries ago, you may find that you share some of her feelings. As you read, think about how her experiences and opinions **relate to your own experiences.** Compare feelings you have had to those the author describes.

from The Pillow Book

Sei Shōnagon

Translated by Ivan Morris

Summary Through her personal observations, Sei Shōnagon gives readers a look into Japanese life during the 10th century. In "In Spring It Is the Dawn," Shōnagon Shares her feelings about the special qualities of each season. "The Cat Who Lived in the Palace" tells how a dog is sent away from the palace as punishment but returns only to be beaten nearly to death. In the end, the ladies and the empress show sympathy to the poor beaten creature. "Things That Arouse a Fond Memory of the Past" describes things that bring happy thoughts about bygone days. In "I Remember a Clear Morning," the author remembers a lovely morning in late summer.

Note-taking Guide

Use the diagram below to record details from *The Pillow Book* that show what life in 10th century was like.

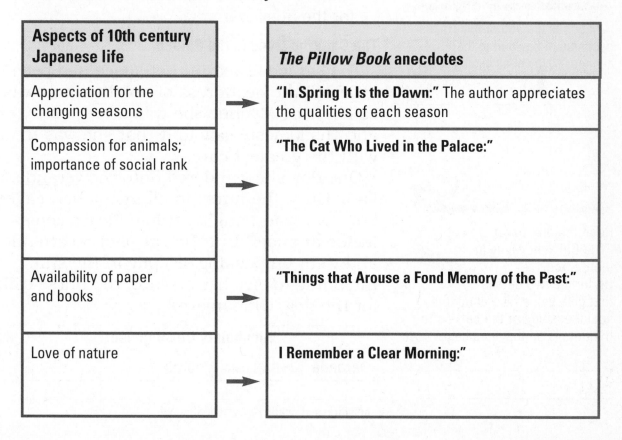

Aspects of 10th century Japanese life		*The Pillow Book* anecdotes
Appreciation for the changing seasons	→	**"In Spring It Is the Dawn:"** The author appreciates the qualities of each season
Compassion for animals; importance of social rank	→	**"The Cat Who Lived in the Palace:"**
Availability of paper and books	→	**"Things that Arouse a Fond Memory of the Past:"**
Love of nature	→	**I Remember a Clear Morning:"**

TAKE NOTES

Activate Prior Knowledge

What are some reasons people record their thoughts and feelings?

_____

_____

_____

Literary Analysis

Read the bracketed passage of this **journal**. How does the author feel about dawn?

_____

_____

Reading Check

What does the author think is the best time of day during the summer? Why does she think so?

_____

_____

Read Fluently

Read the first paragraph of "The Cat Who Lived in the Palace." Underline two details that give you a clue about the social position of the cat. Write the details on the lines below.

_____

_____

from The Pillow Book

Sei Shōnagon
Translated by Ivan Morris

In Spring It Is the Dawn

In spring it is the dawn that is most beautiful. As the light creeps over the hills, their outlines are dyed a faint red and wisps of purplish cloud trail over them.

In summer the nights. <u>Not only when the moon shines, but on dark nights too, as the fireflies flit to and fro, and even when it rains, how beautiful it is</u>!

◆ ◆ ◆

Autumn evenings are beautiful for their flocks of birds; low, glittering sun; and the hum of insects. Winter mornings are most beautiful after snowfall or frost cover. When it is very cold, charcoal fires keep the rooms warm. As the day warms, the sun takes over for the fires' warmth.

The Cat Who Lived in the Palace

The cat who lived in the Palace had been awarded the headdress of nobility[1] and was called Lady Myōbu. She was a very pretty cat, and His Majesty saw to it that she was treated with the greatest care.

One day she wandered onto the <u>veranda</u>, and Lady Uma, the nurse in charge of her, called out, "Oh, you naughty thing! Please come inside at once." But the cat paid no attention and went on basking sleepily in the sun. Intending to give her a scare, the nurse called for the dog, Okinamaro.

Vocabulary Development

veranda (vuh RAN duh) *n.* porch

---

1. **headdress of nobility** a symbol of honor.

<u>"Okinamaro, where are you?" she cried. "Come here and bite Lady Myōbu!"</u>

♦ ♦ ♦

Okinamaro thought the nurse was serious, and he ran toward the cat to bite her. Lady Myōbu raced behind the blind and surprised the Emperor. The Emperor demanded that Okinamaro be punished and sent away to Dog Island. He also demanded that Lady Uma no longer be permitted to care for the royal cat.

The guards caught Okinamaro and took him away. This was very sad because he used to be the pride of the palace. He had been decorated with peach blossoms and willow leaves at the festival of the dogs.

♦ ♦ ♦

We all felt sorry for him. "When Her Majesty was having her meals," recalled one of the ladies-in-waiting, "Okinamaro always used to be in attendance and sit opposite us. How I miss him!"

♦ ♦ ♦

Several days later, the palace attendants heard a great howling and crying that lasted for a very long time. They were told that two officials were beating a dog horribly. The dog was being punished for returning from Dog Island.

♦ ♦ ♦

Obviously the victim was Okinamaro. I was absolutely wretched and sent a servant to ask the men to stop; but just then the howling finally <u>ceased</u>. "He's dead," one of the servants informed me. "They've thrown his body outside the gate."

Vocabulary Development

ceased (SEEST) *v.* stopped

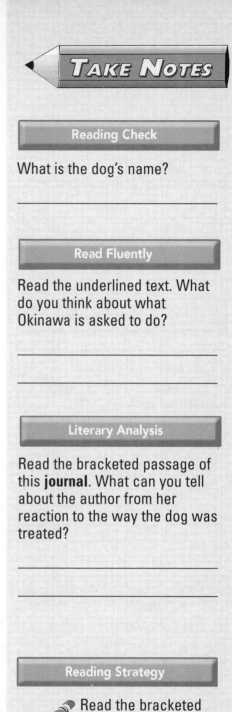

TAKE NOTES

Reading Check

What is the dog's name?

_____

_____

Read Fluently

Read the underlined text. What do you think about what Okinawa is asked to do?

_____

_____

_____

Literary Analysis

Read the bracketed passage of this **journal**. What can you tell about the author from her reaction to the way the dog was treated?

_____

_____

_____

Reading Strategy

Read the bracketed passage. Underline the sentence that tells what Shōnagon does when she learns that the officials are beating a dog. **Relate** Shōnagon's experience to yourself. What would you have done if you had been in Shōnagon's position?

_____

_____

Does Okinamaro deserve the treatment he receives? Explain.

_____

_____

_____

Background

Shōnagon's religion is Buddhism. Buddhists believe in *reincarnation*, which means that people and animals return after death to live another life as a different creature. In the first bracketed passage, circle where the author refers to reincarnation.

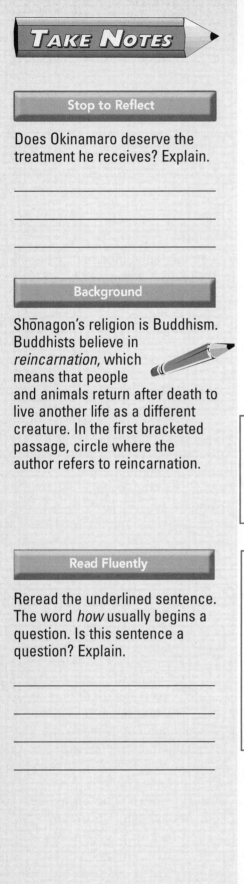

Read Fluently

Reread the underlined sentence. The word *how* usually begins a question. Is this sentence a question? Explain.

_____

_____

_____

That evening a poor, trembling dog crept into the Palace. The attendants wondered if this could be Okinamaro. But when they called to the dog, it did not respond. The Empress ordered a messenger to call for Lady Ukon, who would surely know whether the dog was Okinamaro.

When Lady Ukon arrived, she admitted that the dog looked like Okinamaro, but he did not behave as he always had, by running and wagging his tail. She determined that this was not the same dog. The Empress was very sad.

In the morning, the author went to hold the mirror for the Empress while her hair was being done. The same hurt dog snuck into the room.

◆　◆　◆

"Poor Okinamaro!" I said. "He had such a dreadful beating yesterday. <u>How sad to think he is dead! I wonder what body he has been born into this time.</u> Oh, how he must have suffered!"

◆　◆　◆

At these kind words, the poor dog began to tremble and shake. Then he began to cry. The people in the Palace knew then that he truly was Okinamaro. They were all thrilled. The Empress smiled happily and called all her attendants to share her happiness. When the Emperor came to see the dog, he was amazed to see such deep feelings from an animal.

When the official who had beaten Okinamaro learned of his return, he came looking for the dog. However, the author ordered a maid to tell him that this was not the same dog after all.

Okinamaro was pardoned and permitted to return to the Palace. He became his happy self again.

◆　◆　◆

Yet even now, when I remember how he whimpered and trembled in response to our sympathy, it strikes me as a strange and moving scene; when people talk to me about it, I start crying myself.

Things That Arouse a Fond Memory of the Past

Some objects that bring back old memories are dried flowers, decorations from a doll festival, and special, purple fabric pressed between pages of a book.

◆　◆　◆

It is a rainy day and one is feeling bored. To pass the time, one starts looking through some old papers. And then one comes across the letters of a man one used to love.

Last year's paper fan. A night with a clear moon.

I Remember a Clear Morning

Shōnagon remembers a clear morning after a rain when she saw dew drops on lovely flowers.

◆　◆　◆

On the bamboo fences and criss-cross hedges I saw tatters of spider webs; and where the threads were broken the raindrops hung on them like strings of white pearls. I was greatly moved and delighted.

◆　◆　◆

As the sun rose higher, the dew dried, and branches began to sway with the wind. Shōnagon says that she later explained to others the beauty she saw. She was amazed that no one else shared an appreciation of the beauty she described.

Reading Strategy

Can you **relate** to the emotions Shōnagon expresses in the first bracketed passage?

Stop to Reflect

From "Things That Arouse a Fond Memory of the Past," what can you tell about the author's earlier years?

_____

_____

Reading Strategy

Think about how the memories addressed in "Things That Arouse a Fond Memory of the Past" **relate to your own experiences**. Which of your own fond memories does the selection bring to mind?

_____

_____

Read Fluently

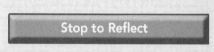

Read the second bracketed passage aloud. To what does the author compare raindrops on spider webs? Underline the answer and write it on the line below.

_____

from The Pillow Book

1. **Interpret:** In "Things That Arouse a Fond Memory of the Past," Sei Shōnagon lists the following items: *dried hollyhocks, material pressed in a notebook, an old love letter, a paper fan,* and *a moonlit night.* Why do you think she will not talk about the memories that these items bring to mind?

_____

_____

2. **Literary Analysis:** In the last paragraph of the **journal** entry "In Spring It Is the Dawn," what detail of day-to-day court life does Sei Shōnagon describe?

_____

_____

_____

3. **Literary Analysis:** Think about the events in "The Cat Who Lived in the Palace" and the way in which the court members are described. Do you think the **anecdote,** or short account of an amusing event, shows the Japanese nobility to be responsible and effective leaders? Explain.

_____

_____

_____

4. **Reading Strategy:** Which of Sei Shōnagon's experiences or reflections could you most easily **relate** to your own? Record your answers in the chart.

Writer's Experience	My Experience	How They Relate

SUPPORT FOR WRITING AND EXTEND YOUR LEARNING

Writing: Journal Entry

"The Cat Who Lived in the Palace" tells the story of Okinamaro from Sei Shōnagon's point of view. Write a **journal entry** describing the same events from the point of view of the Empress. To help you understand the Empress's personality, answer the follow questions.

- How would you describe the Empress' personality?

  _____

- Give an example of something that the Empress does that reveals something about her personality.

  _____

  _____

- What details from the story would the Empress not have known?

  _____

- How might her story be different?

  _____

  _____

Use your responses to write your journal entry.

Research and Technology: Graphic Presentation

"Things That Arouse a Fond Memory of the Past" is about objects that make Sei Shōnagon think of happy memories. Conduct a poll among your classmates to find out some of the things that make them think of happy memories. Then, create a **graphic presentation of poll results** to show your findings. You might show the most popular answers in a bar graph, a pie chart, or a table.

What question or questions will you ask your classmates?
How will you record their answers?
How will you organize and present the information?

Zen Parables

LITERARY ANALYSIS

A **parable** is a short story that teaches a lesson. The lesson is sometimes called a "moral." **Zen parables** teach the ideas of Zen Buddhism. They do so by getting the reader to think rather than by stating a clear moral. As you read these tales, you may see that there is no simple statement of the story's point.

Zen parables often are based on a **paradox**. A paradox is a statement or situation that has two ideas. These ideas seem like opposites. This is a paradox many people find familiar: "The more things change, they more they stay the same." Paradoxes are surprising because they really show the truth.

Some Zen parables have statements that are paradoxes. Others have whole situations that are paradoxes. These types of situations go against what makes sense or what you expect will happen.

READING STRATEGY

To **interpret** the paradox in a Zen parable, find the ideas that seem like opposites. These are sometimes called "contradictions." Look for statements, details, or ideas that do not make sense at first. They may go against what you expect. Then, decide what the contradiction is supposed to make you think about. Use the chart below to help you interpret the paradoxes in the stories.

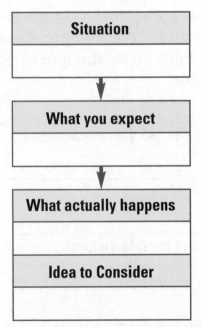

Situation

What you expect

What actually happens

Idea to Consider

Zen Parables

Compiled by Paul Reps

Summaries In "A Parable," a man is chased by a tiger. He escapes by clinging to a vine hanging over a cliff. Another tiger waits below. Two mice start to chew the vine. The man then sees strawberries. He eats one. It is wonderfully sweet. In "Publishing the Sutras," a man named Tetsugen collects money in order to publish the sutras. The sutras are religious writings. Tetsugen gives the money away to people in need. He finally publishes the sutras on his third try. In "The Taste of Banzo's Sword," a man learns to be patient in order to become the greatest swordsman in Japan.

Note-taking Guide

Use the chart below to keep track of the events in these parables.

Parable	Main character(s)	What he or she wants	What he or she does
"A Parable"			
"Publishing the Sutras"			
"The Taste of Banzo's Sword"			

Zen Parables

1. **Interpret:** In "Publishing the Sutras," Tetsugen twice gave his money away to those in need. What do you think the Japanese mean when they say that these were "invisible" sets of sutras?

_____

_____

2. **Draw Conclusions:** In "The Taste of Banzo's Sword," Banzo attacks Matajuro. He does this to train him. Why do you think this form of teaching works so well?

_____

_____

3. **Literary Analysis:** Use the chart below to write what the **paradox** is in each Zen parable. Remember that a paradox will seem like it does not make sense. Write whether the paradox is a statement or a situation.

Parable	Paradox	Statement or Situation
"A Parable"		
"Publishing the Sutras"		
"The Taste of Banzo's Sword"		

4. **Reading Strategy:** Interpret the paradox in "The Taste of Banzo's Sword." Matajuro tells Banzo he will try very hard to learn to sword fight. Banzo says this will make his training take longer. How does Banzo's statement surprise you?

_____

_____

_____

SUPPORT FOR WRITING AND EXTEND YOUR LEARNING

Writing: Annotated Bibliography

Your bibliography must use an approved style for citing your sources. One approved style is called MLA (Modern Language Association). Use the chart below to practice citing sources using MLA style. Use the samples as models and fill in your sources in the spaces given.

Source Type	Book	Source Type	Encyclopedia Article
Sample	Watts, D. T. <u>Zen Lessons of the Zen Masters</u>. New York: Harper and Row, 1966.	Sample	"Koans." <u>Encyclopedia Americana</u>. 1975 ed.
Your Source		Your Source	

Source Type	Article from a Periodical	Source Type	Web Site
Sample	Suzuki, Ellen. "Paradox and Swordfighting." <u>Zen Studies</u> 15.3 (1998): 35-42	Sample	"Wisdom Traditions." <u>Exploring Religion</u>. University of Minnesota. 12 June 2005. <http://www.umn.edu/wis.>
Your Source		Your Source	

Research and Technology: Multimedia Report

Your **multimedia report** will show connections between Zen ideas and the ways the Japanese create buildings (architecture) and gardens (landscaping). Use these questions to start your research:

- What qualities do the Japanese think are important in their buildings?

_____

_____

- What ideas or values do these methods show?

_____

- What qualities do the Japanese think are important in their gardens?

_____

_____

- What ideas or values do these methods show? _____

_____

REFERENCE MATERIALS

About Reference Materials

Reference materials are sources of information on specific topics. You use them to find facts, look up the meanings of words, or learn the steps in a process. Reference materials may come in print form, such as books, or in electronic form, such as Internet Web sites. You can find these materials in libraries and media centers. Here are examples of common reference materials:

- A **dictionary** lists word pronunciations, origins, and definitions.
- A **thesaurus** is a book of synonyms and antonyms.
- An **encyclopedia** provides information on topics such as history, science, and literature.
- An **almanac** contains information on topics such as weather forecasts, astronomical data, and statistics about people, places, and events.
- A **how-to book** gives instructions for making or doing something.

Reading Strategy

Your ability to **follow directions** is an important life skill. Whether the directions are simple or complex, you must follow each step carefully to be successful. Read the tips for following directions below.

Tips for Following Directions
1. Read the directions thoroughly before beginning the task.
2. As you work through the task, do not skip any steps.
3. Study any diagrams or illustrations provided.
4. Consider whether your finished product is what you expected it to be.
5. If there are problems with your product, review the directions and diagrams to determine where you went wrong. Make adjustments as necessary.

BUILD UNDERSTANDING

Knowing these words will help you read this reference material.

origami (or uh GAH mee) *n.* a traditional Japanese art of folding paper to make shapes

kimono (kuh MOH noh) *n.* a traditional Japanese robe for men or women

The Origins Of Origami

Steve and Megumi Biddle

The development of paper folding in the West can be traced back to a company of Japanese jugglers who visited Europe in the 1860s, at the time when the Japanese were beginning to make contact with other cultures. The jugglers brought with them the method for folding the "flapping bird." Soon directions for this and other folds were appearing in various European publications. Magicians, including Harry Houdini, were especially interested in paper folding, attesting to the association between origami and magic, which continues today.

Paper folding, of course, had begun long before—in fact nearly two thousand years before, with the invention of paper in China in 105 A.D. Paper documents were usually rolled and their ends tied. There is a long tradition in China of folding paper into decorative shapes that are tossed onto coffins as symbols of objects for the departed to take with them into the next world.

Read Fluently

Read the title and the underlined sentence. What information do you expect to get from this selection?

_____

_____

_____

Stop to Reflect

Why does the art of origami seem magical to people?

_____

_____

_____

Reading Check

Circle the place in the text that tells when paper was invented in China. Write your answer on the line below.

_____

Some **reference materials** include historical facts. What two historical figures made note of early decorative napkin folds?

_____

_____

_____

Circle the place where you found the answer.

List one reason why paper was considered sacred in sixth-century Japan.

_____

_____

_____

For more than five hundred years, the Chinese kept the paper-making process a secret. Then in the eighth century, Chinese invaders captured in Arabia were forced to reveal the technique. Eventually the process reached southern Europe.

Documents show that the Spanish symbol of paper folding, the *pajarita*, or "little bird," existed in the seventeenth century. Elsewhere in Europe, the art of paper folding was echoed in decorative napkin folds. At a banquet given by the sixteenth-century pope Gregory XIII, the setting included a table "decorated with wonderfully folded napkins." And the English diarist Samuel Pepys wrote in March 1668, "Thence home and there find one laying napkins against tomorrow in figures of all sorts."

The Japanese tradition of folding paper is a long and continuous one. It probably began in the sixth century, when a Buddhist priest brought paper-making methods to Japan from China by way of Korea. At that time, paper was a rare and precious commodity[1], and a formal kind of paper folding developed for use in both religious and secular life. There is perhaps another reason for the importance of paper in Japanese life. The Japanese word *kami* can mean "paper" as well as "God," even though they are written differently. This has given rise to the belief that paper is sacred. It has long been associated with the Shinto religion and the folding of human figures *(hitogata)* that are blessed by God.

---

1. **commodity** (kuh MAHD uh tee) *n.* anything bought and sold.

During Japan's Edo period (1600–1868), a time of development in the arts, paper became inexpensive enough to be used by everyone, and origami became a form of entertainment. Japanese woodblock prints from this period show origami models, people folding paper, and origami in kimono patterns.

In the 1890s, the Japanese government introduced a widespread system of preschool education, and origami was introduced as a tool for bringing minds and hands into coordination. It is still taught to young children today.

Since the 1950s, interest in origami has proliferated[2] in the United States and Great Britain as well as Japan, resulting in a variety of books and articles on the subject and in the founding of many origami societies worldwide.

Despite its popularity, for many years origami generated only a dozen or so noteworthy creations, such as the flapping bird and jumping frog. Today, however, it seems there is no shape that cannot be folded. And it can be tremendously exciting to see a flat piece of paper become transformed into a three-dimensional object. Learning how to fold new models is thrilling: Enjoy the one you encounter on the next page.

TAKE NOTES

Stop to Reflect

How did the price of paper influence the art of origami?

_____

_____

_____

Reading Check

Why was origami taught to preschool children in 1890s Japan?

_____

_____

_____

---

2. **proliferated** (proh LIF er ayt ed) *v.* produced or created quickly.

Helpful Tips

- Before you start, make sure your paper is the correct shape.

- Fold on a smooth, flat surface, such as a table or a book. Make your folds neat and accurate.

- Press your folds into place by running your thumbnail along them. Do not panic if your first few attempts at folding are not very successful. With practice you will come to understand the ways a piece of paper behaves when it is folded.

- Look at each diagram carefully, read the instructions, then look ahead to the next diagram to see what shape should be created when you have completed the step you are working on.

- Above all, if a fold or whole model does not work out, do not give up hope. Go through all the illustrations one by one, checking that you have read the instructions correctly and have not missed an important word or overlooked a symbol. If you are still unable to complete the model, put it to one side and come back to it another day with a fresh mind.

Reading Strategy

When you are **following directions**, it is helpful to read all the instructions before you begin. How do the Helpful Hints prepare you to follow the directions for folding your first dove?

_____

_____

_____

Dove Hato

A passage from the eighth-century chronicle the *Kojiki* describes the mournful sound of the dove like this:

Hasa no yama no hato no shitanaki ni nauku.

I weep with the murmuring sound of doves crying at Mount Hasa.

Making an Origami Dove

Try changing the angle of the head and wings each time you fold this model to see how many different doves you can create. Use a square piece of paper, white side up.

1. Begin with a diaper fold. Fold and unfold it in half from side to side.

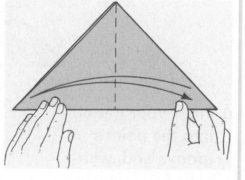

2. Valley fold the top points down two thirds of the way as shown.

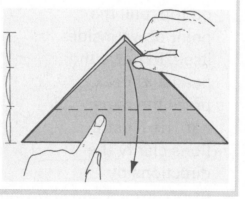

TAKE NOTES

Read Fluently

Read aloud the bracketed passage. What emotions do the words call to mind?

_____

_____

_____

Stop to Reflect

Why do you think the fold in Step 1 is called a "diaper fold"?

_____

_____

_____

Reading Strategy

In what way do the drawings make **following the directions** easier?

_____

_____

_____

TAKE NOTES

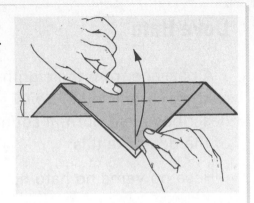

3. Valley fold the front flap of paper up as shown.

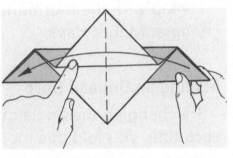

4. To make the wings, valley fold the paper in half from right to left.

5. Now inside reverse fold the top point. This is what you do:

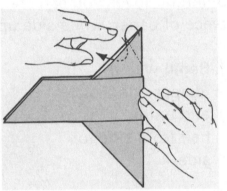

6. Place your thumb into the point's groove and, with your forefinger on top, pull the point down inside itself. To make the head and beak, press the paper flat. The illustrations clarify the directions by using arrows and showing exactly what your hands should do.

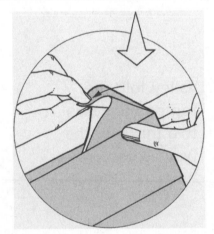

Reading Strategy

In what way do the numbered items make **following the directions** easier?

_____

_____

_____

Stop to Reflect

Why do you suppose the author makes a special point to draw Step 5?

_____

_____

_____

_____

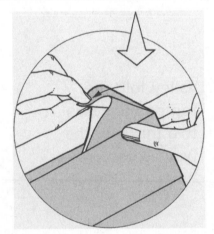

7. Valley fold the front wing over as shown. Repeat behind.

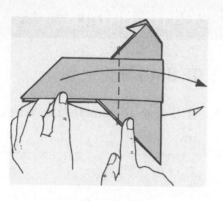

8. Open out the wings slightly.

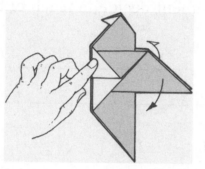

9. To complete the dove, turn the paper around.

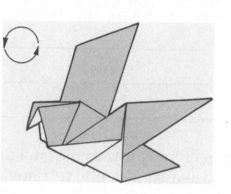

Reading Informational Materials

What might happen if you skipped one of the steps in the process of making the origami dove?

_____

_____

Why is it important to **follow directions** accurately?

_____

_____

THINKING ABOUT THE ORIGINS OF ORIGAMI

1. Origami began in Japan. How did the it reach the West?

_____

_____

2. Why did the Japanese government decide to teach origami in preschools?

_____

_____

READING STRATEGY

3. This selection includes a history of origami, a poem, and diagrams. Which makes it easier to **follow the directions**? Explain.

_____

_____

_____

4. There are at least three types of folds involved in making an origami dove. Which type of fold divides a square into a triangle?

_____

_____

_____

TIMED WRITING: EXPLANATION (30 Minutes)

Write step-by-step instructions for making something or completing a task. Draw at least one diagram to show the steps clearly.

• Choose a project or task that is easy to complete.

_____

_____

• List the materials that are needed to complete the task.

_____

_____

_____

• Explain the first step in completing the task.

_____

_____

_____

from the Iliad: from Book 1 • from Book 6

LITERARY ANALYSIS

The **theme** of a literary work is its main idea or message. Long works such as epics often have more than one theme. At the beginning of the *Iliad*, the theme is the anger of the hero Achilles (a KIL eez). War, peace, honor, duty, life, and death are other themes of the story. Homer tells these themes through the following:

• Characters • Events that happen • Descriptions

The *Iliad*'s opening lines also contain **foreshadowing**. Foreshadowing means giving clues about future events. This makes the reader wonder what is going to happen.

READING STRATEGY

Sentences in the *Iliad* have many details and descriptive words. They may be long, with many parts. To **analyze confusing sentences,** look at one section at a time.

• Find the key (important) parts of the sentence: the words that tell *who* is doing something and *what* they are doing.
• Use the key parts to figure out the main idea of the sentence. Use this chart to analyze confusing sentences as you read.

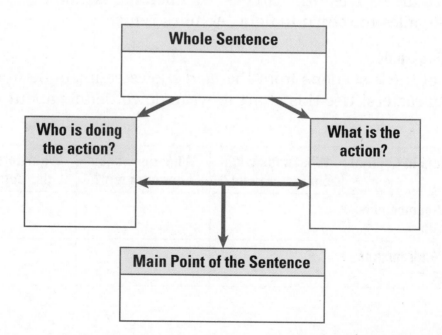

from the Iliad: from Book 1: The Rage of Achilles • from Book 6: Hector Returns to Troy

Homer
Translated by Robert Fagles

Summaries Book I explains Achilles' anger. The Greeks are at war with the Trojans. Greek King Agamemnon (AG uh MEM nahn) has made the god Apollo (Uh PAHL oh) angry. Apollo has sent a terrible disease and the Greeks are dying. To soothe Apollo, Agamemnon must return the girl Chryseis (kri SEE is) to her father. Chryseis is a captive taken from Troy. Achilles also holds a girl captive. Her name is Briseis (bry SEE is). After Agamemnon sends Chryseis home, he takes Briseis. Achilles refuses to fight for Agamemnon anymore. He also begs his mother to ask Zeus (ZOOS) to help the Trojans win. **Book 6** shows the meeting between Hector and his wife Andromache (an DRAHM uh kee). Andromache is afraid that Hector will be killed in the war. Hector soothes her and then returns to battle. The Trojans start to defeat the Greeks. Agamemnon sends two soldiers to beg Achilles to return to fight. Achilles refuses.

Note-taking Guide

Each of these sections from the *Iliad* shows conflicts between two main characters. Use this chart to write down details about each conflict.

Characters in Conflict	What does each character want?	What does each character feel?	What does each character do?
Book I: Agamemnon and Achilles			
Book 6: Andromache and Hector			

from the Iliad: from Book 1 • from Book 6

1. **Analyze Cause and Effect:** How does Agamemnon's choice to take Briseis affect Achilles? Explain.

_____

_____

2. **Literary Analysis:** Use the chart below to write down details that show what Achilles and Hector each feel about war, duty, and being a hero.

	Achilles' Feelings	Hector's Feelings
War		
Duty		
Heroism		

Then, explain how their feelings about these **themes** are the same and how they are different.

_____

_____

3. **Literary Analysis:** In Book I, Thetis begs Zeus to help her son Achilles. She makes one statement that **foreshadows** what will happen to Achilles' later in life. What is that statement?

_____

_____

4. **Reading Strategy:** Find the **sentence** that begins on line 298 of Book 1. Who is doing the action? What is the action?

_____

_____

Writing: Everyday Epic

Ancient epics are about heroes and important events. Some modern epics are about ordinary people and events. They show that everyday life is important. Write an **everyday epic** about something that happened to you. Use methods that Homer uses to make events dramatic. Use the chart to think about details that will help you write your epic.

Event From My Daily Life:

Who Was There: _____

What Happened: _____

Methods Homer Uses:

• **Special Words to Describe Characters:** _____

• **Actions to Tell About in a Long Speech:** _____

Use your notes to help you write your everyday epic.

Research and Technology: Multimedia Map

Make a **multimedia map** of the area of the world in which the *Iliad* takes place. Use drawings, photographs, recordings of music, and recordings of people speaking to make your map. Follow these steps to find materials:

- Find details in the *Iliad* that mention places where events occur.
- Make a list of these places.
- Search the library card catalog and the Internet to find resources that have pictures, videos, or recordings. Use keywords such as "Greece" or "Troy."
- Ask a teacher or librarian to help you find recordings of people speaking Greek. You may even find recordings of the *Iliad* itself.

Choose the best items to include in your map.

from the Iliad: from Book 22 • from Book 24

LITERARY ANALYSIS

Imagery is the use of words that appeal to the senses. Images describe the ideas or actions in a work. They can help you see, hear, feel, smell, and taste what is happening. In the *Iliad* some images are recurring. This means they repeat over and over. These types of images help support the poem's main ideas. Athena's blazing eyes are an example of a recurring image. This image supports the idea of Achilles' anger. Use this chart to connect images in the poem with important ideas.

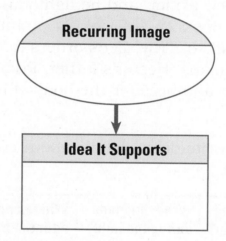

Some of the *Iliad*'s strongest images appear in **epic similes.** An epic simile has these traits:
- It compares two different things.
- It is introduced by the word *like* or *as.*
- It is very long and detailed.
- It may tell an entire little story.

As you read, think about how epic similes add to the story.

READING STRATEGY

The action in the *Iliad* moves quickly. Keep track of what is happening by pausing to **picture the action.** Follow these steps: First, read the details and images. Then, form a picture in your mind of the events.

from the Iliad: from Book 22: The Death of Hector • from Book 24: Achilles and Priam

Homer
Translated by Robert Fagles

Summary Earlier in the *Iliad*, Hector killed Achilles' friend Patroclus [puh TRAK luhs]. Patroclus had been wearing Achilles' armor. A god gives Achilles new armor, and he fights and kills Hector. This fight takes place in Book 22. In Book 24, Achilles drags Hector's body around the walls of Troy. Zeus orders Achilles to give the body back to the Trojans. Hector's father, Priam [PRY uhm], goes to Achilles with gifts and begs for the body of his son.

Note-taking Guide

Use this chart to write down details about events in these sections of the *Iliad*.

Book 22	What happens before the fight?	What happens during the fight?	What happens after the fight?	How do other characters react?
Book 24	What does Priam do?	What does Achilles do?	How does Andromache react?	How does Helen react?

from the Iliad: *from* Book 22 • *from* Book 24

1. **Analyze:** In Book 22, Hector thinks about what he should do with Achilles. He decides to fight. What does this decision show about his character?

   _____

   _____

2. **Literary Analysis:** Read this **image** from line 3 of Book 24: "the sweet warm grip of sleep." Explain which words relate to the sense of touch and which words relate to the sense of taste.

   _____

   _____

3. **Literary Analysis:** In Book 22, there is an **epic simile** about Achilles in lines 59–64. There is one about Hector in lines 258–261. Use the chart below to analyze them. Write down details from the lines about Achilles in the left circle. Write down details from the lines about Hector in the right circle. Write down ideas that apply to both heroes in the middle section.

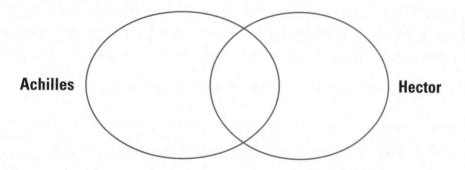

Achilles   Hector

4. **Reading Strategy:** Write down three details that help you **picture the action** in the battle between Hector and Achilles. Explain why you chose each detail.

   _____

   _____

   _____

SUPPORT FOR WRITING AND EXTEND YOUR LEARNING

Writing: Editorial

Decide whether you think Achilles behaves well in the *Iliad*. Write an **editorial** in which you state your opinion and support it with details. In the chart, write a thesis statement. Then, write down your reasons and details that support them. Use these notes to help you write your editorial.

Thesis Statement (my opinion):	
I think Achilles _____ behave well in the *Iliad* because _____.	
Reasons for my opinion:	Details that support my reasons:
1.	
2.	
3.	

Listening and Speaking: Movie Preview

Imagine that "The Death of Hector" has been turned into a movie. Write the script for a **movie preview**. A preview is a type of commercial that shows parts of a film. It makes people want to see the whole movie.

- Decide which parts of the story to put into the preview.

_____

- Copy out dialogue from the poem that you want to use.

_____

_____

_____

- Write down ideas for music and sound effects.

_____

_____

You Know the Place: Then • He is More Than a Hero • Olympia 11

LITERARY ANALYSIS

Lyric poetry expresses the ideas and feelings of one speaker. Lyric poems were originally sung to the music of a stringed instrument called a lyre. Narrative poems tell stories, but lyric poems produce a single effect. Use this chart to record the words and phrases that contribute to a single effect.

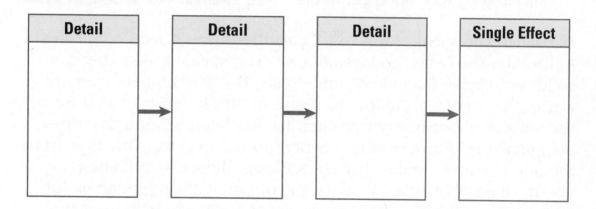

Detail	Detail	Detail	Single Effect

The poems of Sappho and Pindar share the musical quality of lyric poems. Each poem's **form**, however, has a different effect. Form is a poem's organization and structure.

- Sappho's poems take the form of simple lyrics. They are very personal.
- Pindar's poem uses a more complex form known as the **ode**. This form is more public. It is used by Pindar to honor winning athletes.

Think about how each poem's form affects your reaction.

READING STRATEGY

Lyric poems nearly always use images of the senses—taste, touch, sight, hearing, and smell—to get ideas and feelings across. To **respond to imagery,**

- Identify images of the senses in the poems.
- Think about how these images relate to your own life.

As you read, connect your own experiences to the images and ideas that Sappho and Pindar present.

You Know the Place: Then • He is More Than a Hero

Sappho
Translated by Mary Barnard
Translated by Richmond Lattimore

Olympia 11

Pindar
Translated by Richmond Lattimore

Summaries The speaker in **"You Know the Place: Then"** addresses Aphrodite, the Greek goddess of love. The speaker asks the goddess to leave Crete and come to see the worshippers who are waiting for her to bring love to them. In **"He Is More Than a Hero,"** the speaker describes her passion for her beloved. She describes being jealous of a man who sits next to her beloved. One look from the one she loves makes her speechless. She feels as if she is about to die. **"Olympia 11"** is a song of praise for Agesidamos (uh GES i da mose), the boy who won the boxing competition at the Olympian games in 476 B.C.

Note-taking Guide

Use this chart to record examples that support the main idea of each poem.

Poem	Main Idea	Examples From Poem
You Know the Place: Then		
He Is More Than a Hero		
Olympia 11		

You Know the Place: Then • He is More Than a Hero • Olympia 11

1. **Evaluate:** In your opinion, is poetry a good way to express feelings? Explain.

   _____

   _____

   Is poetry a good way to praise a hero? Why or why not?

   _____

   _____

2. **Literary Analysis:** In Ancient Greece, lyrics were meant to be sung to music. How might music have reinforced the images and overall effect of "He Is More Than a Hero"?

   _____

   _____

3. **Literary Analysis:** The **forms**, or organization and structure, of the poems of Sappho and Pindar differ in some ways. How do the forms of the poems of each contribute to their effect?

   _____

   _____

4. **Reading Strategy:** Use this chart to list **images** that describe the precincts of Aphrodite in Crete in "You Know the Place: Then."

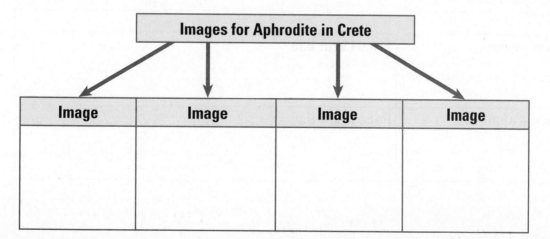

Writing: Comparative Analysis of Translations

Write an **analysis** comparing and contrasting Mary Barnard's and Richmond Lattimore's translations of Sappho's "He Is More Than a Hero."

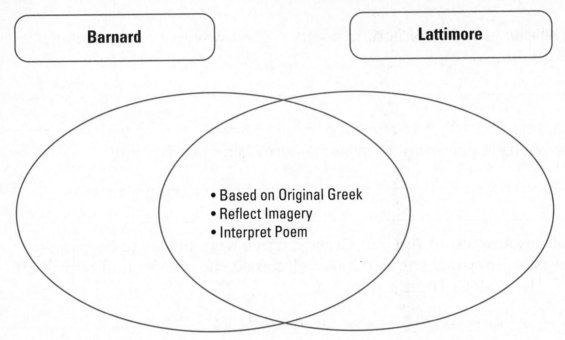

Barnard

Lattimore

- Based on Original Greek
- Reflect Imagery
- Interpret Poem

Use these notes to help you write a comparative **analysis** of the translations.

Listening and Speaking: Recitation

Memorize one of Sappho's poems for a **recitation**. Use this chart to plan your presentation.

Poem:	
Tone of poem:	Pitch I Will Use:
Message of poem:	Pace I Will Use:

from History of the Peloponnesian War: Pericles' Funeral Oration

LITERARY ANALYSIS

A **speech** is an oral presentation on an important issue. Elements of a speech include the following:
- **Purpose:** the reason for giving the speech
- **Occasion:** the event that inspires the speech
- **Audience:** people who hear or read the speech

One form of speech is an **oration**. It is a formal address that is meant to inspire listeners and move them to action. Pericles (PER ik lees) uses different techniques in his oration to achieve a desired effect. One such technique is *restatement.* This is the repeating of an important idea in different words. Pericles also uses *parallelism,* or repeating grammatical structures. This means that he sets up certain phrases or sentences in similar ways. Parallelism can help make ideas easier for the audience to remember.

READING STRATEGY

Speakers often reveal the **cultural attitudes** of their society on important issues. Identifying the things that are important to a society can help you understand it. To recognize cultural attitudes, determine what a speaker suggests is good, bad, important, or necessary. Ask yourself, "What does this society value?" Then, use the chart below to record a passage from "Pericle's Funeral Oration" and decide what cultured attitude the passage reveals.

As you read, look for other passages that reveal Athenian attitudes. Use them to help you understand what life was like in Athens.

Passage	Cultural Attitude It Reveals
	1._____ _____ 2._____ _____

from History of the Peloponnesian War: Pericles' Funeral Oration

Thucydides
Translated by Rex Warner

Summary Pericles was an Athenian general during the Peloponnesian War between Athens and Sparta. In his "Funeral Oration," Pericles praises soldiers who have died for Athens. He begins by saying that Athens is great because it has a democratic government. Also, he says, Athenians are free to live as they choose. Pericles argues that this lifestyle inspires soldiers to be loyal and brave. The men who have died to protect Athens' freedom will be remembered for their courage. Pericles reminds the people that they must continue to fight for freedom. He then offers words of comfort to the families of the dead soldiers.

Note-taking Guide

Pericles' speech has three purposes: to honor the war dead, to inspire Athenian pride, and to move Athenians to positive action. In the chart below, note passages from Pericles' speech that support each purpose.

Purpose of Pericles Speech		
Honor the War Dead	**Inspire Athenian Pride**	**Move to Positive Action**

from History of the Peloponnesian War: Pericles' Funeral Oration

Thucydides
Translated by Rex Warner

Thucydides explains that honoring the war dead is an ancient Athenian tradition. He gives details of Athenian funeral customs. He says that the man chosen to speak at the burial must be highly intelligent. The speaker must be respected in the community. Pericles is chosen.

Pericles begins his speech by admitting that words spoken by one man are unlikely to please all listeners. Relatives may think he does not praise enough. Strangers may think he praises them too much. However, says Pericles, it is his duty to do his best to meet all their expectations.

◆　◆　◆

"I shall begin by speaking about our ancestors, since it is only right and proper on such an occasion to pay them the honor of recalling what they did. In this land of ours there have always been the same people living from <u>generation</u> to generation up till now, and they, by their courage and their virtues, have handed it on to us, a free country. They certainly deserve our praise. Even more so do our fathers deserve it. For to the <u>inheritance</u> they had received they added all the empire we have now, and it was not without blood and <u>toil</u> that they handed it down to us of the present generation."

Vocabulary Development

generation (jen er AY shun) *n.* a single lifespan; the average period between the birth of parents and the birth of their offspring

inheritance (in HEHR uh tens) *n.* something of value; often received from a person of another generation

toil (TOYL) *n.* hard work; exhausting labor

Literary Analysis

Pericles gives his **speech** to honor the Athenians who died in battle. What does Pericles say he will speak about first? Underline the passage in which Pericles tells his audience what he will speak about first.

Reading Strategy

Pericles' speech reveals the **cultural attitudes**, or values, of his people. Underline a passage in the bracketed text that reveals Athenians' attitude toward their ancestors.

Reading Check

What is the inheritance that Pericles says has been handed down from generation to generation of Athenians?

_____

_____

One of the **cultural attitudes** of the Athenians is tolerance, or respect, toward others. Underline a passage in this paragraph that shows how Athenians practice tolerance in their daily lives.

Pericles speaks of private life and public life. What does he say is the Athenians' **attitude** toward the law? Check the correct answer from the choices below.

[ ] insulting

[ ] tolerant

[ ] respectful

Pericles continues to explain the nature of his speech. He tells his audience that he will discuss the way of life that has made Athens great. Then he will speak in praise of the dead.

◆　◆　◆

"Let me say that our system of government does not copy the <u>institutions</u> of our neighbors. It is more the case of our being a model to others, than of our imitating anyone else. Our constitution is called a democracy because power is in the hands not of a minority but of the whole people. When it is a question of settling private disputes, everyone is equal before the law; when it is a question of putting one person before another in positions of public responsibility, what counts is not membership of a particular class, but the actual ability which the man possesses. No one, so long as he has it in him to be of service to the state, is kept in political obscurity[1] because of poverty. And, just as our political life is free and open, so is our day-to-day life in our relations with each other. We do not get into a state with our next-door neighbor if he enjoys himself in his own way, nor do we give him the kind of black looks which, though they do no real harm, still do hurt people's feelings. We are free and <u>tolerant</u> in our private lives; but in public affairs we keep to the law. This is because it commands our deep respect."

Vocabulary Development

institutions (IN stuh TOO shenz) *n.* established laws, customs, and practices

tolerant (TOL uhr ent) *adj.* patient and accepting of others' feelings; fair toward those who are different

---

1. **obscurity** (ub SKYOOR uh tee) *n.* state of being unclear and easily misunderstood.

Athenians are law-abiding citizens, Pericles continues, but they also like to have fun. They enjoy contests and sacrifices throughout the year. They decorate their homes tastefully. Pericles says that the Athenians' attitude toward the military is different from that of their opponents. Athenians rely on natural courage and loyalty to defend their city. Spartans, on the other hand, must be trained from a young age to be courageous.

♦ ♦ ♦

"There are certain advantages, I think, in our way of meeting danger voluntarily, with an easy mind, instead of with a <u>laborious</u> training, with natural rather than with state-induced courage. We do not have to spend our time practicing to meet sufferings which are still in the future; and when they are actually upon us we show ourselves just as brave as these others who are always in strict training. This is one point in which, I think, our city deserves to be admired. There are also others:

Our love of what is beautiful does not lead to extravagance; our love of the things of the mind does not make us soft. We regard wealth as something to be properly used, rather than as something to boast about. As for poverty, no one need be ashamed to admit it: the real shame is in not taking practical measures to escape from it. Here each individual is interested not only in his own affairs but in the affairs of the state as well: even those who are mostly occupied with their own business are extremely well-informed on general politics—this is a <u>peculiarity</u> of ours: we do not say that a man who takes no interest in

Vocabulary Development

laborious (luh BOR ee uhs) *adj.* taking much work or effort

peculiarity (pi KYOO lee AHR uh tee) *n.* something unusual or special

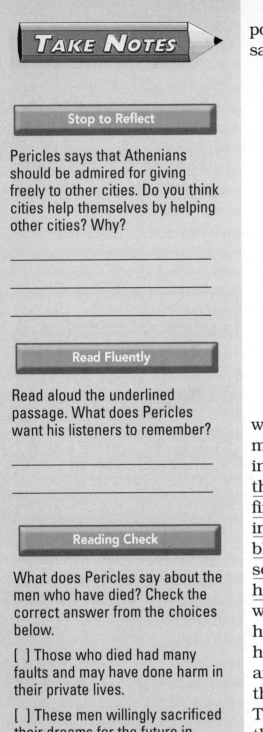

Stop to Reflect

Pericles says that Athenians should be admired for giving freely to other cities. Do you think cities help themselves by helping other cities? Why?

_____

_____

_____

Read Fluently

Read aloud the underlined passage. What does Pericles want his listeners to remember?

_____

_____

Reading Check

What does Pericles say about the men who have died? Check the correct answer from the choices below.

[ ] Those who died had many faults and may have done harm in their private lives.

[ ] These men willingly sacrificed their dreams for the future in order to defend their city against its enemies.

[ ] Many of these men might have escaped poverty and grown rich in the great city of Athens if they had not died at war.

politics is a man who minds his own business; we say that he has no business here at all."

◆　◆　◆

Pericles says that Athenians should also be admired as true friends because they give freely to other cities. They do not expect anything in return. This is one of many things that makes Athens great. Pericles suggests that Greece could benefit from studying Athenian society. Athenians have traveled many seas. They have explored many lands. Wherever they go they leave behind reminders of their generosity and their strength. Pericles notes that it is the courage of its people that has made Athens great.

◆　◆　◆

"To me it seems that the <u>consummation</u> which has overtaken these men shows us the meaning of manliness in its first revelation and in its final proof. <u>Some of them, no doubt, had their faults; but what we ought to remember first is their <u>gallant</u> conduct against the enemy in defense of their native land. They have blotted out evil with good, and done more service to the commonwealth than they ever did harm in their private lives.</u> No one of these men weakened because he wanted to go on enjoying his wealth: no one put off the awful day in the hope that he might live to escape his poverty and grow rich. More to be desired than such things, they chose to check the enemy's pride. This, to them, was a risk most glorious, and they accepted it, willing to strike down the enemy and <u>relinquish</u> everything else. As for

---

Vocabulary Development

consummation (KAHN soo MAY shun) *n.* state of highest perfection or skillfulness

gallant (GAL uhnt) *adj.* brave and noble-minded

relinquish (ree LING kwish) *v.* to give up or let go of success or failure, they left that in the doubtful hands of Hope, and when the reality of battle was before their faces, they put their trust in their own selves. In the fighting, they thought it more honorable to stand their ground and suffer death than to give in and save their lives."

◆　◆　◆

When they fought, these men were willing to trust themselves and to stand up to the enemy. Pericles says these men were worthy of their great city. Those left behind should always remember how great Athens is. They should realize that they owe this greatness to those who died to protect her. The glory of these men will live forever in the hearts and minds of people throughout the world.

◆　◆　◆

"It is for you to try to be like them. Make up your minds that happiness depends on being free, and freedom depends on being courageous. Let there be no relaxation in face of the perils of the war. The people who have most excuse for despising death are not the wretched and unfortunate, who have no hope of doing well for themselves, but those who run the risk of a complete reversal in their lives, and who would feel the difference most intensely, if things went wrong for them. Any intelligent man would find a <u>humiliation</u> caused by his own <u>slackness</u> more painful to bear than death, when death comes to him unperceived, in battle, and in the confidence of his patriotism."

◆　◆　◆

Stop to Reflect

Pericles says the war heroes believed it was better to fight and die than to give in and save themselves. Do you agree with this attitude?

_____

Why, or why not?

_____

_____

_____

Literary Analysis

Why do you think Pericles tells his listeners in his **speech** to try to be like the war heroes?

_____

_____

_____

Vocabulary Development

humiliation (hyoo MIL ee AY shun) *n.* embarrassment; loss of pride or self-respect

slackness (SLAK nes) *n.* lack of discipline; carelessness; laziness

Complete the following sentence:

Athenians feel it is _____ to show patriotism and to die in defense of one's city.

Why does Pericles believe that the sons and brothers of the dead will struggle the most? Underline the answer in this paragraph.

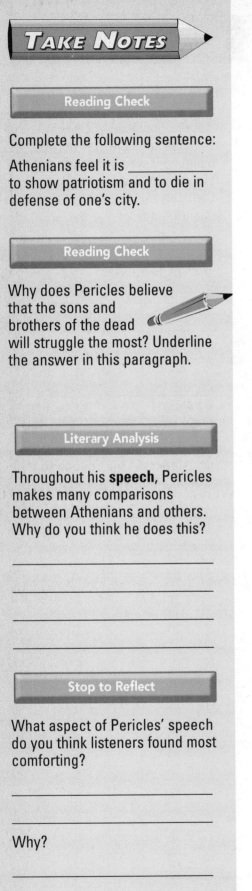

Throughout his **speech**, Pericles makes many comparisons between Athenians and others. Why do you think he does this?

_____

_____

_____

_____

What aspect of Pericles' speech do you think listeners found most comforting?

_____

_____

Why?

_____

_____

_____

Pericles notes that he wishes to comfort the parents of the dead. He reminds them that the dead have ended their lives with honor. He urges the parents to consider having more children. He explains that having more children will distract them from their sorrow. New children will also assure the future of Athens. Older listeners, he says, should take comfort in their memories. They should be proud of the way their loved ones died.

♦　♦　♦

"As for those of you here who are sons or brothers of the dead, I can see a hard struggle in front of you. Everyone always speaks well of the dead, and, even if you rise to the greatest heights of heroism, it will be a hard thing for you to get the reputation of having come near, let alone equaled, their standard. When one is alive, one is always liable to the jealousy of one's competitors, but when one is out of the way, the honor one receives is sincere and unchallenged."

♦　♦　♦

Pericles briefly addresses the widows of the dead. He advises them that the highest goal for women should be not to be the object of gossip. They should desire not to be talked about through praise or criticism.

Pericles concludes his speech by saying that the children of the dead will be supported by the city until they become adults. This is the reward offered to the dead and to their children for their noble sacrifice.

from History of the Peloponnesian War: Pericles' Funeral Oration

1. **Draw Conclusions:** What comfort does Pericles offer to the parents of the dead?

   _____

   What does this tell you about the Athenian attitude toward honor?

   _____

   _____

2. **Literary Analysis: Restatement** is the repeating of an idea in different words. **Parallelism** is the use of repeated grammatical structures. Use the chart below to analyze these techniques that Pericles uses in his **speech.**

Technique	Example	Effect
Restatement		
Parallelism		

3. **Literary Analysis:** What is Pericles' main purpose in this **oration?**

   _____

   _____

4. **Reading Strategy:** Explain the Athenian **cultural attitudes** toward wealth and poverty that are revealed in this selection.

   _____

   _____

   _____

SUPPORT FOR WRITING AND EXTEND YOUR LEARNING

Writing: Essay about Leadership

Discuss the qualities of a good leader in an essay. Use details from the funeral oration to support your arguments.

In the chart below, list four qualities of a good leader. Then, beside each quality, note an example from "Pericles' Funeral Oration" in which Pericles demonstrates that quality.

Leadership Quality	Example from "Pericles' Funeral Oration"

Research and Technology: Rights Chart

Pericles claims that everyone is equal under Athenian law. Evaluate the truth of this claim through research. Present your findings in the form of a **rights chart.**

Asking questions can help you focus your research. For example, you might ask, "What rights did children have in Pericles' Athens?" Think of three questions that will help guide your research, and write them on the lines below.

- ______________________________
  ____
- ______________________________
  ____
- ______________________________
  ____

Use the answers to your questions to develop your rights chart.

from the Apology

LITERARY ANALYSIS

A **monologue** is a long and revealing speech by one character. In this monologue from the *Apology*, Socrates [SAHK ruh teez]
- explains and defends his thoughts and beliefs.
- talks about his life's work, which has been the search for knowledge.

Socrates often makes an idea clear by using an **analogy.** An analogy is a comparison of relationships. An analogy shows how the relationship between one pair of things is like the relationship between another pair of things. One analogy Socrates makes is that he is like a gadfly. Notice how he uses other comparisons to explain his ideas.

READING STRATEGY

You do not have to just accept the idea someone states in a text. You can challenge it. To **challenge a text,** follow these steps:
- Make a judgment about the argument and the ideas that support it. That means you decide if you think the idea is reasonable.
- Compare the argument with your own knowledge and experience. Also compare it with other things you have read.
- Decide whether you agree or disagree with the argument.

Use this chart to record your thinking.

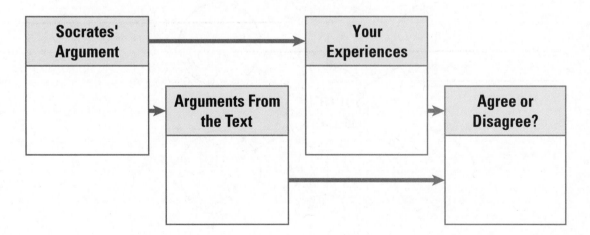

from the Apology

Plato
Translated by Benjamin Jowett

Summary Socrates was an ancient Greek philosopher. In this speech, he defends his life at a trial. He has been accused of not believing in the gods and of giving young people bad ideas. Socrates vows to tell the entire truth. His story began when the god Apollo said that no one was wiser than Socrates. Socrates did not believe this was true and set out to find a wiser man. Instead, he found that people were foolish. He made many enemies after he showed these people that they really knew nothing. He proclaims that only God is wise. Socrates explains that he does believe in the gods. He also says he will never stop questioning things. Believing that no evil can happen to a good man, he urges his friends to be cheerful.

Note-taking Guide

Use this diagram to record statements from the *Apology* that show what Socrates believes.

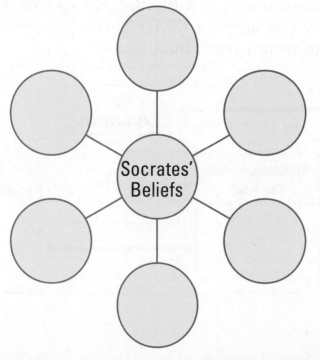

Socrates' Beliefs

from the Apology

1. **Deduce:** Socrates traveled around, trying to find a wise person. He questioned many people about their knowledge and beliefs. Why did his questioning make so many people his enemies?

   _____

   _____

2. **Define:** Socrates says he is wiser than others. This is not because he knows more than other people do. What kind of person does Socrates say is wisest?

   _____

   _____

3. **Literary Analysis:** Use this chart to study the character of Socrates. Choose three statements Socrates makes. Explain what each one tells you about his personality and beliefs.

Statement	What It Tells You About Socrates
1.	1.
2.	2.
3.	3.

4. **Reading Strategy: Challenge** Socrates' statement that "he who will fight for the right ... must have a private station and not a public one." A "private station" means that the person is a private citizen, not a politician. Do you agree with Socrates when he says that politicians cannot fight for what is right? Explain.

   _____

   _____

   _____

Writing: Account of a Remarkable Person

Write a paper describing a special person you know. Choose a person you admire. Fill in the chart with details about that person.

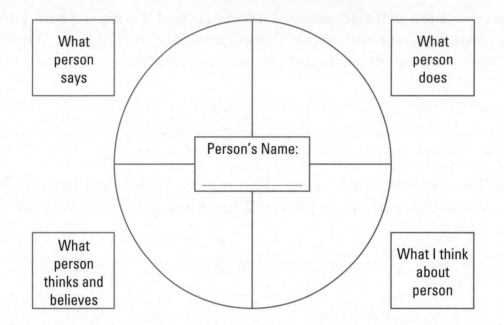

Use your notes to help you write your paper about the person.

Listening and Speaking: Interview

Choose a partner. Pretend you are interviewing someone who was at the trial of Socrates. Have one person ask the questions (interviewer). The other person should answer (subject). Use your answers to these questions to plan the **interview**:

- Was the subject a member of the audience or a member of the jury?

_____

- Write down two questions the interviewer will ask about the crowd at the trial. Also, write down the subject's answers.

_____

_____

- Write down two statements by Socrates that the interviewer will quote.

_____

Use these notes to plan your interview.

Oedipus The King, Part I

LITERARY ANALYSIS

A **tragedy** is a type of play. It shows the downfall of a person. This person is the *protagonist*, or main character. He or she

- is usually of high birth, such as a king.
- is often a leader who is loved and respected by his or her people.
- often starts a chain of events that lead to his or her own destruction.

Tragedies explore powerful feelings. These include love, hate, revenge, and loyalty. Aristotle wrote that tragedy makes the audience feel pity and fear. We feel sorry for the protagonist's suffering. At the same time we fear for him or for ourselves.

The main character of a tragedy is also known as the **tragic hero**. The tragic hero usually has a weakness that causes his or her downfall. This weakness is called a **tragic flaw**. As you read, pay attention to details in Oedipus' actions and statements. These details may offer hints about his heroic qualities or flaws. Use this chart to organize your observations about his character.

Heroic Qualities	Actions	Flawed Qualities	Actions
	Statements		Statements

READING STRATEGY

Try to picture a live performance when you **read drama**. Pay attention to stage directions. These are usually printed in italics, *a slanted printing style that sets them off from the rest of the text*. They tell about characters' thoughts, attitudes, and behavior. As you read stage directions and characters' words, try to picture how the characters look, sound, move, and talk to one another.

Oedipus The King, Part I
Sophocles
Translated by David Grene

Summary In Part I, Oedipus is concerned about the problems in his kingdom. Crops are failing, women are not able to have children, and disease is spreading. Oedipus learns that the cause of these problems is a curse. The curse was placed on the kingdom by a man who had killed the former king, Laius. Oedipus does not believe the seer, or fortune-teller, who tells him that he is the murderer. The seer also tells him that the murderer has married his own mother. Instead, Oedipus suspects that the seer and his brother-in-law, Creon, are trying to take away his kingdom. Oedipus' wife Jocasta tries to keep him from getting angry by telling him about the death of her first husband, Laius. Oedipus begins to imagine that he was involved in Laius' murder and starts looking into the crime.

Note-taking Guide

Use a chart like the one shown to record information about the story of King Oedipus.

Setting	Characters	Problem	Events

Oedipus The King, Part I

1. **Infer:** In the opening scene, what does Oedipus' response to the problems in the kingdom tell you about how he views his people?

   _____

2. **Literary Analysis:** The main figure in a **tragedy** is usually a person of high position in society. This person also has unusual personal qualities. In what ways does Oedipus fit this description?

   _____

3. **Literary Analysis:** Oedipus wants to know the truth about the murder of Laius, even if he will suffer personally when he finds out. How does this affect your view of Oedipus as a **tragic hero**?

   _____

4. **Literary Analysis:** Which of Oedipus' negative qualities might be considered a **tragic flaw**?

   _____

5. **Reading Strategy:** As you **read drama,** stage directions give important information. In a chart like the one shown, list three details that appear in the stage directions in Part I. Then, explain how they help the reader imagine the action. Finally, write a brief comment on the importance of each detail.

Stage Direction	What it Shows	Importance
1.		
2.		
3.		

Writing: News Article

Write a **news article** about events in *Oedipus the King*, Part I.

5 W's				
Who is the main character?	**What** problem does he or she face?	**When** do events take place?	**Where** do events take place?	**Why** do events develop as they do?

Use your notes to help you write a **news article** about events in the play so far.

Listening and Speaking: Dramatic Reading

Prepare a **dramatic reading** of a speech from Part I of *Oedipus the King*.

- Write the line numbers of the speech you will prepare.

_____

- Identify the character who is speaking.

_____

- Describe the mood, or feeling, the speech creates.

_____

- Describe the tone of voice you will use.

_____

- List facial expressions and gestures you will use.

_____

- List ideas for music that fits the mood of the speech.

_____

Use these notes to rehearse your **dramatic reading** and present it to the class.

Oedipus the King, Part II

LITERARY ANALYSIS

Irony results from the difference between what you expect and reality. In literature, there are three main types of irony:

- **Verbal irony** is the use of words to mean the opposite of their usual meaning.
- **Situational irony** occurs when the result of an action or event is exactly opposite to what you would expect.
- **Dramatic irony** occurs when readers or audience members are aware of truths that the characters themselves do not know.

This play provides one of literature's best examples of dramatic irony. As you read Part II, notice the contrast between what Oedipus believes to be true and what the reader or viewing audience knows to be true.

Sophocles slowly reveals the painful truths to Oedipus as the action in the play continues. That slow process builds **suspense**—a feeling of stress or uncertainty. As you read, notice the way in which Oedipus' pursuit of the truth increases suspense.

READING STRATEGY

Like people in real life, characters in literature are not always what they seem. To gain additional knowledge as you read, **question the characters' motives**—their reasons for behaving as they do. Ask whether characters are motivated by fear, greed, guilt, love, loyalty, revenge, or another emotion or desire. As you read, use this chart to examine the motives of the characters in Part II of the play.

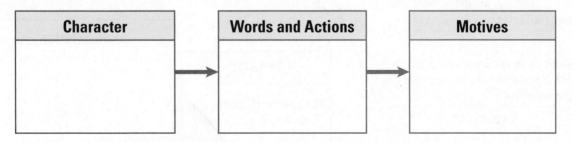

Character	Words and Actions	Motives

Oedipus the King, Part II

Sophocles

Translated by David Grene

Summary In Part II, Oedipus learns that his father, Polybus of Corinth, has died of old age. At first Oedipus is relieved. He thinks that he cannot be the son in the prediction who killed Laius and then married his mother. However, Oedipus discovers that Polybus and his wife were not his real parents. He learns that he was found on a mountain and brought to them. The herdsman who left Oedipus to die as a baby tells him that Jocasta is his mother and Laius was his father.

Note-taking Guide

Use this diagram to record the events in Part II.

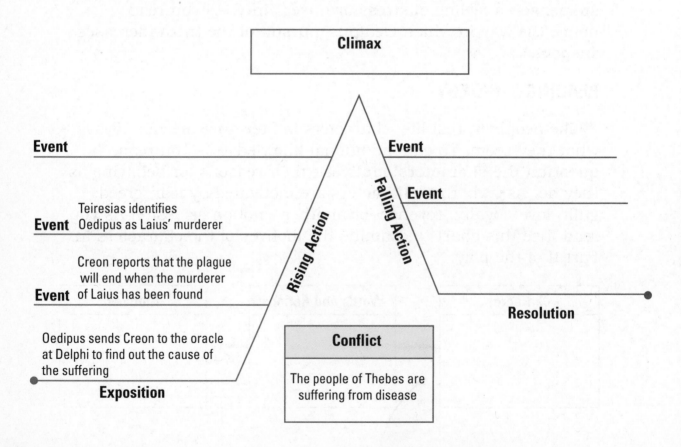

Climax

Event _____

Event _____

Event _____

Event Teiresias identifies Oedipus as Laius' murderer _____

Event Creon reports that the plague will end when the murderer of Laius has been found _____

Oedipus sends Creon to the oracle at Delphi to find out the cause of the suffering

Rising Action

Falling Action

Exposition

Resolution

Conflict

The people of Thebes are suffering from disease

Oedipus the King, Part II

1. **Analyze:** Why does Oedipus insist that he is better off blind and living than dead?

   _____

2. **Literary Analysis:** The Messenger attempts to cheer Oedipus by telling him that Polybus and Merope were not his true parents. How are the Messenger's efforts an example of **situational irony**?

   _____

3. **Literary Analysis:** What information about Oedipus' past provides **dramatic irony** in the scene involving Oedipus, Jocasta, and the Messenger from Corinth?

   _____

4. **Reading Strategy:** Fill in a chart like the one shown to compare and contrast the attitudes of the Corinthian Messenger and the Herdsman. What **motives** do each of the characters have for giving information to Oedipus? Write motives they share in the center of the two circles and different motives in each of the separate circles.

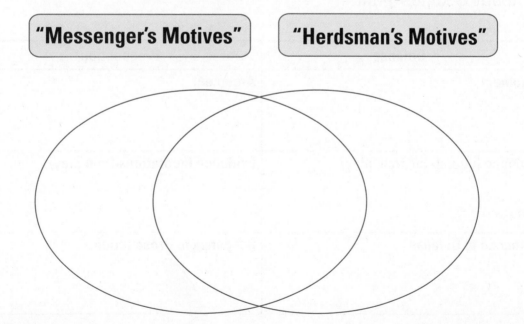

"Messenger's Motives"   "Herdsman's Motives"

SUPPORT FOR WRITING AND EXTEND YOUR LEARNING

Writing: Character Study

Use the following tips to help you write a **character study** of Oedipus in which you judge Oedipus' character and guilt.

- List passages that describe or show Oedipus' reactions, statements, and decisions.

_____

_____

_____

_____

- Explain what each passage tells about Oedipus.

_____

_____

_____

_____

- Write a thesis statement about Oedipus' character based on the passages.

_____

_____

Listening and Speaking: Debate

Fill in the chart below. Use these notes to help prepare for either side of your **debate** about Oedipus. The debate will take the form of a mock trial about Oedipus' guilt.

Defense	Prosecution
Argument	**Argument**
Evidence (quotations from play)	**Evidence (quotations from play)**
Response to Defense	**Response to Prosecution**

WEB RESEARCH SOURCES

About Web Research Sources

A Web site is a collection of Web pages—text and graphics on a topic that can be found on the Internet. **Web research sources** include any Web site that provides information for researchers.

When you conduct research, it is important to review the information on a Web site carefully. Some information may not be accurate. The authors of the Web site may not be well qualified, or they may present misleading information.

Reading Strategy

Analyzing the Usefulness and Credibility of Web Sources When you find a Web site on a subject, you should **analyze the usefulness and credibility of the source.** A useful site is one that is easy to understand and to navigate, or move through. A credible site gives trustworthy, up-to-date information. Use the information in the chart below to evaluate, the sites you find.

A Useful Web Site . . .	A Credible Web Site . . .
• has vocabulary and information suitable for your research needs and your audience	• presents thorough coverage of a subject
• includes interesting and easy-to-follow graphics, such as charts and maps	• may be sponsored by a college or university or approved by subject-matter specialists
• offers a clear site map	• includes a bibliography or identifies the source of its information
• has a search engine within the site so you can easily get more information	• is updated periodically so the information is current

Build Understanding

Knowing these terms will help you understand the information on this Web site.
digital (DIJ i tuhl) **library** (Ly brer ee) *n.* an online set of materials on various topics
database (DAYT uh bays) *n.* a collection of information on a particular subject, usually stored on a computer

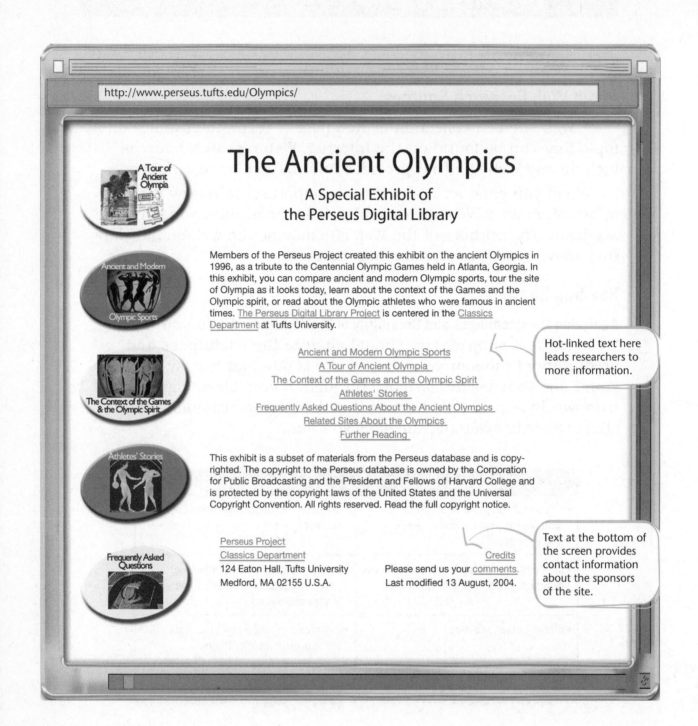

http://www.perseus.tufts.edu/Olympics/

The Ancient Olympics

A Special Exhibit of
the Perseus Digital Library

Members of the Perseus Project created this exhibit on the ancient Olympics in 1996, as a tribute to the Centennial Olympic Games held in Atlanta, Georgia. In this exhibit, you can compare ancient and modern Olympic sports, tour the site of Olympia as it looks today, learn about the context of the Games and the Olympic spirit, or read about the Olympic athletes who were famous in ancient times. The Perseus Digital Library Project is centered in the Classics Department at Tufts University.

Ancient and Modern Olympic Sports
A Tour of Ancient Olympia
The Context of the Games and the Olympic Spirit
Athletes' Stories
Frequently Asked Questions About the Ancient Olympics
Related Sites About the Olympics
Further Reading

Hot-linked text here leads researchers to more information.

This exhibit is a subset of materials from the Perseus database and is copyrighted. The copyright to the Perseus database is owned by the Corporation for Public Broadcasting and the President and Fellows of Harvard College and is protected by the copyright laws of the United States and the Universal Copyright Convention. All rights reserved. Read the full copyright notice.

Perseus Project
Classics Department
124 Eaton Hall, Tufts University
Medford, MA 02155 U.S.A.

Credits
Please send us your comments.
Last modified 13 August, 2004.

Text at the bottom of the screen provides contact information about the sponsors of the site.

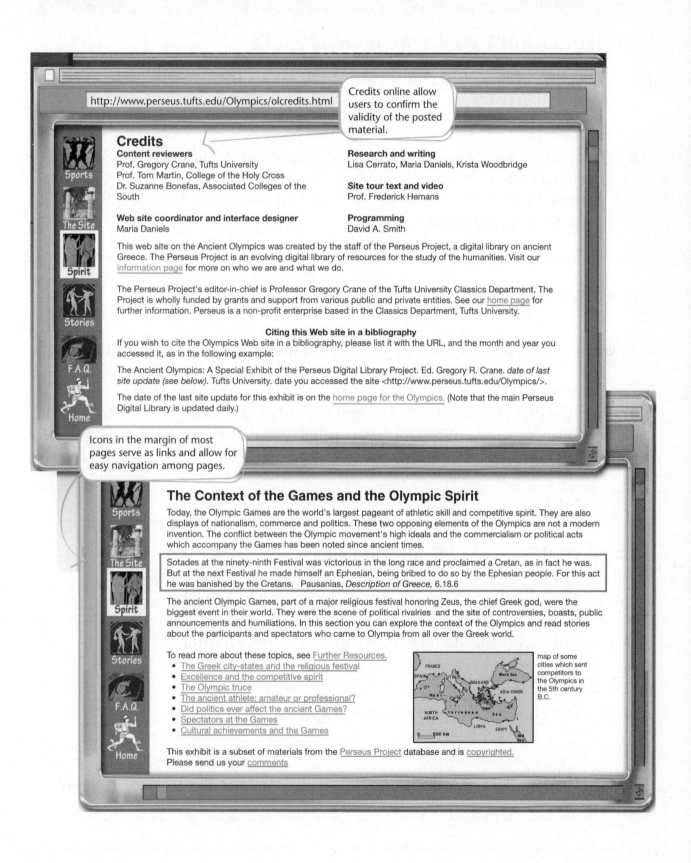

http://www.perseus.tufts.edu/Olympics/olcredits.html

Credits online allow users to confirm the validity of the posted material.

Credits

Content reviewers
Prof. Gregory Crane, Tufts University
Prof. Tom Martin, College of the Holy Cross
Dr. Suzanne Bonefas, Associated Colleges of the South

Research and writing
Lisa Cerrato, Maria Daniels, Krista Woodbridge

Site tour text and video
Prof. Frederick Hemans

Web site coordinator and interface designer
Maria Daniels

Programming
David A. Smith

This web site on the Ancient Olympics was created by the staff of the Perseus Project, a digital library on ancient Greece. The Perseus Project is an evolving digital library of resources for the study of the humanities. Visit our information page for more on who we are and what we do.

The Perseus Project's editor-in-chief is Professor Gregory Crane of the Tufts University Classics Department. The Project is wholly funded by grants and support from various public and private entities. See our home page for further information. Perseus is a non-profit enterprise based in the Classics Department, Tufts University.

Citing this Web site in a bibliography

If you wish to cite the Olympics Web site in a bibliography, please list it with the URL, and the month and year you accessed it, as in the following example:

The Ancient Olympics: A Special Exhibit of the Perseus Digital Library Project. Ed. Gregory R. Crane. *date of last site update (see below)*. Tufts University. date you accessed the site <http://www.perseus.tufts.edu/Olympics/>.

The date of the last site update for this exhibit is on the home page for the Olympics. (Note that the main Perseus Digital Library is updated daily.)

Icons in the margin of most pages serve as links and allow for easy navigation among pages.

The Context of the Games and the Olympic Spirit

Today, the Olympic Games are the world's largest pageant of athletic skill and competitive spirit. They are also displays of nationalism, commerce and politics. These two opposing elements of the Olympics are not a modern invention. The conflict between the Olympic movement's high ideals and the commercialism or political acts which accompany the Games has been noted since ancient times.

Sotades at the ninety-ninth Festival was victorious in the long race and proclaimed a Cretan, as in fact he was. But at the next Festival he made himself an Ephesian, being bribed to do so by the Ephesian people. For this act he was banished by the Cretans. Pausanias, *Description of Greece*, 6.18.6

The ancient Olympic Games, part of a major religious festival honoring Zeus, the chief Greek god, were the biggest event in their world. They were the scene of political rivalries and the site of controversies, boasts, public announcements and humiliations. In this section you can explore the context of the Olympics and read stories about the participants and spectators who came to Olympia from all over the Greek world.

To read more about these topics, see Further Resources.
- The Greek city-states and the religious festival
- Excellence and the competitive spirit
- The Olympic truce
- The ancient athlete: amateur or professional?
- Did politics ever affect the ancient Games?
- Spectators at the Games
- Cultural achievements and the Games

map of some cities which sent competitors to the Olympics in the 5th century B.C.

This exhibit is a subset of materials from the Perseus Project database and is copyrighted. Please send us your comments

THINKING ABOUT WEB RESEARCH SOURCES

1. What two links could you use to learn about the way Ancient Olympia looked?

_____

2. The page called "The Context of the Games and the Olympic Spirit" is an interior page. It provides information on one of the topics that you can link to from the home page. How can you move between this interior page and the home page?

_____

READING STRATEGY:

3. What is one feature that helps you **evaluate the site's credibility?**

_____

4. The "Credits" page contains a section entitled "Citing this Web site in a bibliography." What can you infer about the site from this information?

_____

_____

TIMED WRITING: EVALUATION (25 minutes)

Write a brief evaluation of this Web site, based on the three pages shown here and your ratings of the site's usefulness and credibility.

• Does the Web site list credible sources of information?

_____

• Is the Web site easy to navigate? Explain.

_____

• What might you change about the Web site to make it more useful?

_____

_____

BUILD SKILLS

from the Aeneid

LITERARY ANALYSIS

An epic is a long story or poem about the adventures of gods or of a hero. A **national epic** tells about the founding of a nation or culture. In the *Aeneid* (ee NEE id), Virgil writes about the founding of Rome. With the noble deeds of the hero Aeneas (i NEE uhs), Virgil shows that the Romans are honest, fair, and devoted to duty.

As you read the *Aeneid*, identify the details that would make Romans proud of their origins and culture.

READING STRATEGY

When you read certain selections, you must **apply background information** to help you understand them. Writers often refer to famous characters and events from other pieces of literature. For example, Virgil refers to characters and events in the Greek epic the *Iliad*, by Homer.

It may be useful to apply background information about the *Iliad* to your reading of the *Aeneid*. To recognize references to the Iliad, be sure to read the footnotes at the bottom of each page. Then complete the chart below to apply background information.

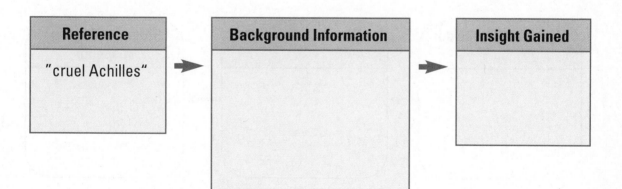

Reference	→	Background Information	→	Insight Gained
"cruel Achilles"				

from the Aeneid, Book II: How They Took the City

Virgil

Translated by Robert Fitzgerald

Summary The *Aeneid* tells the story of the fall of Troy from the point of view of the hero Aeneas. In Book I, Aeneas arrives in Carthage and begins to tell the story of Troy to Queen Dido. He explains that the Greeks built a large wooden horse and had hid soldiers inside its belly. The Greeks then pretended to retreat from Troy and left the horse behind as a gift.

Book II begins with Aeneas telling what happened after the Trojans discovered the horse. Aeneas explains that some Trojans advised against taking the horse inside the city walls. However, Sinon, a Greek spy, lied and told the Trojans that the Greeks built the horse in order to please Athena. He told the Trojans that the horse was a gift, or offering. The Trojans believed Sinon and brought the horse inside Troy's walls.

Note-taking Guide

Use the diagram below to record the main events in this story.

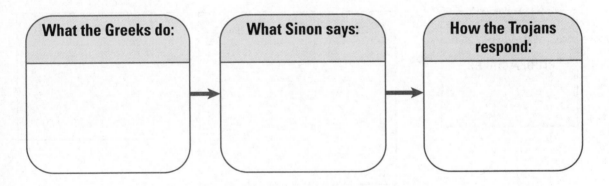

What the Greeks do:	What Sinon says:	How the Trojans respond:

from the Aeneid
Virgil

Book II: How They Took the City
Translated by Robert Fitzgerald

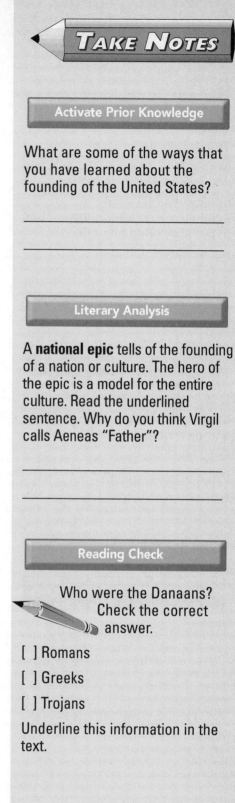
Book I of the *Aeneid* begins: "I sing of warfare and a man at war." That man at war is the Trojan prince Aeneas, who embodies the Roman ideal of devotion to duty as he performs his mission to found the Roman people. He and his men set sail from Troy, only to encounter a series of adversities on their way to Italy.

After a storm stirred up by jealous Juno, Aeneas and his men reach Carthage, where Queen Dido holds a banquet in the Trojans' honor. Disguised as Aeneas' son, Cupid (Amor) attends the banquet and causes Dido to fall in love with Aeneas. To prolong his stay, Dido asks Aeneas to recount the fall of Troy and his subsequent wanderings, which he does as Book II begins.

The room fell silent, and all eyes were on him,
<u>As Father Aeneas from his high couch began:</u>

"Sorrow too deep to tell, your majesty,
You order me to feel and tell once more:
How the Danaans[1] leveled in the dust
The splendor of our mourned-forever kingdom—

◆ ◆ ◆

---

1. Danaans (DAY nay unz) *n.* tribal name for Greeks.

Activate Prior Knowledge

What are some of the ways that you have learned about the founding of the United States?

_____

_____

Literary Analysis

A **national epic** tells of the founding of a nation or culture. The hero of the epic is a model for the entire culture. Read the underlined sentence. Why do you think Virgil calls Aeneas "Father"?

_____

_____

Reading Check

Who were the Danaans? Check the correct answer.

[ ] Romans

[ ] Greeks

[ ] Trojans

Underline this information in the text.

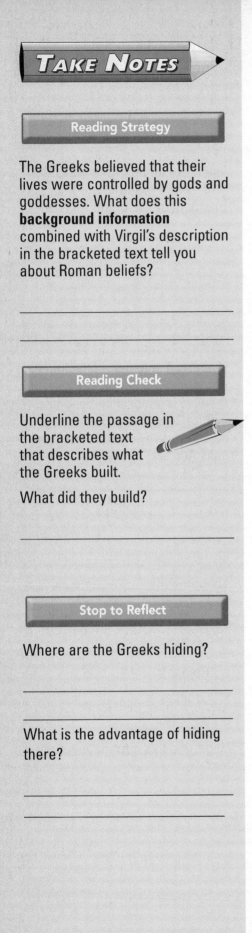
Reading Strategy

The Greeks believed that their lives were controlled by gods and goddesses. What does this **background information** combined with Virgil's description in the bracketed text tell you about Roman beliefs?

_____

_____

Reading Check

Underline the passage in the bracketed text that describes what the Greeks built.

What did they build?

_____

_____

Aeneas continues to speak to Queen Dido. He explains that he will overcome his grief and tell her the story of the fall of his city, Troy.

◆ ◆ ◆

Knowing their strength broken in warfare,
  turned
Back by the fates, and years—so many years—
Already slipped away, the Danaan captains
By the divine <u>handicraft</u> of Pallas[2] built
A horse of <u>timber</u>, tall as a hill,
And <u>sheathed</u> its ribs with planking of cut pine.
This they gave out to be an offering
For a safe return by sea, and the word went
  round.
But on the sly they shut inside a company
Chosen from their picked soldiery by lot,
Crowding the vaulted caverns in the dark—
The horse's belly—with men fully armed.

◆ ◆ ◆

Aeneas describes how the men of Troy went out, thinking the enemy was gone. The Trojans wander along the beach and look at the deserted campsites. But the Greeks have not really left. Some of their soldiers are hidden in the wooden horse. When the Trojans see the huge horse, some of them want to bring it inside their city gates. Other Trojans oppose this idea, thinking the horse is part of a Greek trick.

◆ ◆ ◆

Vocabulary Development

handicraft (HAN di kraft) *n.* skill working with the hands
timber (TIM buhr) *n.* wood
sheathed (SHEETHD) *v.* put into a protective covering

---

2. **Pallas** (PAHL uhs) *n.* a goddess, hostile to the Trojans and helpful to the Greeks.

Contrary <u>notions</u> pulled the crowd apart.
Next thing we knew, in front of everyone,
Laocoön[3] with a great company
Came furiously running from the Height[4]
And still far off cried out: "O my poor people,
Men of Troy, what madness has come over you?
Can you believe the enemy truly gone?
<u>A gift from the Danaans, and no ruse[5]?</u>
<u>Is that Ulysses' way, as you have known him?</u>
Achaeans[6] must be hiding in this timber,
Or it was built to butt against our walls,
Peer over them into our houses, pelt
The city from the sky. Some <u>crookedness</u>
Is in this thing. Have no faith in the horse!
Whatever it is, even when Greeks bring gifts
I fear them, gifts and all."

◆ ◆ ◆

After Laocoön gives the warning that the horse is a trick of the Greeks, he throws his spear into the horse. Aeneas cries that if the gods had been with them, the Trojans would have then discovered the Greeks hidden in the horse and Troy would still stand.

Aeneas now describes how Trojan shepherds find an unknown Greek. This is Sinon, a Greek spy who lets the Trojans take him as prisoner. Sinon pretends to be helpless and makes a pitiful speech.

◆ ◆ ◆

The whimpering speech brought us up short;
  we felt
A twinge for him. Let him speak up, we said,
Tell us where he was born, what news he
  brought,
What he could hope for as a prisoner.

Vocabulary Development

notions (NOH shunz) *n.* ideas
crookedness (KROOK ehd nes) *n.* dishonesty; deceit

---

3. **Laocoön** (lay AHK uh wahn) *n.* Trojan priest of the god Neptune.
4. **the Height** *n.* the Acropolis.
5. **ruse** (ROOZ) *n.* trick.
6. **Achaeans** (uh KEE uhnz) *n.* Greeks.

TAKE NOTES

Reading Check

Does Laocoön believe the wooden horse is a gift or a trick?

_____

Underline the words and phrases that support your answer.

Reading Strategy

In the *Iliad*, Homer portrays Ulysses as a noble warrior. Apply this **background information**. Read the underlined text. How does Homer's portrayal of Ulysses contrast with Virgil's?

_____

_____

_

Literary Analysis

Read the bracketed text of the **national epic**. What Roman values does Aeneas reveal?

_____

_____

Stop to Reflect

Do you think the Trojans' feelings toward Simon will lead to trouble? Why or why not?

_____

_____

_____

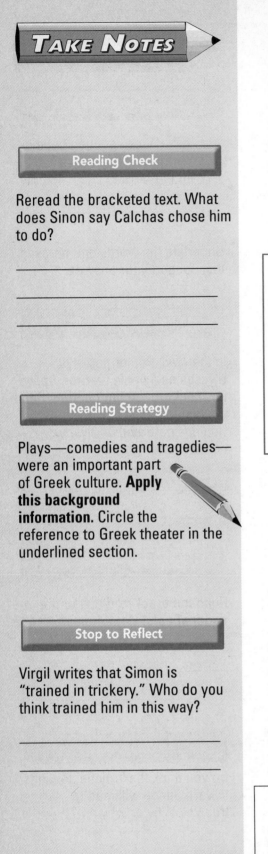

Reading Check

Reread the bracketed text. What does Sinon say Calchas chose him to do?

_____

_____

_____

Reading Strategy

Plays—comedies and tragedies—were an important part of Greek culture. **Apply this background information.** Circle the reference to Greek theater in the underlined section.

Stop to Reflect

Virgil writes that Simon is "trained in trickery." Who do you think trained him in this way?

_____

_____

Sinon now speaks. He claims he is telling the truth. Sinon describes how he became an enemy of Ulysses. Then he continues his deceit, saying it is useless to tell his story to the Trojans. Since he is a Greek, he is considered an enemy as are all Greeks. He says he expects punishment.

The Trojans, says Aeneas, ask Sinon to continue his story. They do not believe that he is lying to them.

Sinon continues his false story. He claims the Greeks have consulted the seer Calchas to determine the will of the gods. Sinon says he was chosen by Calchas to be sacrificed and that all the rest of the Greeks agreed. He claims he broke free and hid from them. Sinon says he fears that his family will be punished for his escape, and he begs the Trojans to take pity on him.

Aeneas speaks again. He says the Trojan king, Priam, ordered the chains to be removed from Sinon. Priam then questions Sinon about the purpose of the wooden horse.

◆ ◆ ◆

These were his questions. Then the captive, trained
In trickery, in the stagecraft of Achaea,
Lifted his hands unfettered to the stars.
"Eternal fires of heaven," he began,
"Powers inviolable, I swear by thee,
As by the altars and blaspheming swords
I got away from, and the gods' white bands[7]

Vocabulary Development

unfettered (uhn FET urd) *adj.* unchained; unrestrained
blaspheming (blas FEEM ing) *adj.* irreverent; showing a lack of respect

---

7. **god's white bands** *n.* narrow bands or ribbons used to tie up or fasten something.

I wore as one chosen for sacrifice,
This is justice, I am justified
In dropping all <u>allegiance</u> to the Greeks—
As I had cause to hate them; I may bring
Into the open what they would keep dark.
No laws of my own country bind me now."

◆ ◆ ◆

Sinon now makes up a lie about how and why the Greeks retreated. He tells the Trojans how the Greeks angered the goddess Pallas Athene and claims that she is now against the Greeks. Therefore, the Greeks have gone home to get new troops and new powers. The huge wooden horse, Sinon says, is meant as an offering to the great goddess Pallas Athene (also called Minerva). He tells the Trojans that if they pull the horse into their city, they will be saved and the Greeks will be conquered.

Aeneas concludes his tale, admitting the Trojans were fooled.

◆ ◆ ◆

This <u>fraud</u> of Sinon, his accomplished lying,
Won us over; a tall tale and fake tears
Had captured us, whom neither Diomedes
Nor Larisaean Achilles[8] overpowered,
Nor ten long years, nor all their thousand ships.

Vocabulary Development

allegiance (uh LEE juns) *n.* loyalty; devotion
fraud (FRAWD) *n.* dishonest deception; trick

---

8. Larisaean Achilles (luh RIS ee in uh KIL eez) *n.* Achilles, the foremost Greek warrior, was so called after Larissa, a town in his homeland of Thessaly.

◀ **TAKE NOTES**

Reading Check

Why does Simon say that he is justified in dropping all allegiance to the Greeks?

_____

_____

_____

Underline the text that supports your answer.

Stop to Reflect

Can you understand why the Trojans trusted Sinon? Why or why not?

_____

_____

_____

Literary Analysis

How do the last five lines of this **national epic** allow the Romans to remain proud even though the Greeks have conquered Troy?

_____

_____

_____

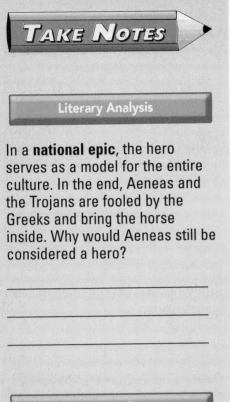

Literary Analysis

In a **national epic**, the hero serves as a model for the entire culture. In the end, Aeneas and the Trojans are fooled by the Greeks and bring the horse inside. Why would Aeneas still be considered a hero?

_____

_____

_____

Stop to Reflect

If you were a Trojan listening to Sinon's story, would you have believed him? Would you have sympathy for him?

Explain.

_____

_____

_____

_____

Despite warnings that Greeks are hiding in the horse, the Trojans bring the horse inside the walls of Troy. During the night, the horse emits the Greeks, who are ready for combat. Aeneas is also ready. In a fierce spirit, he and his men fight against desperate odds. Toward daybreak, Aeneas finds a crowd of refugees gathered for exile, waiting for him to lead them to safety. He does so, with characteristic courage.

from the Aeneid

1. **Analyze:** Sinon says that the Danaans built the wooden horse as an offering. Its purpose was to aplogize for stealing Athena's sacred statue, the Palladium. To what Trojan feelings might Sinon be trying to appeal with this story?

_____

2. **Literary Analysis:** Aeneas is the son of the goddess Aphrodite. Why might this have prompted pride for Romans reading their **national epic?**

_____

3. **Literary Analysis:** Aeneas is the **epic hero** of Virgil's *Aeneid*. Ulysses (Odysseus) is the epic hero of Homer's *Odyssey*. Use the Venn diagram below to compare and contrast the two epic heroes.

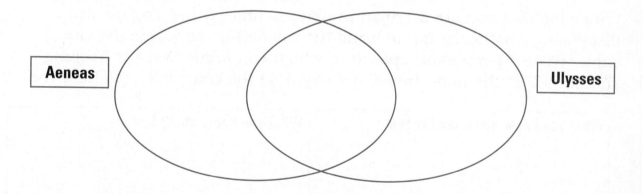

Aeneas   Ulysses

4. **Reading Strategy:** Ulysses is the Roman name for Odysseus, a Greek warrior. He is known in Homer's epics as a smart and resourceful warrior. **Apply this background information** to explain what is meant by the following lines, spoken by Laocon:
   a. A gift from the Danaans, and no ruse?
   b. Is that Ulysses' way, as you have known him?

_____

Writing: Analysis of Storytelling Technique

The Aeneid is made up of Aeneas' account of the fall of Troy and long speeches by Sinon. However, the book itself is written by Virgil. Virgil, Aeneas, and Sinon are all tellers of this story. To help you analyze Virgil's storytelling, fill in the chart below. Write down details about characters and events from both Aeneas' and Sinon's points of view.

Point of view	Characters	Events
Aeneas		
Sinon		

Use your answers to write an analysis of Virgil's storytelling technique.

Listening and Speaking: Persuasive Speech

Imagine that you are a Trojan in Aeneas' time. Other Trojans are discussing whether or not to bring the wooden horse inside the city gates. Write a **persuasive speech** in which you argue that the Trojans should not let the horse inside the city. Use the chart below to help you.

What you know about the Greeks:	What you know about Sinon:
What you know about the wooden horse:	What might happen if the horse is let in:

Use your notes to write your speech and deliver it to your class.

from the Metamorphoses:
The Story of Daedalus and Icarus

LITERARY ANALYSIS

A **narrative poem** tells a story. Narrative poems are different from lyric poems, which express the thoughts or feelings of the speaker. Ballads are one type of narrative poetry. Epic poems like Virgil's *Aeneid* (uh NEE id) are another. In the *Metamorphoses*, Ovid (AHV id) uses the epic form. However, he does not tell the story of an important historical event. Instead, he tells entertaining tales about gods, demigods, and mortals. As you read "The Story of Daedalus (DED uh les) and Icarus (IK ar es)" from the *Metamorphoses*, notice how Ovid uses both narrative and poetic techniques.

A **myth** is a fictional tale that comes out of a culture's oral tradition and usually involves supernatural characters or events. Myths often teach the values and ideals of a culture. Sometimes, they attempt to explain unknowns, such as the following:

- Causes of natural occurrences or the origins of earthly life
- Origins of place names
- Reasons for certain customs

READING STRATEGY

As you read this story, you will probably find yourself **anticipating events**. That means that you look forward to what happens next. Anticipating events focuses on your emotional reaction to events, rather than on logical prediction. This process leads you to connect with characters as you watch their lives unfold. Use this chart as you read "The Story of Daedalus and Icarus." In it, note clues that cause you to anticipate later events in the story.

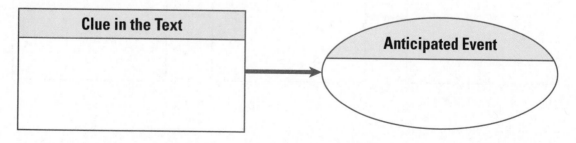

Clue in the Text	Anticipated Event

from the Metamorphoses: The Story of Daedalus and Icarus

Ovid
Translated by Rolphe Humphries

Summary In this myth, a boy pays a terrible price for ignoring his father's advice. Daedalus and his son, Icarus, are trapped on the island of Crete. To escape, Daedalus builds wings for himself and his son. He builds the wings from feathers and wax. Daedalus warns his son not to fly too close to the sun. The joy of flying causes Icarus to forget his father's warning. Soon, the sun melts the wax on Icarus' wings. The boy falls from the sky and into the sea.

Note-taking Guide

Use this chart to record the sequence of events in the myth.

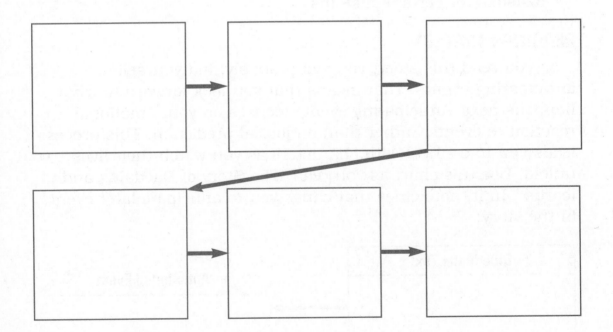

from the Metamorphoses:
The Story of Daedalus and Icarus

1. **Apply:** What warning does Daedalus give his son as the two prepare to take off?

   _____

   _____

   In what way might this advice apply to life in general?

   _____

   _____

2. **Literary Analysis:** What does Ovid do to make this **narrative poem** interesting and suspenseful even for readers who are familiar with the story? Explain.

   _____

   _____

3. **Literary Analysis:** Using this chart, show how certain details in "The Story of Daedalus and Icarus" teach lessons or convey values.

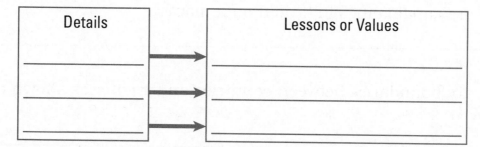

4. **Reading Skill:** At what point in the story can readers first **anticipate** that Daedalus' plan might lead to disaster? List specific lines.

   _____

   _____

Writing: Script for a Multimedia Presentation of a Story

Use the chart below as an aid in planning a **script for a multimedia presentation** of "The Story of Daedalus and Icarus." Record your ideas for different types of media that you could use to illustrate different lines in the poem.

	Ideas for Media	Lines in Poem
Photographs		
Artwork		
Music		
Video Clips		
Sound Effects		

Research and Technology: Map of the Roman Empire

Answer these questions to help you as you prepare to draw a **map of the Roman Empire** in Ovid's time.

1. How are mountains indicated on a map?

   _____

2. How are capital cities indicated on a map?

   _____

3. How are boundaries between countries and territories shown on a map?

   _____

from the Annals: *from* The Burning of Rome

LITERARY ANALYSIS

Annals are nonfiction works of history. They tell about events that happen year-to-year. In the *Annals*, the writer Tacitus [TAS uht uhs] tells about events that happened during the first century of the Roman Empire. He also includes these elements:
- descriptions that make events clear to the reader
- explanations of the reasons for events
- explanations of the effects of events

Tacitus uses **descriptive details** to explain what happened. These details appeal to the senses, give an exact fact, or name something specific. One exact fact that Tacitus shares is the price of corn. This type of detail brings the story to life. Look for descriptive details as you read.

READING STRATEGY

Bias is an opinion that affects how a writer treats a topic. If you **recognize the author's bias** you will be able to understand why he or she stresses some facts or makes certain statements. For example when Tacitus' talks about Nero, he uses many negative words. One negative word he uses is *brutality*. To see bias, use the chart below as you read.

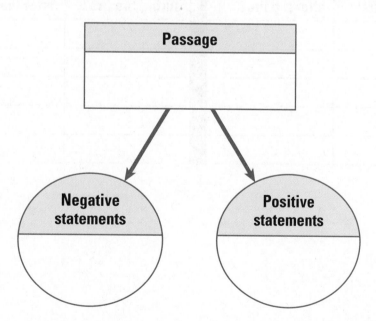

from the Annals: The Burning of Rome

Tacitus

Translated by Michael Grant

Summary Tacitus describes a great fire that destroys much of Rome. The people's grief and anger is made worse by rumors that the Emperor Nero started the fire. The rumor says Nero wanted an excuse to build a new palace and gardens. Nero tries to stop the rumor by blaming the Christians for starting the fire. He orders many Christians to be arrested and killed. He tries to get back the public's support but people do not trust him.

Note-taking Guide

Use this chart to keep track of the events described in the *Annals*.

What happens to the city...		What does Nero do...	
during the fire?	after the fire?	during the fire?	after the fire?

from the Annals: The Burning of Rome

1. **Analyze:** How did the way the city was set up help the fire spread?

   _____

   _____

2. **Literary Analysis:** This chart lists traits common to **annals.** Complete the chart by writing in details from the selection that show each trait.

Element of an Annal	Examples from the Annals of Tacitus
Review of a year's important events	
Explanation of the reasons for events	
Explanation of the causes of events	
Vivid descriptions	

3. **Literary Analysis:** Facts are statements that can be proved true. Does Tacitus only report facts, or does he also report rumors? Explain.

   _____

   _____

4. **Reading Strategy: Recognize the author's bias.** What are two phrases Tacitus uses that tell you his opinion about Christianity.? Explain.

   _____

   _____

   _____

SUPPORT FOR WRITING AND EXTEND YOUR LEARNING

Writing: Eyewitness Narrative Essay

Use the Annals as a model to write an eyewitness narrative essay about an event you have witnessed.

Event you will write about:

- Is the event you witnessed famous? Is it something only your friends or family know about?

_____

- What details will you use to make it clear to your readers how you feel about what happened?

_____

_____

_____

Use these notes as you write your essay.

Listening and Speaking: Skit

Write a skit, or short dramatic scene, in which a group of Romans gossip about the fire. Prepare to work on your skit by following these steps:

- Decide what kind of Romans you will be. For example, you could be workers, children, or business owners.

_____

_____

_____

- Write down details that show how the fire affected people.

_____

_____

- Write down details from the *Annals* that tell you what daily life was like for Romans.

_____

Use these details as you plan and write your skit.

from the Song of Roland • from The Nibelungenlied

LITERARY ANALYSIS

Medieval epics began in the great halls of Germany. They celebrated important qualities like being loyal and brave. In addition, medieval epics

- made clear what was important to a group of people.
- were based on history but stretched the truth for excitement.
- were performed long before they were written down.

The **epic hero** is a special person who shows a culture's highest values. The hero in most epics also has a **heroic flaw**. This weakness of character may lead to suffering or even death.

READING STRATEGY

Feudalism is the name for the way that work, government, and other social relationships were set up in Europe during the Middle Ages. Under this system, farmers called serfs worked the land. The land was owned by people known as vassals. Vassals vowed to be loyal to their lords. Most people of the time felt that military skill, loyalty, and honor were the most important virtues. As you read, use this chart to identify **feudal values**.

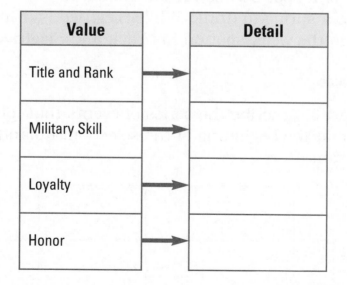

Value	Detail
Title and Rank	
Military Skill	
Loyalty	
Honor	

from the Song of Roland • *from* The Nibelungenlied

Translated by Fredrick Goldin, A. T. Hatto

Summaries The *Song of Roland* is an epic about Roland, a great knight under the French King Charlemagne [SHAHR luh MAYN]. Charlemagne is fighting the Spanish Muslims, or Saracens [SA ruh SENZ]. Roland leads the rear guard of the French army. They are outnumbered by the Saracens. During the battle, Roland's men are slaughtered. Roland himself is fatally wounded. He blows his horn, or *olifant* [OH li FAWNT], to summon help, but it is too late. Charlemagne arrives with his army. The Saracens flee. Before Roland dies, he tries to destroy his sword so that no unworthy person will take it.

In this section of the *Nibelungenlied* [NEE buh LooNG en LEED], Hagen [HAH gen] and King Gunther [GooN ter] kill the hero Siegfried [SEEG freed]. Hagen and Gunther make a plan to trick Siegfried while they are all out hunting. During the hunt, Siegfried kills many animals. He is skilled and powerful. He is also invulnerable except for a spot between his shoulder blades. The hunting party goes to a spring to drink. While Siegfried is drinking, Hagen spears him in the weak spot on his back and Siegfried dies.

Note-taking Guide

Use this chart to describe the series of events that follow from the hero's action at the beginning of the selection. Roland's action is filled in for you.

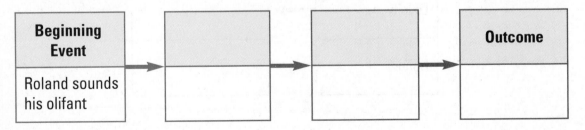

Beginning Event			Outcome
Roland sounds his olifant			

from the Song of Roland • from The Nibelungenlied

1. **Interpret:** Why does Oliver think Roland is not a good vassal?

   _____

   _____

2. **Make a Judgment:** Siegfried boasts that he is strong and brave. Do you think his personality contributes to his death? Explain.

   _____

   _____

3. **Literary Analysis:** Tellers of **medieval epics** felt that a good story was more important than facts. How might this have affected what people knew about their own history?

   _____

   _____

4. **Literary Analysis:** Each story has many details that show what Roland and Siegfried are like. Use this chart to write down details that show different parts of each **epic hero**'s personality.

Hero	Appearance	Abilities and Skills	Others' Opinions of Him	Opinion of Himself
Roland				
Siegfried				

5. **Reading Skill:** Loyalty was an important **feudal value**. How do both Siegfried and Roland show they are loyal to the kings that they serve?

   _____

   _____

   _____

SUPPORT FOR WRITING AND EXTEND YOUR LEARNING

Writing: Persuasive Essay on Values

Roland and Siegfried have courage and strength. However, neither is very prudent, or cautious. Write an essay about courage and prudence. Use details from these stories. Some virtues have a negative side:

- Having courage means being brave. A brave person may be reckless.

- Acting with prudence means being careful. A careful person may not take needed risks.

Use the chart below to analyze details from each story. Then, use your notes to help you as you write your essay.

	Detail	Trait it Shows	Why is it good? Why is it bad?
Details about Roland	He does not call for help in time.	Courage	It is good because Roland is brave. It is bad because he really needed help.
	He fights even though he is hurt.		
	He protects his sword.		
Details about Siegfried	He does not listen to his wife.	Courage	It is good because Siegfried is brave. It is bad because he is too confident.
	He kills the most animals.		
	He lets Gunther drink first.		

Listening and Speaking: Press Conference

Run a **press conference** at which Charlemagne tells what happened to Roland and the French army. Use these questions to start your work:

- Where is Charlemagne at the start of the battle and at the end?

_____

- Where is Roland at the start of the battle and at the end?

_____

- What do the Saracens do during the battle?

_____

INTERVIEWS

About Interviews

An **interview** is a record of a conversation between two or more people. Usually, one person (the interviewer) asks questions and the other person (the subject) answers. The purpose of an interview is to get information about a person, an event, or a topic. The subject usually has special knowledge. He or she may offer an expert opinion or a firsthand account of an event.

Interviews can be found in magazines, on the Internet, on the radio, and on television. Most print interviews include these elements to help readers tell apart the words of the interviewer and subject:
- the names or initials of the interviewer and the subject
- special formatting, such as colons (:) after each person's name

Reading Strategy

People interview other people for many reasons. They may want to entertain, to inform, to inspire, or to persuade the audience. When you **analyze the purpose** of an interview, you determine the reason the interview took place. To do this, begin by looking carefully at the language in the interview. Notice the words, details, and descriptions that point to a particular purpose.

As you read the *ComicFan* interview, use the chart below to list the details that help you determine the purpose of the interview.

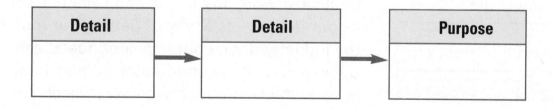

Detail	Detail	Purpose

BUILD UNDERSTANDING

Knowing these terms will help you read this interview.

Middle Ages *n.* a period of European history after the fall of ancient Rome and before the Renaissance (A.D. 476 c.–1450)

medieval (meh DEE vul) *adj.* relating to, or characteristic of, the Middle Ages

---

In what publication did this interview appear?

_____

_____

Circle the place where you found the answer.

1. Who is being interviewed in this selection?

_____

_____

2. What work did the person write?

_____

_____

What two elements of this interview help you to determine who is speaking?

1. _____

_____

2. _____

_____

from ComicFan

INTERVIEW WITH SHANE L. AMAYA,
Writer of the comic *Roland: Days of Wrath*

Slated for release in July [1999], Shane L. Amaya's *Roland: Days of Wrath* has all the ingredients to be a hit. Recently chosen worthy of the Small Press Snapshot and Certified Cool mentions in May's Previews catalog, *Roland: Days of Wrath* promises beautiful art and an epic storyline. We recently caught up with the busy writer for a little one-on-one.

ComicFan: I understand that *Roland: Days of Wrath* is your first published work. Do you see this series as a springboard to other projects or have you committed yourself to this project for the long run?

Shane: The Roland comic is my first self-published work. My artists and I see this comic as our debut[1]—as a way of getting our foot in the industry door. I hope to continue to self-publish and write comics after *Roland*: I am already thinking about two new projects for next year; I know my artists, Gabriel Ba and Fabio Moon, have stories to tell as well. Since our collaboration[2] on the Roland comic has gone so well, we will definitely work together again, and sooner rather than later.

---

1. **debut** (day BYOO) *n.* first appearance.
2. **collaboration** (kuh lab uy RAY shuhn) *n.* a situation in which people work together.

ComicFan: Now for those not familiar with your upcoming comic *Roland: Days of Wrath*. How would you describe the story and characters?

Shane: The Roland comic is based on the early medieval French war epic the *Song of Roland*. It was probably written late in the 11th century but the action is set in a glorified past— Charlemagne's[3] 8th century Holy Roman Empire. It is the story of Roland's sacrifice, his stepfather's betrayal, and Charlemagne's eternal embattlement.[4] The story is incredibly powerful and the language—having been refined orally for over three hundred years—is strong and beautiful. The characters are all warriors, feudal[5] lords, kings and vassals.[6] They are cut sharply: Roland is brave and Oliver is wise; they boast and betray; they weep and roar with anger—and these men fight, with all the strength in their hearts, and kill and die on the battlefield.

ComicFan: So what do you think fuels your passion for comic books? Is there a particular aspect?

Shane: Comic books tell more powerful, more emotionally evocative[7] and more stimulating stories than any other medium. Comics are capable of the best storytelling art and literature can offer: they feature the best of two infinitely productive universes—the imagination literature

Reading Check

What is the setting of *Roland: Days of Wrath*?

_____

_____

Circle the place where you found the answer.

Reading Strategy

When you **analyze the purpose** of a written work, you look for details that tell why the author is writing. From the details provided so far, what do you think is the purpose of this interview?

_____

_____

_____

_____

---

3. **Charlemagne** (SHAR luh mayn) (A.D. 742-814) the first ruler of the Holy Roman Empire.
4. **embattlement** (em BAT tul ment) *n.* the positioning for war.
5. **feudal** (FYOO dul) *adj.* of the social system of feudalism in which land was worked by serfs and owned by vassals who owed military service to an overlord.
6. **vassals** (VAS uhls) *n.* the servant or subject of an overlord.
7. **evocative** (ee VAHK uh tiv) *adj.* tending to call forth, or elicit.

Read aloud the underlined text. In your own words, tell why Shane likes comic books better than any other form of media.

_____

_____

Underline the words and phrases in the bracketed text that show that Shane's purpose is to give readers a preview of the comic.

What is Shane's opinion about the Middle Ages?

_____

List two details from the text to support your answer.

1. _____

_____

2. _____

_____

---

relate, share and encourage the creativity of two art forms in one unique—and amazing—medium.

ComicFan: I know you've done a lot of research into the historical aspects of the *Song of Roland*, which your comic is based on. What do you find so captivating about the *Song of Roland*?

Shane: The Middle Ages are an incredibly fascinating, important and—despite popular belief—creatively astounding period. I love the medieval imagination; medieval imagination has, I think, influenced the modern world in profound, unshakeable ways. The *Song of Roland* captivates me in more ways than I can say here: but for one, it is an amazing example of medieval ingenuity. How does Charlemagne's actual, historical and shameful defeat become a poem that, throughout time, transforms this skirmish into a story of apocalyptic[8] struggle and Christ-like sacrifice; of battlefields packed with hundreds of thousands of warriors; of Anti-Gods and Judas figures;[9] and where the stakes are no higher than the fate of the entire universe?!

ComicFan: Which writers do you think have had the most influence on you?

Shane: The works I enjoy reading most of all are those created by countless, anonymous authors. These include ancient epics and sagas[10], much of medieval literature, folk tales and other oral narratives. I enjoy medieval literature especially for the way it is created: through the hands and voices of many, . . . through marginalia[11] and glosses[12] upon

---

8. **apocalyptic** (uh PAHK uh lip tik) *adj.* pertaining to the end of the world where evil is destroyed and goodness overcomes all.

9. **Judas figures** *n.* traitors.

10. **sagas** (SAH guhs) *n.* stories.

11. **marginalia** (mar juh NAY le uh) *n.* words or pictures in the margin of a text.

12. **glosses** (GLAHS us) *n.* words of explanation in a text.

glosses, and because of the way it is constantly interpreted, translated—and forever changing. <u>To a medieval mind, authorship is wholly unimportant: it is only the story that matters, and still more important than the story is the way that it is well told. . . .</u>

ComicFan: What do you think you enjoy more, the creating of Roland or the reading of it?

Shane: I never get tired of reading either the *Song of Roland* or my comic! Though the process of creation is a lot of fun, there's nothing like seeing the finished product.

ComicFan: Finally, what can readers expect to see in the coming issues of *Roland: Days of Wrath*?

Shane: The Roland comic is a moving and poignant[13] story of war and vengeance, fraternity and betrayal, faith and wisdom. Readers can expect a beautifully drawn and colored mini-series that will take them into a vivid medieval world of tenuous[14] politics and treacherous pagan citadels[15]; they will witness justice, bloody vengeance, epic battle-storm and battlefields choked with dying warriors; readers will know the depths of Charlemagne's terrible grief, and the heart of one of the world's greatest heroes!

ComicFan: Thanks again for your time, Shane, and good luck with your great comic! You've got what looks like a hit on your hands, keep it up.

Roland: Days of Wrath **from Terra Major debuts in July [1999] at comic-book shops everywhere.**

---

13. **poignant** (POYN yunt) *adj.* emotionally touching or moving.
14. **tenuous** (TEN yoo us) *adj.* flimsy; insubstantial.
15. **citadels** (SIT uh dels) *n.* forts; places of safety.

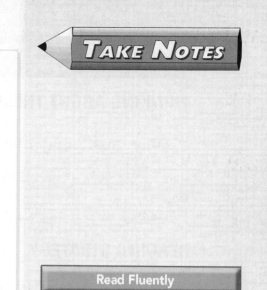

TAKE NOTES

Read Fluently

Read aloud the underlined text. Do you agree that a story is more important than its author? Explain your answer.

_____

_____

_____

_____

Reading Informational Materials

What words or phrases in the selection let you know that the **interview** is ending?

_____

_____

_____

THINKING ABOUT THE INTERVIEW

1. Why does Amaya love comic books?

_____

_____

READING STRATEGY

2. Find two details that make you think the **purpose** of this interview is to entertain. Explain your choices.

_____

_____

3. Find two details that make you think the purpose of the interview is to inform. Explain your choices.

_____

_____

TIMED WRITING: EXPOSITION (25 minutes)

Write an explanation of how you could turn a literary work into a comic book or cartoon. Use the chart below to write down the title of a literary work that you like. List the main characters. Then, write down one event from the story. List three reasons that it would be powerful if shown in pictures.

Title of Literary Work	Main Characters
Event	**Reasons**

from Perceval • The Lay of the Werewolf

LITERARY ANALYSIS

An **archetype** [AR kuh TYP] is a detail, character type, or theme (message) that appears in the literature of many cultures. One common archetype is the *quest* [KWEST]. This is a search by a hero for something important. Most quests also have these elements:

- The hero must travel long distances.
- The hero has much to learn. He or she becomes wiser during the quest.
- The hero faces many obstacles (problems).
- The hero may be helped. This help may involve magical powers.

Another common archetype is **disguised identity**. This means that a character uses tricks, different clothing, or even magic to hide his or her true self.

As you read, look for details in these stories that fit the archetype of the quest or of disguised identity.

READING STRATEGY

Many stories that have archetypes also use symbols. A symbol is a person, a place, an animal, or an object that has its own meaning but also stands for something else. Interpreting something means to think about and understand it. **Interpreting symbols** can help you to understand a literary work. To do this, notice objects, people, or even places that seem important in a story. Look at details that describe them. Also, think about your own ideas about these kinds of objects, people, or places. As you read, use the chart below to interpret symbols.

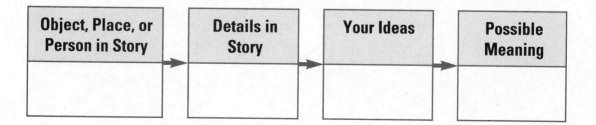

Object, Place, or Person in Story	Details in Story	Your Ideas	Possible Meaning

from Perceval

Chrétien de Troyes
Translated by Ruth Harwood Cline

Summary Perceval is a young knight who goes on a journey to find the Holy Grail (sacred cup). During the journey, he comes to a mysterious castle. Inside, Perceval meets a man who lets him stay the night. As they talk and eat, Perceval sees and hears many strange, wonderful things. He asks no questions about them because he has been trained not to talk too much. The next morning, there is no one at the castle to answer Perceval's questions.

Note-taking Guide

Use the chart below to record the main events and details from story.

Before Perceval reaches the castle	At the castle	The next morning

from Perceval: The Grail

Chrétien de Troyes

Translated by Ruth Harwood Cline

A young knight named Perceval began a journey. He traveled alone. He prayed that he would find his mother alive and well. He stopped when he came to a wide, deep river and cried out to God.

◆ ◆ ◆

"Oh God Almighty! It would seem,
if I could get across this stream,
I'd find my mother, if she's living."
He rode the bank with some misgiving
and reached a cliff, but at that place
the water met the cliff's sheer face
and kept the youth from going through.
A little boat came into view;
it headed down the river, floating
and carrying two men out boating.
The young knight halted there and waited.

◆ ◆ ◆

Perceval watched the fishermen, hoping they would float near him. He saw them drop their anchor. Then one fisherman baited his hook. Perceval called loudly asking if there was a bridge nearby. The fisherman answered that there was no bridge, ferry, or shallow place to ride across. In fact, his boat was the only one for twenty miles. In reply, the knight asked where he might stay for the night. The fisherman directed him to his own castle on the other side of the great cliff. Perceval happily set off for the castle.

◆ ◆ ◆

The knight rode up the cliff until
he reached the summit of the hill.

© Pearson Education, Inc., publishing as Pearson Prentice Hall.

Reading Strategy

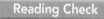 A **symbol** is something that stands for another thing. For example, raging ocean waves might stand for anger. Read the underlined sentence. Then, circle an object that may have a symbolic importance. On the lines below, suggest what this object may **symbolize.**

_____

_____

_____

_____

Reading Check

What does Perceval pray for at the beginning of the tale?

_____

_____

Read aloud the underlined passage. The words *see* and *trickery* are rhyming words. Their similar sounds give emphasis to the meaning. Read the bracketed text. Then, circle two other words that rhyme at the ends of the lines.

The **quest archetype** usually involves a journey in search of a special person or object. In what way does the story so far fit the quest archetype?

_____

_____

_____

What might the fireplace **symbolize?** Circle the letter of the answer below.

a. kind hospitality

b. fierce war

c. great sadness

What details in the text help you answer?

_____

_____

_____

He looked around him from that stand
but saw no more than sky and land.
He cried, "What have I come to see?
Stupidity and trickery!

◆　◆　◆

As Perceval rode further, however, he began to see a tower in the valley. He rode closer and saw the fisherman's castle. Perceval took back his unkind words and was happy again. At the castle, the drawbridge was down. Four servants greeted him, cared for his horse, and brought him a new, silk cloak. Then they led him to a beautiful hallway. Perceval stayed there until two servants led him to the main hall.

The hall was square, and on one side was the handsome lord of the castle. The lord sat on a bed wrapped in a robe and blankets. Perceval was astonished when he saw the great fireplace in the center of the room.

◆　◆　◆

Between four columns, burning bright,
a fire of dry logs cast its light.
In order to enjoy its heat,
four hundred men could find a seat
around the outsized fire, and not
one man would take a chilly spot.
The solid fireplace columns could
support the massive chimney hood,
which was of bronze, built high and wide.

◆　◆　◆

Two servants presented Perceval to the lord. The lord greeted him warmly and apologized for not standing. He explained that he was ill and could not stand. Then, he invited Perceval to sit beside him. A servant brought a sword to the lord. The lord noted that it was made of fine, strong steel. Then the servant explained where the sword had come from.

The <u>squire</u> said, "Sir, if you permit,
<u>your lovely blonde niece sent this gift,</u>
<u>and you will never see or lift</u>
<u>a sword that's lighter for its strength,</u>
<u>considering its breadth and length.</u>
Please give the sword to whom you choose,
but if it goes to one who'll use
the sword that he is given well,
you'll greatly please the <u>demoiselle</u>.
No sword will be quite like this sword."
Immediately the noble lord
bestowed it on the newcomer,
who realized that its hangings were
a treasure and of worth untold.

◆　◆　◆

Perceval looked at the sword carefully. It was made of gold. It had splendid decorations on its case and on its handle. The lord explained that it had been made for Perceval alone, and asked him to try it out. Perceval thanked the lord, pulled the blade out, and then admired how it looked at his waist and in his fist.

◆　◆　◆

It seemed as if it would assist
the youth in any time of need
to do a brave and knightly deed.

◆　◆　◆

The knight gave the sword and its case to the servants who were caring for the rest of his armor.

◆　◆　◆

Out of a room a squire came, clasping
a lance of purest white: while grasping
the center of the lance, the squire
walked through the hall between the fire
and two men sitting on the bed.

Vocabulary Development

squire (SKWYR) a servant or helper
demoiselle (dem wa ZEL) a young woman

Read Fluently

Read aloud the underlined text. Then, on the lines below, write what the squire said in your own words.

_____

_____

_____

_____

_____

Reading Strategy

Circle two words or phrases that suggest that the sword is a **symbol** for strength and goodness.

Literary Analysis

Read the bracketed passage. How does the sword fit into Perceval's **quest**?

_____

_____

_____

_____

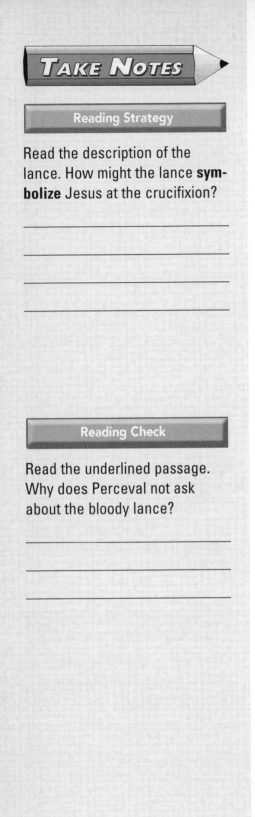

Read the description of the lance. How might the lance **symbolize** Jesus at the crucifixion?

_____

_____

_____

_____

Reading Check

Read the underlined passage. Why does Perceval not ask about the bloody lance?

_____

_____

_____

All saw him bear, with measured tread,
the pure white lance. From its white tip
a drop of crimson blood would drip
and run along the white shaft and
drip down upon the squire's hand,
and then another drop would flow.

♦   ♦   ♦

The white lance amazed the knight. But he did not ask why it dripped with blood. The lord had warned him not to be too talkative. The knight did not want to be impolite, so he stayed silent as he watched. He saw two servants enter. They each held a golden candelabra with ten candles. Next Perceval saw a beautiful young woman carrying a brilliant grail, or cup. It was decorated with the rarest of gems and shone brightly. Following her was another young woman with a platter.

♦   ♦   ♦

The young man saw the maids' procession
and did not dare to ask a question
about the grail or whom they served;
the wise lord's warning he observed,
for he had taken it to heart.
I fear he was not very smart;
I have heard warnings people give:
that one can be too talkative,
but also one can be too still.
But whether it was good or ill,
I do not know, he did not ask.

♦   ♦   ♦

The servants began preparing for a meal. They washed their hands. Then they brought in an ivory tabletop and put it on top of table legs made of ebony. This black wood is remarkable because it will not burn and it will not rot. The servants put the white table on the black legs and spread a sparkling white cloth over it all.

The meal served on the table was grand. Servants sliced peppered meat from a large roast. They poured wine and served hunks of bread. As they ate, Perceval watched servants carry the grail back and forth in front of the bed. He still did not ask whom the servants were feeding.

◆ ◆ ◆

So he would ask: before he spoke
he'd wait until the morning broke,
and he would ask a squire to tell,
once he had told the lord farewell
and all the others in his train.

◆ ◆ ◆

He put it out of his mind and continued to eat. Servants brought a kingly meal with wine, fruit, and gingerbread. After dinner special liquors and medicines were offered to calm Perceval's stomach. The many foods and splendid display impressed Perceval greatly. After dinner, the lord said goodnight. The servants set up a bed for the knight in the great hall. Then four strong servants carried the lord to his rest. Other servants helped the knight take off his clothes and prepared him for bed. He slept peacefully.

In the morning, Perceval woke to find that the castle was completely empty. There were no servants to help him dress, so he pulled on his clothes by himself and saw that his armor had been placed near his bed.

◆ ◆ ◆

When he had armed himself at last,
he walked around the great hall past
the rooms and knocked at every door
which opened wide the night before,
but it was useless: juxtaposed[1]

---

1. juxtaposed (JUKS tuh pohzd) *adj.* put side by side or close together.

from Perceval: The Grail **183**

TAKE NOTES

Reading Check

In your own words, explain Perceval's plan for learning about the grail.

_____

_____

_____

_____

Literary Analysis

The **quest archetype** involves a challenge or struggle. What challenge does Perceval face in the morning?

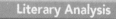

_____

_____

_____

_____

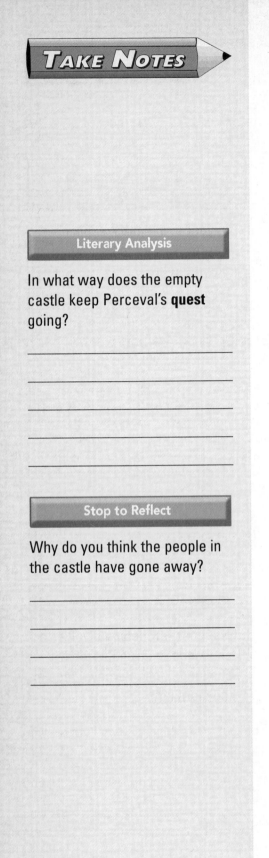
the doors were tightly locked and closed.
He shouted, called, and knocked outside,
but no one opened or replied.

♦ ♦ ♦

Finally, the knight stopped calling
and decided to leave the castle. At the
foot of the stairs, he found his horse sad-
dled. He saw his shield and lance leaning
against the wall for him. On his horse, he
searched the castle once more but found
no one. He rode to the gate and saw that
the drawbridge had been left open for
him. Perceval decided that he would
search the woods around the castle for
anyone with information about the lance
or grail. But as he rode out, he realized
that the drawbridge was being raised
slowly. His horse reached the end of the
bridge and had to make a great leap onto
the bank. Surprised, Perceval swerved
around quickly to see who had raised the
bridge so mysteriously.

♦ ♦ ♦

He shouted, hearing no reply,
"Whoever raised the bridge," said he,
"where are you? Come and talk to me!
Say something to me; come in view.
There's something I would ask of you,
some things I wanted to inquire,
some information I desire."
His words were wasted, vain and <u>fond</u>;
no one was willing to respond.

Literary Analysis

In what way does the empty
castle keep Perceval's **quest**
going?

_____

_____

_____

_____

_____

Stop to Reflect

Why do you think the people in
the castle have gone away?

_____

_____

_____

Vocabulary Development

fond (FAHND) *adj.* foolish

© Pearson Education, Inc., publishing as Pearson Prentice Hall.

The Lay of the Werewolf

Marie de France,
Translated by Eugene Mason

Summary In this story, a wife learns that her husband is a werewolf. She makes a plan to get rid of him. She asks a knight to steal her husband's clothes. Without them, the husband cannot return to his human form. Later, a king makes friends with the werewolf. He returns the clothes to the werewolf. The werewolf uses the clothes to become human again. The king tells the wife and the knight to leave the kindom, never to return.

Note-taking Guide

Use the chart below to take notes about the story.

Character	What He/She Wants	What He/She Does	What happens as a result
Wife			
Werewolf			
Knight			
King			

from Perceval • The Lay of the Werewolf

1. **Analyze:** In *Perceval*, the fisherman tells Perceval to go to his home. Perceval follows directions and comes to a castle. Are the fisherman and the lord of the castle the same person? Explain.

_____

2. **Interpret:** In *The Lay of the Werewolf*, the husband does not want to tell his secret. The wife keeps asking him anyway. What does this show about her?

_____

3. **Literary Analysis:** One common **archetype** is the **quest**. The story of Perceval has all the traits of a quest. Some of them are listed below. Complete the last two rows of the chart with details from the story.

Quest Trait	Story Detail from *Perceval*
Hero	Perceval
Wise teacher	the Fisher-King
Goal (purpose of the quest)	To find the Holy Grail
Obstacles (problems the hero faces)	1. _____ 2. _____
Magical objects the hero sees or uses	1. _____ 2. _____

4. **Reading Strategy:** When you interpret **symbols**, you think about the deeper meaning of details. Jesus has been called a "fisher of men." Think about this information. Then, write down your ideas about what the Fisher King might symbolize.

_____

_____

Writing: Modern Symbolic Tale

Write a story of a quest. Set your story in today's world. This means you should include modern places, tools, words, and ideas. Use the chart to think about details to include in your story.

Use your notes to guide you as you write your story.

Hero	Write down ideas about your hero: 1. Name:_____ 2. Age:_____ 3. Type of Person:_____
Setting	Write where the quest begins and ends:
Goal	Write the name of the person or object your hero wants to find: Write the reason your hero wants to find it:
Obstacles	Write down two problems your hero must overcome: 1._____ 2._____
Help	Write down the name of a person who helps your hero: Write down how the person helps:

Research and Technology: Research Presentation

The story of Perceval is part of a group of stories about King Arthur and his Knights. They are called the Arthurian legends. Some scholars believe that Arthur was a real person. Others feel he is totally fictional. Write a **research presentation** about how the legends of King Arthur began. Use these steps to start your research.

- Write down three key words or phrases you can use to search the Internet. These may include "King Arthur," or "Arthurian Legends."

- List two Web sites that you find in your search.

- Do a search for "King Arthur" in a library card catalog. List three books, magazines, or other print sources that you find.

Take notes from these sources to use in your research presentation.

from the Divine Comedy, Inferno: Canto I • Canto III

Dante Alighieri
Translated by John Ciardi

LITERARY ANALYSIS

An **allegory** is a story with two levels of meaning. The first level is the literal meaning (what the words say). The second level is the symbolic meaning (the idea the words represent). This chart shows two levels of meaning of some words in the *Inferno*:

Literal Meaning	Symbolic Meaning
Mountain	A difficult task
A fierce animal	A sinful temptation
Sunlight	God's love

READING STRATEGY

Imagery is the use of words that appeal to the senses: sight, hearing, taste, smell, and touch. To **interpret an image**, think about how the words involve your senses. Identify the feeling or idea the image brings to mind. Use this chart to help you interpret images from the *Inferno*.

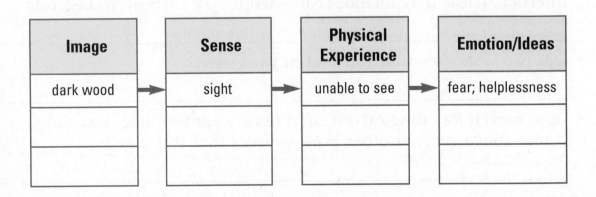

Image	Sense	Physical Experience	Emotion/Ideas
dark wood	sight	unable to see	fear; helplessness

from the Divine Comedy, Inferno: Canto I: The Dark Wood of Error

Dante Alighieri
Translated by John Ciardi

Summary Midway through his life, Dante finds himself lost in a terrible forest. It is the Dark Wood of Error. Dante tries to leave this forest but he cannot do so. The ghost of an ancient Roman poet named Virgil appears. Virgil says he will lead Dante out of the woods. First, they must travel through Hell. This is where sinners are punished. Then, they must pass through Purgatory. This is where sinners learn to give up their sins. A saintly young woman named Beatrice will then guide Dante to Paradise. This is where spirits rejoice in the presence of God. Dante agrees to go with Virgil, and they set off.

Note-taking Guide

Use the diagram below to keep track of events in Canto I.

Situation at the beginning of Canto I	Dante sees...	Dante is scared by...	Dante meets...	Situation at the end of Canto I
Dante is lost in a dark wood.				

In the underlined passage, the word astray means "off the right path." Keeping in mind the meaning of astray, what is the **symbolic meaning** of "dark wood" in the passage?

_____ a sinful and careless time in life

_____ an exciting trip through the jungle

_____ an area filled with trees

Read the bracketed passage. Underline the words that form an **image** of the hill. To which senses does this image appeal? Explain below.

_____

_____

_____

What helps calm Dante's fears?

_____

_____

from the Divine Comedy, The Inferno:

Canto I: The Dark Wood of Error

Dante Alighieri
Translated by John Ciardi

Midway in our life's journey,[1] I went astray
from the straight road and woke to find myself
alone in a dark wood. How shall I say
what wood that was! I never saw so drear,
so rank, so arduous[2] a wilderness!
Its very memory gives a shape to fear.

♦ ♦ ♦

Dante explains that the place was almost as bad as death. He could not remember how he had arrived at such a terrible place. His life had become sinful. He had wandered away from the path of goodness. And although he was afraid at every step, he walked through this evil valley.

♦ ♦ ♦

I found myself before a little hill
and lifted up my eyes. Its shoulders glowed
already with the sweet rays of that planet[3]
whose virtue leads men straight on every road,

♦ ♦ ♦

The sunshine helped calm Dante's fears, just as morning does after a dark night. He turned around to look at the path he had just traveled. Then he rested. He lay down until his heartbeat was slower. Then he rose and began to climb the hill quickly. Yet just as he began, he came upon a spotted leopard. He tried to get around the leopard, but his path was

---

1. **Midway in our life's journey** The Bible says that a life span is threescore years and ten, or seventy years. In this story, Dante is halfway through his seventy years. He is thirty-five, i.e., A.D. 1300.
2. **so rank, so arduous** so overgrown, so difficult to cross.
3. **that planet** the sun. Medieval astronomers considered it a planet. It is also symbolic of God as He who lights man's way.

blocked at every turn. He thought of turning back the way he had come. But then he remembered that this was the Easter season, the time of hope and rebirth. This thought calmed him.

◆ ◆ ◆

Yet not so much but what I shook with dread
   at sight of a great Lion that broke upon me
   raging with hunger, its enormous head
held high as if to strike a mortal terror
   into the very air. And down his track,
   a She-Wolf drove upon me, a starved horror
ravening and wasted beyond all belief.

◆ ◆ ◆

The wolf was skinny with hunger, and she snarled savagely. Dante was so afraid that he lost all hope of climbing the great sunny mountain. He fell back down into the dark woods. There, he saw a ghostly figure forming. He asked the figure if it were a ghost or a man. The figure gave Dante some clues: he was once a man who was born in Mantua, Italy, during Caesar's rule. He had lived in the Northern Italian city of Lombardy. He was the poet who wrote the *Aeneid*.

◆ ◆ ◆

"And are you then that Virgil and that fountain
   of purest speech?" My voice grew <u>tremulous</u>:
Glory and light of poets! now may that zeal
   and love's apprenticeship that I poured out
   on your heroic verses serve me well!
For you are my true master and first author,
   the sole maker from whom I drew the breath
   of that sweet style whose measures have
brought me honor.

◆ ◆ ◆

Vocabulary Development

tremulous (TREM yoo lus) *adj.* trembling; fearful or timid

TAKE NOTES

Read Fluently

Read aloud the first bracketed text. Underline the words or phrases that create a vivid **image** of the She-Wolf.

Literary Analysis

In an **allegory**, the characters often represent other people or ideas. In the second bracketed passage Dante calls Virgil "the sole maker from whom I drew the breath of that sweet style." To what or whom is Dante comparing Virgil?

_____

_____

_____

Reading Check

How does Dante feel when he meets Virgil? Circle the letter of the correct answer.

a. peaceful

b. overjoyed

c. indifferent

d. angry

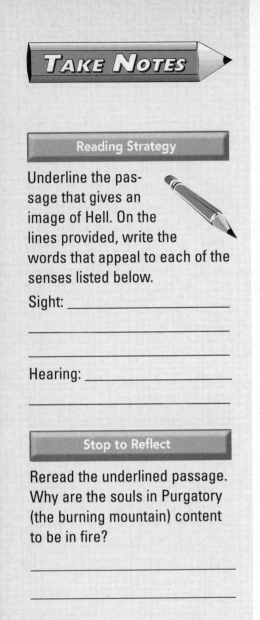
Reading Strategy

Underline the passage that gives an image of Hell. On the lines provided, write the words that appeal to each of the senses listed below.

Sight: _____

_____

_____

Hearing: _____

_____

Stop to Reflect

Reread the underlined passage. Why are the souls in Purgatory (the burning mountain) content to be in fire?

_____

_____

_____

_____

Reading Check

Does Dante follow Virgil?

_____

Where are they headed?

_____

_____

Dante explained to Virgil that he ran back to the dark woods because of the She-Wolf. Then he asked Virgil to protect him from the beast. Virgil said that anyone who wanted to escape the three wild animals must take a longer path. He offered to guide Dante on this longer path that would take him first through Hell and then through Purgatory.

◆　◆　◆

There you shall see the ancient spirits tried
in endless pain, and hear their lamentation
as each bemoans the second death[4] of souls.
Next you shall see upon a burning mountain[5]
souls in fire and yet content in fire,
knowing that whensoever it may be
they yet will mount into the blessed choir.

◆　◆　◆

Virgil told Dante that if he still wished to climb beyond Purgatory, a worthier spirit named Beatrice would be his guide. Virgil explained that he was forbidden to enter Heaven because he lived before the time of Christianity. He did not know the Christian God. Dante agreed to follow Virgil, and together they began their journey into Hell.

Vocabulary Development

lamentation (lam en TAY shun) *n.* a weeping or wailing

---

4. **the second death** damnation. "This is the second death, even the lake of fire." (the Bible, Revelation 20:14)
5. **a burning mountain** The Mountain of Purgatory, described in the second book of Dante's *Divine Comedy*.

from the Divine Comedy, Inferno: Canto III: The Vestibule of Hell

Dante Alighieri
Translated by John Ciardi

Summary Dante and Virgil arrive at the Gate of Hell. They hear the cries of the Opportunists. These are people who cared only for themselves when they were alive. These people cannot enter Hell itself. They are tortured forever at its entrance. Dante and Virgil go to the river *Acheron* [AK uh rahn]. There, Dante sees crowds of souls waiting at the riverbank. The souls are waiting for the boatman *Charon* [KER uhn], who will ferry them across the river to Hell. Charon says he cannot take Dante because he is a living man. Virgil says that Charon must take Dante.

Note-taking Guide

In this Canto, Dante sees two separate groups of sinners. Use the chart below to write down details that describe each group. One detail for each group has been done for you.

The Opportunists	The "throng" at the River
live neither in Hell nor out of Hell	are waiting to enter Hell

1. **Analyze:** In the Dark Wood, Dante sees a leopard, a lion, and a wolf. What emotion or idea does each beast stand for? Explain.

   _____

   _____

   _____

2. **Analyze Cause and Effect:** Think about the words carved on the Gate of Hell. How do you think Dante wants readers to feel when they read this passage? Explain.

   _____

3. **Literary Analysis:** The *Inferno* is an **allegory**. Every detail has two levels of meaning. The literal meaning is what the words say. The **allegorical** meaning is what the words symbolize. Use the chart below to write down your ideas about the meanings of details in Cantos I and III.

Detail	Literal Meaning	Allegorical Meaning
straight road		
dark wood		
leopard		
wasps and hornets		

4. **Reading Strategy:** Reread the last three stanzas of Canto III. What senses do the **images** in these stanzas bring to mind? Explain your answers.

   _____

   _____

Writing: Writing from Another Point of View

Write a new version of Cantos I and III as though Virgil were telling the story. Keep the same events and details, but show everything the way Virgil would see it. Answer these questions to get started:

- What does Virgil think of Dante when they first meet?

_____

_____

- Why do you think Virgil helps Dante?

_____

_____

- Why does Virgil know the way through Hell?

_____

_____

- How does Virgil feel about the awful things he and Dante see in Hell?

_____

_____

Use your answers to guide you as you write your story.

Listening and Speaking: Presentation

Dante became lost "midway" through life. This is another way of saying "at middle age." Make a **presentation** about middle age. You will need to do some research. Use these questions to guide your work.

Questions to Answer:
• What age is the middle of life today?
• Did people in the past have the same idea?
• What kind of life do many people in middle age have today?
• What kind of life did middle-aged people have in the past?
• Your question:
• Your question:

Inferno, Cantos V and XXXIV

LITERARY ANALYSIS

Characterization is the art of showing what characters are like. There are two ways that writers make characters seem real:

- *Direct characterization*: A writer tells the reader what a character is like.
- *Indirect characterization*: A writer hints at what a character is like. The writer shows what the character says and does, or how other characters treat or talk about the character.

When a character in a literary work talks about something outside the work, it is called an **allusion**. For example, in Canto V Francesca talks about Lancelot, a famous knight. When Francesca talks about Lancelot, she connects her story to his.

READING STRATEGY

The *Inferno* uses the first-person point of view. The reader sees everything through Dante's eyes. Yet, Dante the poet and Dante the speaker are not the same. In the poem, Dante is just a character. Dante the poet uses Dante the character to tell his ideas. As you read, use the chart to **distinguish between the speaker and the poet.**

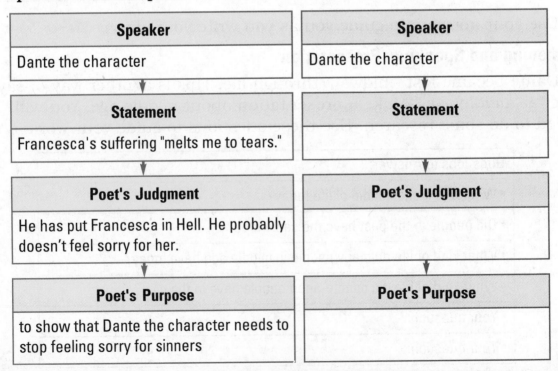

Speaker	Speaker
Dante the character	Dante the character

Statement	Statement
Francesca's suffering "melts me to tears."	

Poet's Judgment	Poet's Judgment
He has put Francesca in Hell. He probably doesn't feel sorry for her.	

Poet's Purpose	Poet's Purpose
to show that Dante the character needs to stop feeling sorry for sinners	

Inferno, Cantos V and XXXIV

Dante Alighieri
Translated by John Ciardi

Summary In Canto V, Dante and Virgil visit the second circle of Hell. They see souls who are carnal (bodily) sinners. Dante speaks to Francesca [Fran CHES kah]. Francesca travels this circle of Hell with her lover Paolo [POW loh]. In Canto XXXIV, Dante and Virgil enter the lowest circle of Hell. They see Satan himself. He is huge and frozen in the ice. Dante and Virgil now must find a way out of Hell.

Note-taking Guide

In these Cantos, Dante describes some characters more than others. Use this chart to write down details about these important characters.

Character	Appearance	Behavior	How Dante Reacts	What Dante Learns
Francesca				
Satan				

Inferno, Cantos V and XXXIV

1. **Evaluate:** In Canto V, what kind of love does Dante say is bad?

   _____

2. **Evaluate:** In Canto XXXIV, does Dante still feel sad about the sinners he sees? Explain.

   _____

   _____

3. **Literary Analysis:** You learn what Dante is like in a number of ways. Use the chart to write down what each example of **indirect characterization** tells you about Dante.

Method of Characterization	Example	Trait Revealed
Dante's Actions	He questions Francesca.	Interest in others; sympathy
Dante's Words	"i cowered for shelter."	
Other Characters' Behavior Toward Dante	Virgil carries him.	

4. **Literary Analysis:** In Canto XXXIV, Virgil makes an allusion when he says this line from a hymn: "On march the banners of the King." Virgil adds words that change the line. How do the words he adds change the meaning?

   _____

   _____

   _____

5. **Reading Strategy:** Dante, the **speaker of the poem,** faints when he and Virgil are about to move from one part of Hell to another. How does this make it easier for Dante the **poet** to tell the story?

   _____

   _____

SUPPORT FOR WRITING AND EXTEND YOUR LEARNING

Writing: Response to Criticism

Your response to Dorothy Sayers's ideas depends on what you think about Francesca. Use the chart below to write down details in the poem that tell about Francesca. Decide what trait each detail shows. In the third column, write "good" if you think it is a good trait and "bad" if you think it is bad. Then, decide if you think good and evil are balanced in Francesca.

Detail About Francesca	Trait it Shows	Is it good or bad?

Use these notes to help you write your response to criticism.

Research and Technology: Biographical Analysis Chart

Your **biographical analysis** chart will link the events of Dante's life with his writing. Fill in the chart below to help understand major events in Dante's life. Use library and Internet sources to learn the date of each event. Write the date in the correct slot on the timeline.

Date	Event
	Dante is born.
	The Ghibelline party is banned in Florence.
	Dante's friend Guido Cavalcanti is sent away from Florence and not allowed to return.
	Dante is sent away from Florence and not allowed to return.
	Dante works on his poem, the *Divine Comedy*.
	Dante dies.

from Canzoniere • To Hélène • Roses

LITERARY ANALYSIS

Petrarch was a poet who made the **sonnet** popular during the Italian Renaissance. The Petrarchan sonnet has these features:
- It is a highly structured poem with 14 lines.
- The poem focuses on a single theme.
- It begins with an eight-line *octave*.
- It ends with a six-line *sestet*.
- The octave often poses a question that is answered in the sestet.

All of the five love poems in this grouping are Petrarchan sonnets. Each poem uses different images to describe the speaker's beloved. **Imagery** is descriptive language that appeals to the five senses. Use this chart to compare imagery in the poems.

Senses	Image
Touch	
Sight	
Hearing	
Smell	
Taste	
Overall Effect of the Images	

READING STRATEGY

Reading in sentences will help you understand the meaning of a poem. In poems, the end of each sentence is not always at the end of each poetic line. A sentence may extend for several lines or end in the middle of a line. Pay attention to punctuation as you read. Do not pause or make a full stop at the end of a line unless there is a period, comma, colon, semicolon, or dash.

from Canzoniere: Laura • The White Doe • Spring
Petrarch

To Hélène • Roses
Pierre de Ronsard

Summary In "**Laura**," the speaker describes the beauty that young Laura once had. Now that she is older and less beautiful, he still loves her. In "**The White Doe**," the speaker describes how he admires a female deer (that represents Laura) from a distance. In "**Spring**," he explains how the return of spring reminds him of Laura. It makes him sad because Laura is dead.

In "**To Hélène**," the speaker advises the woman he loves to live for the moment. He tells her she will eventually regret her rejection of his love. In "**Roses**," the speaker compares a beautiful woman's life and death to a rose.

Note-taking Guide

Each of these poems makes a statement about love. Record the statement of each poem in the chart below.

	"Laura"	"The White Doe"	"Spring"	"To Hélène"	"Roses"
Statement about Love	Love, unlike beauty, does not fade.				

from Canzoniere • To Hélène • Roses

1. **Relate:** Petrarch's poems are about love and suffering. Do you think the feelings or situations Petrarch describes in his poems are still relevant today? Why or why not?

_____

_____

_____

2. **Hypothesize:** How do you think Hélène might have responded to the poem about her? Explain.

_____

_____

3. **Literary Analysis:** A **sonnet** has fourteen lines and is made up of two parts. In what way does the two-part structure of the **sonnet** "Laura" reflect the speaker's recollections of Laura?

_____

_____

4. **Reading Strategy:** Analyze how **reading in sentences,** affects the meaning of a poem. Choose a sentence from the poem "Spring" to complete the chart below. Explain the meaning of the sentence and relate its meaning to the poem.

Sentence	Meaning	Relationship to Poem

Writing: Journal Passage

Write a **journal passage** responding to any of the poems from this section. You will write in the voice of the beloved in the poem (such as Laura in "Laura"). Focus on the following questions to get started:

- What details from the poem tell you about the relationship between the speaker and his beloved?

_____

- What details from the poem reveal how the beloved feels about the speaker?

_____

- What details from the poem suggest how the beloved might respond to the poem?

_____

_____

Use your notes as you write your journal passage.

Research and Technology: Informative Essay

William Butler Yeats adapted Ronsard's poem "To Hélène." Yeats' poem is called "When You Are Old." Use the Internet or other sources to find this poem. Write an **informative essay** about these two poems. Answer these questions, then use your notes as you write your essay:

- How many lines are in each poem?

_____

- What do the two poems have in common?

_____

_____

- In what ways are the two poems different?

_____

_____

from the Decameron
Federigo's Falcon

LITERARY ANALYSIS

A **novella** is a short novel. It usually teaches a lesson or a moral to the reader. The novella is a very old form of writing. It was a model for what we know today as the short story. Boccaccio's work is a series of 100 novellas, including "Federigo's Falcon." This story is like other short stories because it contains the following elements:

- a setting (time and place of the story)
- well-developed characters (people who take part in the action of the story)
- a plot that includes the conflict (struggle), climax (high point), and resolution (end of story when a change is shown)
- a theme (message about life)

Use the chart below to identify the details of the novella.

Novella: "Federigo's Falcon"			
Setting:	Characters:	Plot:	Theme:

READING STRATEGY

A good way to help you connect to your reading is to **identify with characters**. This means you put yourself in a character's situation and consider how you would feel. As you read "Federigo's Falcon," pay attention to each character's experiences and choices. Then, consider your reactions to what is happening.

from the Decameron
Federigo's Falcon

Giovanni Boccaccio
Translated by G. H. McWilliam

Summary "Federigo's Falcon" is the story of what young Federigo does for love. Federigo loses his entire fortune in an unsuccessful effort to win Monna Giovanna's love. All he has left is a small farm in the country and a magnificent falcon. One summer, Monna Giovanna and her son go to their country estate. Her son becomes Federigo's friend. He admires Federigo's falcon. The son becomes very ill. He tells Monna Giovanna that having the falcon may help him feel better. Monna Giovanna goes to Federigo's home to ask for his falcon. While she is there, she learns the true extent of Federigo's generosity, but with an unexpected turn of events.

Note-taking Guide

Use this chart to follow the major events in "Federigo's Falcon." Begin with Federigo spending his fortune to show his love for Monna Giovanna.

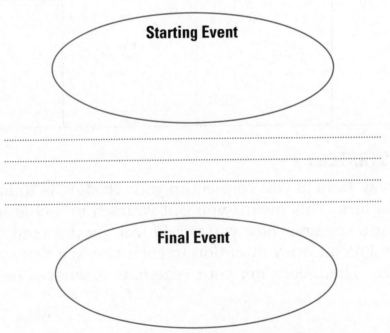

Starting Event

....

....

....

Final Event

from the Decameron
Federigo's Falcon

Giovanni Boccaccio
Translated by G. H. McWilliam

Once Filomena had finished, the queen, finding that there was no one left to speak apart from herself (Dioneo being excluded from the reckoning because of his privilege), smiled cheerfully and said:

It is now my own turn to address you, and I shall gladly do so, dearest ladies, with a story similar in some respects to the one we have just heard.

◆ ◆ ◆

This is a story about a beautiful woman and a generous man. The main character is a young man from Florence, Italy, named Federigo. He was known for his fine manners and good deeds.

◆ ◆ ◆

In the manner of most young men of gentle breeding, Federigo lost his heart to a noble lady, whose name was Monna[1] Giovanna, and who in her time was considered one of the loveliest and most adorable women to be found in Florence.

◆ ◆ ◆

In order to win her love, Federigo held great feasts. He rode fine horses and bought many gifts. He spent his money without thinking at all. However, Monna Giovanna had great virtue, and she did not take notice of his many gifts. She did not so much as look at her admirer Federigo.

Therefore, by trying to win her attention, he spent every penny that he

1. **Monna** lady.

Literary Analysis

A **novella** contains a setting, characters, plot, and a theme. What is the setting of "Federigo's Falcon"?

_____

_____

Underline the passage where you found the answer.

Reading Strategy

Identify with Federigo. How would you have felt if someone you loved did not notice you?

_____

_____

_____

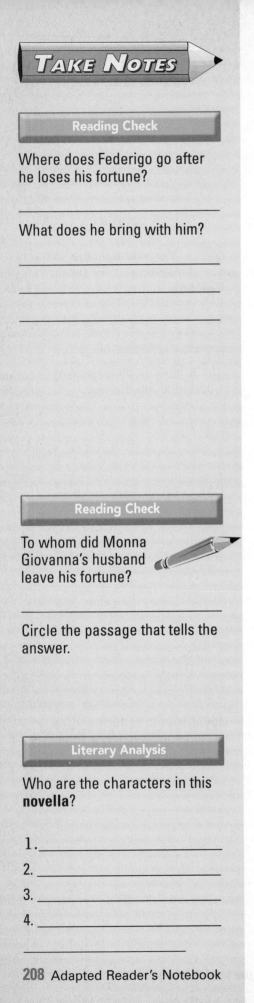

TAKE NOTES

Where does Federigo go after he loses his fortune?

_____

What does he bring with him?

_____

_____

_____

To whom did Monna Giovanna's husband leave his fortune?

_____

Circle the passage that tells the answer.

Who are the characters in this **novella**?

1._____
2._____
3._____
4._____

_____

had. He was finally left with nothing except for a small farm in the country as well as one falcon, which was considered the finest in the world. He decided in his poverty to move out to his farm, live on his small income, and hunt with his fine bird as often as he liked.

One day, after Federigo had moved out to the country, Monna Giovanna's husband fell ill. When he realized that he was about to die, he made his will. He was a very rich man, and he left everything he had to his son. His will stated that if his son died, all the money should go to his wife, whom he loved dearly.

◆ ◆ ◆

Shortly afterward he died, leaving Monna Giovanna a widow, and every summer, in accordance with Florentine custom, she went away with her son to a country estate of theirs, which was very near Federigo's farm. Consequently this young lad of hers happened to become friendly with Federigo, acquiring a passion for birds and dogs; and, having often seen Federigo's falcon in flight, he became fascinated by it and longed to own it, but since he could see that Federigo was deeply attached to the bird, he never ventured to ask him for it.

◆ ◆ ◆

Some time later, the boy grew sick. His mother was terribly worried about him and sat with him day and night. She often asked whether there was something he would like to have that might help him get better.

After hearing the question over and over, the boy finally told his mother that he would like Federigo's falcon. He thought that perhaps this bird might help him get better.

On hearing this request, the lady was somewhat taken aback, and began to consider what she could do about it. Knowing that Federigo had been in love with her for a long time, and that she had never <u>deigned</u> to cast so much as a single glance in his direction, she said to herself: "How can I possibly go to him, or even send anyone, to ask him for this falcon, which to judge from all I have heard is the finest that ever flew, as well as being the only thing that keeps him alive? And how can I be so heartless as to deprive so noble a man of his one remaining pleasure?"

♦ ♦ ♦

She said nothing, but she knew that Federigo would give it to her if she asked for it. After thinking the matter over, she decided that she could not refuse her son. She told him she would go for the falcon in the morning.

♦ ♦ ♦

"Bear up, my son, and see whether you can start feeling any better. I give you my word that I shall go and fetch it for you first thing tomorrow morning."

♦ ♦ ♦

The next morning, Monna Giovanna took a friend and went to Federigo's cottage. Since the weather was not good for hunting, Federigo was at home in his garden. He was very happy and surprised with her visit. She greeted him gracefully. She told him that she had come to make up for the great harm he had suffered because of her. She explained that she had come to show her respect for him

Vocabulary Development

deigned (DAYND) *v.* condescended; stooped

TAKE NOTES

Reading Strategy

Read the bracketed passage. **Identify with the character** of Monna Giovanna. How would you have felt if you had to ask Federigo for his prize falcon?

_____

_____

_____

Reading Check

List the two reasons why Monna Giovanna does not want to ask Federigo for the falcon.

1. _____

_____

2. _____

_____

Reading Strategy

Identify with the character of Federigo. Monna Giovanna has never paid attention to him. How would you greet Monna Giovanna if you were in Federigo's place?

_____

_____

_____

_____

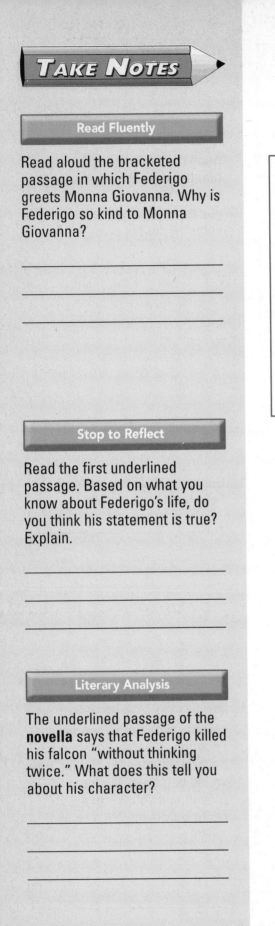

TAKE NOTES

Read Fluently

Read aloud the bracketed passage in which Federigo greets Monna Giovanna. Why is Federigo so kind to Monna Giovanna?

_____

_____

_____

Stop to Reflect

Read the first underlined passage. Based on what you know about Federigo's life, do you think his statement is true? Explain.

_____

_____

_____

Literary Analysis

The underlined passage of the **novella** says that Federigo killed his falcon "without thinking twice." What does this tell you about his character?

_____

_____

_____

had come to show her respect for him and to share a breakfast meal with him. She insisted that he must not go to trouble on account of her visit.

◆ ◆ ◆

"My lady," replied Federigo in all <u>humility</u>, "<u>I cannot recall ever having suffered any harm on your account.</u> On the contrary I have gained so much that if ever I attained any kind of excellence, it was entirely because of your own great worth and the love I bore you. Moreover I can assure you that this visit which you have been generous enough to pay me is worth more to me than all the money I ever possessed, though I fear that my hospitality will not amount to very much."

◆ ◆ ◆

He led her into the house and then asked her to wait while he arranged the breakfast. However, he soon realized that he had become so poor that he had nothing in the house to serve to her. He raced around the house looking for some way to solve the problem. As he was worrying and charging about, his eye fell on his precious falcon.

◆ ◆ ◆

And having discovered, on picking it up, that it was nice and plump, he decided that since he had nowhere else to turn, it would make a worthy dish for such a lady as this. So <u>without thinking twice about it he wrung the bird's neck</u> and promptly handed it over to his housekeeper to be plucked, dressed, and roasted carefully on a spit. Then he

---

Vocabulary Development

humility (hyoo MIL ih tee) *n.* lack of pride

---

covered the table with spotless linen, of which he still had a certain amount in his possession, and returned in high spirits to the garden, where he announced to his lady that the meal, such as he had been able to prepare, was now ready.

♦ ♦ ♦

Federigo served the meal modestly and did not tell his guests that they were eating his prized falcon. After the meal, they chatted for a short while. Then Monna Giovanna decided to tell Federigo the real reason for her visit.

She told Federigo that her request went against all rules of proper behavior because she was asking him for something that was the only pleasure in his life. She then told him that the gift she was requesting was his falcon because her son had taken a strong liking to it. She explained that she was afraid her son would die if she did not bring him the falcon. She said that she was appealing to Federigo's noble heart. She then made a final request for the falcon.

♦ ♦ ♦

"Do me this favor, then, so that I may claim that through your generosity I have saved my son's life, thus placing him forever in your debt."

♦ ♦ ♦

When Federigo realized what she was asking for and that he could not give it to her, he burst into tears. At first, Monna Giovanna thought he was crying at the idea of losing the falcon, and she was about to tell him that she did not want it after all. She decided instead to stay silent and wait for his answer.

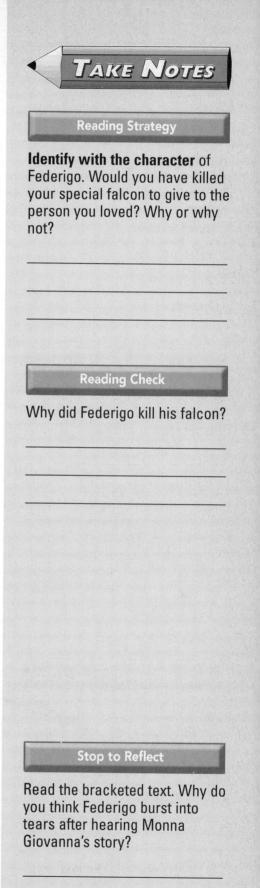

TAKE NOTES

Reading Strategy

Identify with the character of Federigo. Would you have killed your special falcon to give to the person you loved? Why or why not?

_____

_____

_____

Reading Check

Why did Federigo kill his falcon?

_____

_____

_____

Stop to Reflect

Read the bracketed text. Why do you think Federigo burst into tears after hearing Monna Giovanna's story?

_____

_____

_____

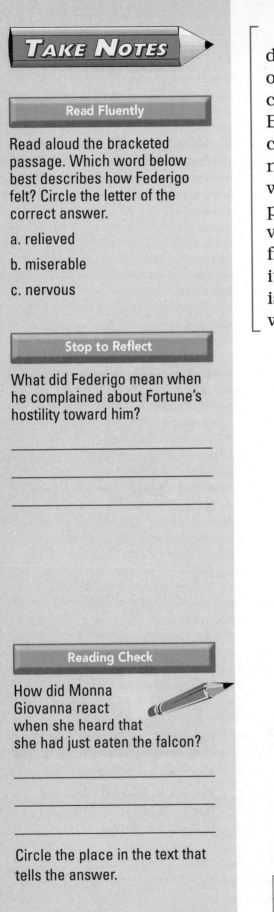

Read aloud the bracketed passage. Which word below best describes how Federigo felt? Circle the letter of the correct answer.

a. relieved

b. miserable

c. nervous

What did Federigo mean when he complained about Fortune's hostility toward him?

_____

_____

_____

How did Monna Giovanna react when she heard that she had just eaten the falcon?

_____

_____

_____

Circle the place in the text that tells the answer.

"My lady," he said, "ever since God decreed that you should become the object of my love, I have repeatedly had cause to complain of Fortune's hostility towards me. But all her previous blows were slight by comparison with the one she has dealt me now. Nor shall I ever be able to forgive her, when I reflect that you have come to my poor dwelling, which you never deigned to visit when it was rich, and that you desire from me a <u>trifling</u> favor which she has made it impossible for me to concede. The reason is simple, and I shall explain it in few words.

♦   ♦   ♦

Federigo said that when Monna Giovanna was so kind to come to his door for breakfast, he thought it was only proper to serve her an excellent meal. So, he roasted the falcon. Now that Federigo discovered that the falcon was the very thing Monna Giovanna wanted, he would never forgive himself for not being able to grant her only wish.

At first, the lady scolded Federigo for killing such a fine bird. Then she told him how she admired his generosity and nobility. However, now she began to worry about her son. She thanked Federigo for the fine meal and returned to tell the disappointing news to her son.

Just as Monna Giovanna had feared, the boy's illness grew worse and after only a few days, he passed away. She wept for her dear, lost boy. After some time had passed, Monna Giovanna's

---

Vocabulary Development

trifling (TRY fling) *adj.* small; simple

---

brothers began to urge her to marry again. Finally she told her brothers that the only man she would marry was Federigo.

Monna Giovanna remembered Federigo's generosity when he killed his fine falcon in her honor. Her brothers laughed at her for being so silly. After all, Federigo was a poor man and owned almost nothing at all. Monna Giovanna remained firm and answered her brothers.

◆   ◆   ◆

"My brothers," she replied, "I am well aware of that. But I would sooner have a gentleman without riches, than riches without a gentleman."

Seeing that her mind was made up, and knowing Federigo to be a gentleman of great merit even though he was poor, her brothers fell in with her wishes and handed her over to him, along with her immense fortune. Thenceforth, finding himself married to this great lady with whom he was so deeply in love, and very rich into the bargain, Federigo managed his affairs more prudently, and lived with her in happiness to the end of his days.

TAKE NOTES

Literary Analysis

Read the bracketed passage of the **novella**. What does Monna Giovanna's statement reveal about her character?

_____

_____

_____

Literary Analysis

A **novella** contains a theme, or message about life. Reread the bracketed passage. Underline the words that reveal the theme. Then, in your own words, state the theme.

_____

_____

_____

Reading Strategy

Identify with the character of Monna Giovanna. Would you choose to marry a person like Federigo? Explain.

_____

_____

_____

Vocabulary Development

thenceforth (THENS forth) *adv.* from that day on

---

from the Decameron
Federigo's Falcon

1. **Draw Conclusions:** Do you think "Federigo's Falcon" contains all the elements of a **novella**? Explain.

_____

_____

_____

2. **Literary Analysis:** How does the setting reflect Federigo's change of fortune?

_____

_____

3. **Literary Analysis:** What lesson about loss and restoration does this story teach? Use details from the tale to support your answer.

_____

_____

_____

4. **Reading Strategy:** In the chart below, choose two events involving Federigo and two involving Monna Giovanna. Then **identifying with each character**, explain what your reaction might be if you experienced similar events.

	Their Experiences	My Reactions
Federigo	1. 2.	1. 2.
Monna Giovanna	1. 2.	1. 2.

SUPPORT FOR WRITING AND EXTEND YOUR LEARNING

Writing: Literary Analysis

Prepare an essay supporting the theme of this story: people should preserve their nobility of spirit at all costs. Use the following chart to expand on the theme.

Theme:	People should preserve their nobility of spirit at all costs.
Restate the theme in your own words:	
Give three examples of how this relates to readers today:	

Listening and Speaking: Storytelling Circle

Prepare a story for a **storytelling circle**. Your story will be on the theme that your group chooses. Use this chart to help you create your story.

My Story			
Setting:	Characters:	Plot:	Theme:

from Starry Messenger • from The Assayer

LITERARY ANALYSIS

A **narrative account** tells the story of real-life events. Narrative accounts are often told by the writer and are usually about personal experiences. Sometimes, however, the writer's feelings or experiences can affect the story. As you read, look for clues in Galileo's writing that describe his excitement of discovery and why his work was important to him.

Narrative accounts often have some special features, which we call the story's **narrative style**. For example, the words an author chooses or the way an author puts words or sentences together help to make one writer's story different from another's. As you read the selections, pay attention to the narrative style that Galileo uses.

READING STRATEGY

You can analyze meaning by **breaking down long sentences.** Separate a sentence's key parts (the *who* and the *what*) from the difficult language to get to the main idea. Use the diagram below to analyze the long sentence shown.

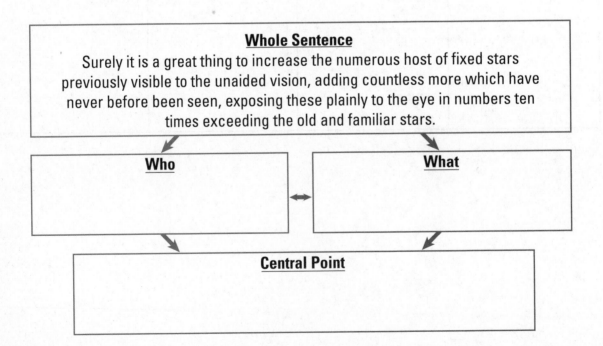

Whole Sentence
Surely it is a great thing to increase the numerous host of fixed stars previously visible to the unaided vision, adding countless more which have never before been seen, exposing these plainly to the eye in numbers ten times exceeding the old and familiar stars.

Who

What

Central Point

from Starry Messenger • from The Assayer

Galileo Galilei
Translated by Stillman Drake

Summary In the selection from *Starry Messenger*, Galileo describes his observations of the surface of the moon and his discovery of the nature of the Milky Way. He tells of learning about the telescope and of his excitement upon seeing objects in space closer than ever before. In *The Assayer*, Galileo relates the tale of a man who was sure that the source for all music was birds. As he traveled, he discovered more sources for song than he had imagined. He then became cautious about claiming much knowledge about the sources of songs.

Note-taking Guide

Use this chart to analyze the author's purposes in the two selections.

Author's Purpose	Examples from *Starry Messenger*	Examples from *The Assayer*
To inform		
To entertain		
To persuade		
To reflect		

from Starry Messenger • *from* The Assayer

1. **Speculate:** Both the man in *The Assayer* and Galileo come to realize that there are many questions that they cannot answer. Do you think this makes the work of scientists easier or harder? Explain.

   _____

   _____

2. **Literary Analysis:** Use the chart below to find examples of the key features of **narrative accounts** in both *Starry Messenger* and *The Assayer*.

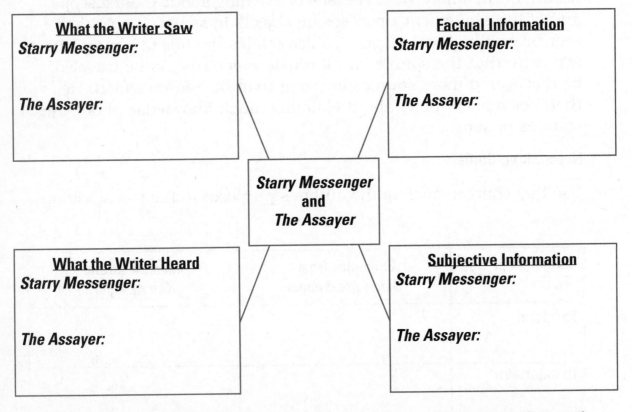

What the Writer Saw
Starry Messenger:

The Assayer:

Factual Information
Starry Messenger:

The Assayer:

Starry Messenger and The Assayer

What the Writer Heard
Starry Messenger:

The Assayer:

Subjective Information
Starry Messenger:

The Assayer:

3. **Literary Analysis:** Galileo uses transitions as part of his **narrative style**. Identify four transitional words or phrases in "Starry Messenger."

   _____

   _____

4. **Reading Strategy:** Reread the third paragraph in "Astronomical Message," (which begins with "It is a very beautiful thing . . ."). In your own words, write the meaning of the two sentences.

   _____

SUPPORT FOR WRITING AND EXTEND YOUR LEARNING

Writing: Response to Literature

In an **essay**, explain whether the emotions Galileo expresses make his findings more or less scientifically trustworthy.

Before beginning your essay, think of what the central idea, or **thesis statement,** of your essay will be. To start, decide which side of the argument you will take, and explain below why you chose that side.

_____

_____

_____

_____

Now write some possible ideas for a thesis statement.

_____

_____

_____

Research and Technology: Scrapbook

List the astronomical sights that Galileo describes in *Starry Messenger.* Then, using the Internet or other electronic sources, locate images of each item. Use these images to create a **scrapbook**, including a passage describing each image you select.

Begin your scrapbook by using the chart below to locate images on the Internet of the astronomical sights that Galileo describes. For each, note the name of the Web site where you found the image, as well as a description of the image.

	Web site	**Web site**	**Web site**
electronic source			
image			

from Don Quixote

LITERARY ANALYSIS

A **parody** is a humorous imitation of another, usually serious, work. A parody makes fun of the more serious work. *Don Quixote* affectionately pokes fun at the literature of chivalry. During the Middle Ages, this literature included stories of brave knights who had great adventures. In *Don Quixote*, the author parodies tales of chivalry through the words and actions of his foolish hero.

Parodies often have a clear **theme**, or central message. *Don Quixote* explores the theme of reality versus fantasy. As you read, think about the following questions:

- At what point do fantasies get in the way of reality?
- Is a life focused strictly on reality more rewarding than a life filled with fantasy and adventure?

READING STRATEGY

Compare and **contrast** an ideal knight and Don Quixote. Look for similarities and differences between the two. Before you read, use the chart shown to list the details that you know about an ideal knight. As you read, record details about Don Quixote. Identify any conclusions you can draw from comparing and contrasting the details.

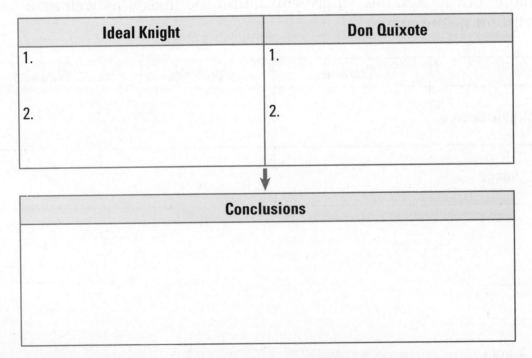

Ideal Knight	Don Quixote
1.	1.
2.	2.

Conclusions

from Don Quixote

Miguel de Cervantes
Translated by Samuel Putnam

Summary *Don Quixote* is a humorous imitation of traditional stories about knights. Don Quixote is a man who reads so many books about knights that he loses his mind. He believes that these stories are true and decides that he will become a knight and travel the world in search of adventure. In preparation, he polishes some old armor and renames himself and his skinny, old horse. He also chooses a pretty girl to be his lady love.

Don Quixote persuades Sancho Panza to be his squire. As the two men travel, they see a group of windmills. Don Quixote thinks that the windmills are giants. Sancho Panza warns him to leave the windmills alone. Don Quixote attacks them and gets hurt.

Note-taking Guide

On the chart, note the actions Quixote takes and the real situation.

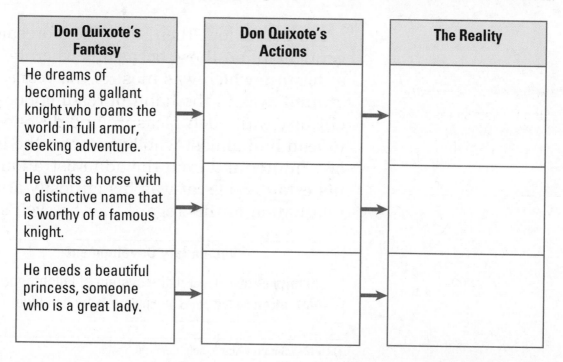

Don Quixote's Fantasy	Don Quixote's Actions	The Reality
He dreams of becoming a gallant knight who roams the world in full armor, seeking adventure.		
He wants a horse with a distinctive name that is worthy of a famous knight.		
He needs a beautiful princess, someone who is a great lady.		

from Don Quixote

Miguel de Cervantes
Translated by Samuel Putnam

CHAPTER I
Which treats of the station in life and the pursuits of the famous gentleman, Don Quixote de la Mancha.

♦ ♦ ♦

In a village called La Mancha[1] there lived a man who owned a lance, a shield, a skinny horse, and a hunting dog. He had enough money to feed himself well and to wear fine clothes for festival days. He lived with a housekeeper and his niece. He also employed a young farm boy to care for his horse and orchards.

This man was nearly fifty years old. He was a healthy man, but he was skinny and bony. He usually got up early in the morning to hunt. His name may have been Quijada or Quesada, although no one knows for sure.

♦ ♦ ♦

You may know, then, that the aforesaid gentleman, on those occasions when he was at leisure, which was most of the year around, was in the habit of reading books of <u>chivalry</u> with such pleasure and devotion as to lead him almost wholly to forget the life of a hunter and even the administration of his estate. So great was his curiosity and <u>infatuation</u> in this regard that he even sold

Vocabulary Development

chivalry (SHIV uhl ree) *n.* the system of knighthood
infatuation (in FACH oo AY shun) *n.* a foolish love

---

1. **La Mancha** province in south central Spain.

TAKE NOTES

Reading Strategy

In the literature of chivalry, the ideal knight was usually young and strong. Read the bracketed text. **Compare and contrast** the description of Don Quixote with the description of an ideal knight. Does Don Quixote fit the description? Why, or why not?

_____

_____

_____

Reading Check

What is Don Quixote's greatest interest?

_____

_____

many acres of tillable land in order to be able to buy and read the books that the loved, and he would carry home with him as many of them as he could obtain.

❖   ❖   ❖

His favorite writer was Feliciano de Silva. Silva's words of love and great challenges were complicated and difficult to understand. However, they were so precious to Don Quixote that he read them over and over. The poor man would lie awake at night thinking about his heroes and trying to make sense of the words of the stories.

Don Quixote worried about the wounds of his heroes and wondered how they would live to appear in another adventure. Sometimes he even thought of writing his own ending to the stories. He would have done just that if his time had not been taken up with other things.

He often discussed the stories with the pastor in his town. They held debates over which knight was better than the other. The village barber often joined them and argued that his own favorite knight was better than any other knight.

Don Quixote became so taken up with books about knights and chivalry that he would stay awake all night reading. Eventually, all of the reading and lack of sleep caused him to go out of his mind. His imagination was filled with adventures, battles, and tales of love. He began to believe that these stories were all true. In time, they became more real to him than anything else.

❖   ❖   ❖

Stop to Reflect

Read the bracketed text. Why do you think Don Quixote is so upset by the events in these stories?

_____

_____

_____

Reading Check

Who is Don Quixote's favorite writer?

_____

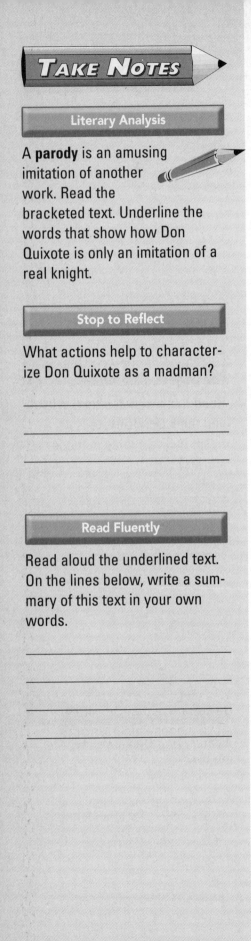

Literary Analysis

A **parody** is an amusing imitation of another work. Read the bracketed text. Underline the words that show how Don Quixote is only an imitation of a real knight.

Stop to Reflect

What actions help to characterize Don Quixote as a madman?

_____

_____

_____

Read Fluently

Read aloud the underlined text. On the lines below, write a summary of this text in your own words.

_____

_____

_____

_____

At last, when his wits were gone beyond repair, he came to conceive the strangest idea that ever occurred to any madman in this world. It now appeared to him fitting and necessary, in order to win a greater amount of honor for himself and serve his country at the same time, to become a <u>knight-errant</u> and roam the world on horseback, in a suit of armor; he would go in quest of adventures, by way of putting into practice all that he had read in his books; he would right every manner of wrong, placing himself in situations of the greatest <u>peril</u> such as would <u>redound</u> to the eternal glory of his name. <u>As a reward for his valor and the might of his arm, the poor fellow could already see himself crowned Emperor of Trebizond[2] at the very least; and so, carried away by the strange pleasure that he found in such thoughts as these, he at once set about putting his plan into effect.</u>

◆ ◆ ◆

First, Don Quixote pulled out some old pieces of his grandfather's armor and polished them. He realized that his helmet had no visor. It was the type for a foot soldier, not for a knight. He decided to make a visor out of cardboard. When it was done, it looked like a real knight's helmet with a full-face visor.

Vocabulary Development

knight-errant (NYT ER uhnt) *n.* a soldier in search of adventures

peril (PER il) *n.* danger

redound (ri DOWND) *v.* to have a result or effect

---

2. Trebizond (TREB uh ZAHND) in Medieval times, a Greek empire off the southeast coast of the Black Sea.

True, when he went to see if it was strong enough to withstand a good slashing blow, he was somewhat disappointed; for when he drew his sword and gave it a couple of thrusts, he succeeded only in undoing a whole week's labor. The ease with which he had <u>hewed</u> it to bits disturbed him no little, and he decided to make it over. This time he placed a few strips of iron on the inside, and then, convinced that it was strong enough, refrained from putting it to any further test; instead, he adopted it then and there as the finest helmet ever made.

◆　◆　◆

After this, he looked carefully at his horse. It was old, skinny and broken-down from many years of hard work on the farm. However, our hero imagined that it was the finest steed of all time. He spent many days thinking of a name for the horse. It needed a name that would be fitting for the famous and worthy knight he planned to become. He worried about the name for some time and finally decided on "Rocinante."

Then he decided that he too needed a worthy name to suit his new life. After a week of thinking about just the right name, he chose "Don Quixote." Then he remembered that many knights were known by their kingdom as well as their name. He decided to add his own city to his name. He would be called "Don Quixote de la Mancha." To him, this sounded very grand and worthy.

After all his planning, he determined that the one thing he lacked was a ladylove. He knew from his books that a

---

Vocabulary Development

hewed (HYOOD) *v.* chopped or hacked

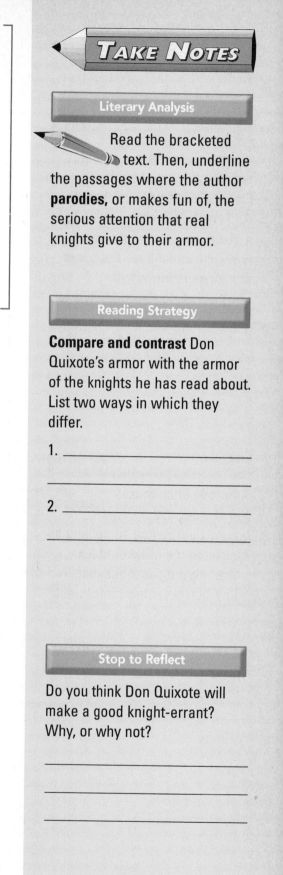

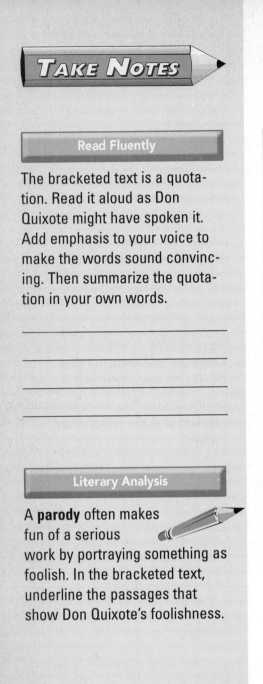
Read Fluently

The bracketed text is a quotation. Read it aloud as Don Quixote might have spoken it. Add emphasis to your voice to make the words sound convincing. Then summarize the quotation in your own words.

_____

_____

_____

_____

Literary Analysis

A **parody** often makes fun of a serious work by portraying something as foolish. In the bracketed text, underline the passages that show Don Quixote's foolishness.

knight must be in love with a lady whom he usually does not know well. He knew that she was important to his plan.

◆ ◆ ◆

"If," he said to himself, "as a punishment for my sins or by a stroke of fortune I should come upon some giant hereabouts, a thing that very commonly happens to knights-errant, and if I should slay him in a hand-to-hand encounter or perhaps cut him in two, or, finally, if I should <u>vanquish</u> and subdue him, would it not be well to have someone to whom I may send him as a present, in order that he, if he is living, may come in, fall upon his knees in front of my sweet lady, and say in a humble and submissive tone of voice, 'I, lady, am the giant Caraculiambro, lord of the island Malindrania, who has been overcome in single combat by that knight who never can be praised enough, Don Quixote de la Mancha, the same who sent me to present myself before your Grace that your Highness may dispose of me as you see fit'?"

◆ ◆ ◆

Don Quixote happily began planning a name for his lady. It so happened that there was a pretty farm girl in his town, named Aldonza Lorenzo. He had once admired her, although she had never known it. He determined that this girl would be his ladylove. He knew that she needed a beautiful name, such as a princess would have. He thought for some time, and finally decided to call her "Dulcinea del Toboso." He felt this musical name fit well with his own name and the name of his horse.

Vocabulary Development

vanquish (VANG kwish) *v.* to overcome

---

from Don Quixote

1. **Compare:** In what ways does Aldonza Lorenzo fulfill the stereotype of a knight's ladlylove?

_____

_____

2. **Literary Analysis**: Identify three characteristics of a medieval romance that *Don Quixote* **parodies.** What details show that this parody is affectionate or gentle?

_____

_____

_____

_____

3. **Literary Analysis**: Using the chart below, identify details from the selection that parody elements of a real knight's life. Indicate how Don Quixote's personality or circumstances influence the parody.

Real Knight	Details	Don Quixote's Influence
Training		
Weapons		
Ladylove		

4. **Reading Strategy: Compare and contrast** Don Quixote and Sancho Panza. Explain how the two men are alike, and how they are different.

_____

_____

_____

SUPPORT FOR WRITING AND EXTEND YOUR LEARNING

Writing: Profile of a Comic Hero

A hero in literature is often a serious character on an important quest. Cervantes reinvents this character by creating a comic hero in *Don Quixote*. Create your own comic hero and write a **profile**, or description, of his or her traits and achievements.

To introduce your character, begin your profile with a brief, humorous incident involving your character. Answer the questions below to help you find ideas for your introduction.

- What was the setting of the incident? Give background information so that readers can visualize the situation.

  ____

  ____

  ____

- What did your character do? How did the particular traits of your character influence the way he or she reacted?

  ____

  ____

  ____

- What was the outcome of the situation?

  ____

  ____

Research and Technology: Create a Visual Essay

Create a **visual essay** on the subject of heroes. Before you begin your research, answer the questions in the chart below. Use these notes to help guide and focus your research.

What specific aspects of heroes and heroism would you like to discuss in your essay?	
What types of images will help you address these topics?	
What are some resources you might use to find or create these images?	

The Fox and the Crow •
The Oak and the Reed

LITERARY ANALYSIS

A **fable** uses a short story or poem to show a simple lesson or principle of behavior. Most fables share the following elements:
- creatures—animals or objects—who speak and interact as though they were human
- a clearly worded moral
- a plot that includes only one event
- an implied fault of character that is addressed in the moral of the fable

These works often use **personification**, giving a nonhuman subject human characteristics. La Fontaine uses personification to teach readers life lessons through the experiences of talking, thinking creatures. As you read these fables, look for examples of personification and other elements common to fables.

READING STRATEGY

La Fontaine does not state the morals, or lessons, that his fables teach. Instead, he allows readers to **draw conclusions** about his meaning. To draw conclusions, consider the message suggested by the fable's details. Use the chart to help you.

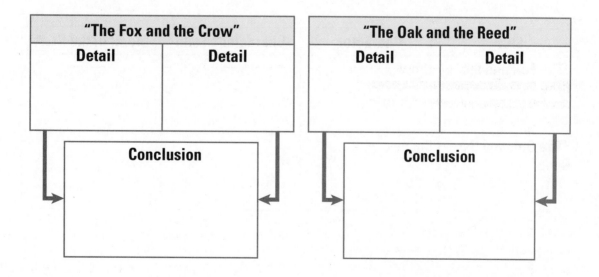

"The Fox and the Crow"	
Detail	**Detail**

Conclusion

"The Oak and the Reed"	
Detail	**Detail**

Conclusion

The Fox and the Crow •
The Oak and the Reed

Jean de La Fontaine
translated by Marianne Moore

Summaries "The Fox and the Crow" shows the dangers of believing flattery, or excessive compliments. A fox wants cheese that a crow has in its beak. The fox compliments the crow's beauty and asks whether the crow's voice is as beautiful as its looks. Flattered, the crow opens its mouth to sing and drops the cheese. The fox immediately grabs it.

In **"The Oak and the Reed,"** an oak tree brags about its strength. The tree criticizes its neighbor, the reed, for being weak. The reed replies that it is stronger than the oak tree. Because it is flexible, the reed can withstand great storms, unlike the oak.

Note-taking Guide

Both **fables** contain such elements as morals, or lessons, and characters with faults. Record these elements from each fable in the chart below.

Story	Character	Character's Fault	Moral of the Story
"The Fox and the Crow"	Crow		
"The Oak and the Reed"	the oak		

The Fox and the Crow • The Oak and the Reed

1. **Connect:** In what ways do the morals of these two fables apply to readers' lives today?

   _____

   _____

2. **Literary Analysis:** Compare the elements found in each of the fables using the Venn diagram shown below.

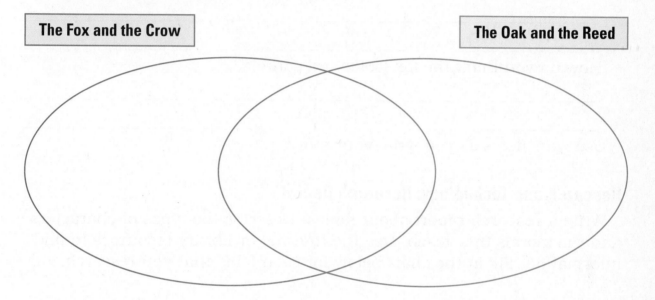

| The Fox and the Crow | | The Oak and the Reed |

3. **Literary Analysis:** List three examples of **personification** in "The Fox and the Crow."

   _____

   _____

4. **Reading Strategy:** What **conclusions** can you draw from the crow's experience in "The Fox and the Crow"?

   _____

   _____

   _____

SUPPORT FOR WRITING AND EXTEND YOUR LEARNING

Writing: Children's Story

Write a **children's story** based on "The Fox and the Crow." Focus on the following questions to develop details for your story:

- How is the crow described in La Fontaine's poem?

____

____

- How do you think the crow looks and sounds?

____

____

- How is the fox described in La Fontaine's poem?

____

____

- How do you think the fox looks and sounds?

____

____

Use your notes as you write your story.

Research and Technology: Research Report

Write a **research report** about fables. Describe the types of characters and the morals they teach. Use the Internet or library resources to find information. Fill in the chart below for each fable that you research.

Fable	Author or Source	Characters	Moral

Use your notes as you write your research report.

from Candide

LITERARY ANALYSIS

Satire is writing that uses humor to show human foolishness and make fun of it. Individual people, institutions, ways of acting, or society in general can all be the subject of satire. The goal of a piece of satire is to bring about change for the better.

Writers of satire use tools such as **exaggeration or hyperbole**, **understatement**, and **faulty logic** to make fun of their subjects. Exaggeration or hyperbole means describing things as larger or more extreme than they are in real life. Understatement means describing things in a way that makes them seem less important or significant than they are. Faulty logic uses the language of logic to make ridiculous statements. Look at these examples from the reading:

- *Exaggeration or hyperbole*: ". . . The Baron's castle was the best of castles. . . ."
- *Understatement*: ". . . the next day he drilled not so badly and received only twenty strokes [of the lash]."
- *Faulty logic*: "Observe that noses were made to wear spectacles and so we have spectacles."

READING STRATEGY

When you **connect a work to its historical context**, you look at the ideas and events in a piece of literature that may be a response to the time when it was written. Use the chart below to list details from the story that reflect the time period. Ask yourself what the detail shows about the time period in which the work was written.

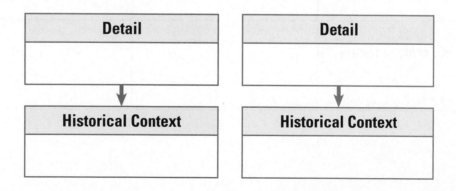

Detail	Detail

↓	↓
Historical Context	Historical Context

from Candide

Voltaire
Translated by Richard Aldington

Summary Candide is a gentle young man who has been raised on the estate of Baron Thunder-ten-tron-ckh (THUN dur TRONK). Candide and the Baron's daughter Cunegonde have both been taught by the famous Dr. Pangloss. Dr. Pangloss taught them to believe in the innocence and goodness of all things. When the Baron discovers Candide and Cunegonde kissing, he throws Candide off of the estate. Candide travels to Bulgaria, where he is forced into service in the Bulgarian army. The excerpt ends with Candide being caught trying to escape the army and facing execution.

Note-taking Guide

Candide believes that this is the best of all possible worlds, and so sees only the good in everything. As a result, Candide's innocence often brings him trouble. Use the chart below to compare Candide's beliefs about the situations he encounters with the reality of those situations.

Event	Candide's Belief	Actual Situation
Candide meets two men who buy him dinner at an inn.		
Candide leaves the Bulgarian army to take a walk.		

from Candide

1. **Analyze:** How does Candide show his innocence as he speaks with the "men dressed in blue" at the inn?

   _____

   _____

   _____

2. **Literary Analysis:** Two types of social injustice that are satirized in _Candide_ are the fact that a woman cannot marry a man who is not a nobleman and the fact that men are forced into the military. What types of social reform do you think the author wanted to inspire?

   _____

   _____

   _____

3. **Literary Analysis:** Use the chart below to write down at least one example of each of the tools of satire used in _Candide_. These include **exaggeration** or **hyperbole**, **understatement**, and **faulty logic**.

Tool of Satire Used	Detail from _Candide_
Exaggeration or Hyperbole	
Understatement	
Faulty Logic	

4. **Reading Strategy:** What are two details about the Baron's family that show the historical context of Voltaire's era?

   _____

   _____

   _____

SUPPORT FOR WRITING AND EXTEND YOUR LEARNING

Writing: Short Satirical Story

Satirists write about situations they would like to change in the world. Choose a situation that you feel needs to be changed, such as a foolish behavior, a social injustice, or an institution. Then, write a short satirical story that encourages people to bring about change.

Your satirical story will use tools like exaggeration or hyperbole, understatement, and faulty logic to make humorous points. Use the chart shown to plan your use of satirical tools.

Detail to be Satirized	Tool of Satire	Example

Listening and Speaking: Group Discussion

Your **group discussion** will compare a musical version of *Candide* to the written version. After listening to the musical version, use the chart below to organize your comparison.

Topic	Written Version	Musical Version
Overall Mood		
Main Events		
Candide's Character		

FEATURE ARTICLES

About Feature Articles

Newspapers contain articles about current events, world news, and **feature articles**. Feature articles are written to inform and to entertain. The author of a feature article often includes an opinion about the topic. Common topics for feature writers include:

- Fashion
- Entertainment
- Health
- Leisure

The selection that follows, "Leonardo: The Eye, The Hand, The Mind," focuses on a museum exhibit. It tells about the works of Leonardo da Vinci, a great artist of the Renaissance.

Reading Strategy

When a writer offers an opinion about a topic, he or she must give evidence to support that opinion. A reader's job is to **evaluate the support**. Good support consists of the following:

- facts
- statistics
- examples
- observations

Each piece of support should convince a reader of the author's opinion. Use a chart like the one shown to list each opinion in the following feature article. For each, identify the details that support that opinion. Then, evaluate the support to decide whether the writer's opinion is valid.

Opinion	Support	Evaluation of Support
Cotter says Leonardo's strengths lie in art, science, engineering, and aesthetic theory.	Cotter lists Leonardo's accomplishments in hydrodynamics, anatomy, physics, astronomy, invention, and art.	The list of accomplishments supports Cotter's opinion that Leonardo's strengths lie in many areas.

BUILD UNDERSTANDING

Knowing the meaning of these words will help you read this article.

aesthetic (es THET ik) *adj.* of beauty or art

Louvre (LOOV) *n.* a famous art museum in Paris, France

Underline the sentence in the first paragraph in which the author states his opinion about Leonardo da Vinci. Restate his opinion in your own words.

_____

_____

_____

1. Read the bracketed text. What evidence does the author give to support the idea that da Vinci was a genius in many fields?

_____

_____

_____

2. When you **evaluate the support,** you decide whether you think the support is convincing. Do you think the author supports his opinion about da Vinci's genius? Explain your answer.

_____

_____

_____

Leonardo: The Eye, the Hand, the Mind
By Holland Cotter

LEONARDO DA VINCI (1452–1519) is the Great Oz of European art. At least that's the way he sometimes seems, glimpsed through the fogs and fumes of history: a cultural force more than a man, a colossal[1] brain and a sovereign[2] hand at the controls of a multidisciplinary[3] universe.

Where did his supreme gift lie? In art? Science? Engineering? Aesthetic theory? All of the above. We all have our strengths; I have mastered MetroCard dispensers and a home computer. Yet Leonardo understood, described and illustrated the principles of hydrodynamics[4], gross anatomy, physics and astronomy. He invented the helicopter, the armored tank and the submarine. He painted like an angel and despite being phobic[5] about deadlines, wrote often and well. In addition, according to Vasari, he was drop-dead gorgeous.

And, perhaps most confounding, he generated all this near-magical accomplishment from behind a curtain of personal discretion[6] so dense and insulating that no historian or psychologist—and dozens, maybe hundreds, have tried—has been able to pull it aside to reveal the person behind the personage.

---

1. colossal (kuh LAH suhl) _adj._ huge.
2. sovereign (SAHV ruhn) _adj._ excellent; outstanding.
3. multidisciplinary (MUL tee DIS uh pli NAYR ee) _adj._ involving many different branches of learning.
4. hydrodynamics (HY droh dy NAM iks) _n._ the branch of physics involving the motion of water.
5. phobic (FOH bik) _adj._ fearful.
6. discretion (di SKRESH uhn) _n._ modesty; the quality of being discreet.

"Leonardo da Vinci, Master Draftsman" at the Metropolitan Museum of Art also tries, and manages to part the curtain just a crack. We may not learn exactly what made this artist tick, but we can see him ticking away, at length and in some depth.

Naturally, the show had blockbuster written all over it from the word go. With 118 Leonardo drawings, it is the largest gathering of his work in America. The lending institutions are a superstarry lot: the Uffizi, the Louvre, the Vatican[7], the Royal Library at Windsor Castle. And the Met has given it the imperial treatment: crimson walls, acres of space, a catalog as thick as *The Physician's Desk Reference*.

Are the drawings worth the fuss? In a word, totally. Individually, many are glorious; some are workmanlike; a few are just weird, so weird you find yourself wondering: what planet was this guy from? As a package, though, as the datastream output of a single sensibility, they're huge. They are also very alive. People always say that you can't know painting from a book, that you have to experience it. This is at least as true of drawing, a profoundly physical medium, where a smudge or erasure can be a heart-catching event, and a pen stroke can leap like a solar flare.

Reading Feature Articles

Read the bracketed text. What event prompted this **feature article**?

_____

_____

_____

Reading Feature Articles

Feature articles are both informative and entertaining. In the paragraph that begins "Are the drawings worth the fuss?" underline the words or phrases that make this article lively and entertaining.

---

7. Vatican (VAT i kuhn) *n.* the home of the Roman Catholic Pope and the location of many famous pieces of art.

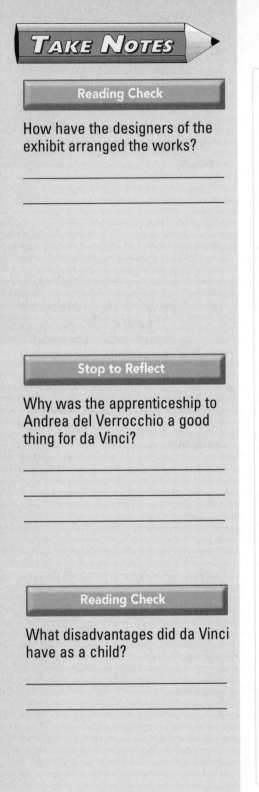

TAKE NOTES

Reading Check

How have the designers of the exhibit arranged the works?

_____

_____

Stop to Reflect

Why was the apprenticeship to Andrea del Verrocchio a good thing for da Vinci?

_____

_____

_____

Reading Check

What disadvantages did da Vinci have as a child?

_____

_____

The show comes with some fresh scholarship, not blindingly revealing, but solid and worthwhile. The curators Carmen C. Bambach and George R. Goldner, both of the Met's department of drawings and prints, have avoided a hit parade approach in their selection, opting instead for some less familiar material. They've also brought related drawings—10 studies for the Florentine mural "The Battle of Anghiari" alone—together, in some cases for the first time. Finally, by arranging the work chronologically, they've created something like an organic picture of the history of one man's polymathic[8] life.

Leonardo was born in 1452 and started life with certain disadvantages. He was a small-town kid, . . . indifferently[9] educated and—a liability[10] for an artist, you would think—left-handed. But he also had luck. His supportive father took him to Florence, by then a major node on the information highway of Renaissance Europe. There he was apprenticed to Andrea del Verrocchio, a leading sculptor but also a painter (five gorgeous drawings of his open the show) from whom Leonardo learned much.

For one thing, he learned to draw sculpturally. This meant drawing with a command of volume, as several early drapery studies demonstrate. It also meant executing fleet[11], notational sketches to capture the look of real things viewed from many angles in actual space, as seen in Leonardo's serial depictions of squirming babies and wide-awake cats. From Verrocchio he also learned to carry a notebook with him at all times and to use it, so that whatever went in through the eye came out through his hand.

---

8. polymathic (PAHL uh MATH ik) *adj.* possessing great and varied learning.
9. indifferently (in DIF er ent lee) *adv.* in a way that is not particularly good or bad.
10. liability (LY uh BIL uh tee) *n.* something that works to one's disadvantage; a hindrance.
11. fleet (FLEET) *adj.* swift.

In 1481, he landed a substantial job, an altar-piece painting of "The Adoration of the Magi." And at that point, he seemed to have settled on a work pattern that, for better or worse, he would follow thereafter. Basically, it entailed conceiving pictorial designs so complex and technically demanding that he would never complete them.

For "The Adoration," for example, he planned to place more than 60 figures in an elaborate perspectival[12] setting. He drew and drew; several well-known studies, one of them madly complicated, are in the show. But the ideas never really gelled, and he eventually headed to Milan in search of different work, leaving an unfinished painting behind.

He stayed in Milan, employed by the city's ruler, Ludovico Sforza, for 15 years, which were among the most productive of his life. His first commission—he proposed it himself—was an outsize equestrian[13] monument to Ludovico's father. Again, he produced studies galore, dashed off and spirited, fastidious[14] and polished. But the monument never materialized, and the plans were abandoned.

In any case, Leonardo was, as usual, working on several other things. One was the unfinished painting, now owned by the Vatican, titled "St. Jerome in the Wilderness." It's at the Met and gives a stark, almost agonizing sense of how he carried his obsessive, draftsmanlike self-correction right into what should have been the final stages of a painting.

Reading Check

Circle the paragraph in which the author describes da Vinci's work pattern. Then, put a square around the paragraph that gives an example of that pattern.

Reading Strategy

1. Read the author's opinion in the underlined passage. Then, circle two examples in the bracketed text that support this opinion.

2. **Evaluate the support.** Does the author convince you of his opinion with these examples? Explain.

_____

_____

_____

_____

---

12. **perspectival** (per SPEK tiv ul) *adj.* appearing to have depth.
13. **equestrian** (ee KWES tree un) *adj.* on horseback.
14. **fastidious** (fas TID ee uhs) *adj.* not easy to please; very critical.

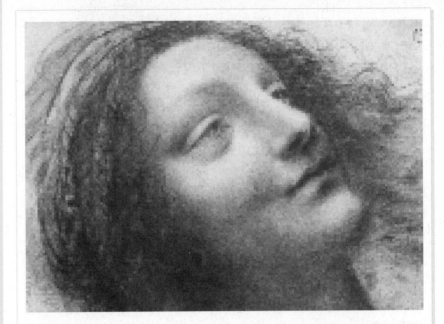

Stop to Reflect

Da Vinci worked on "The Last Supper" for five years. What does this fact tell you about da Vinci's character?

_____

_____

_____

Reading Check

What caused the city government of Florence to decide to hire da Vinci to paint a mural of the Battle of Anghiari?

_____

_____

_____

And there was "The Last Supper," painted from 1493 to 1498 in the refectory of Santa Maria della Grazie. One renowned sheet from Windsor carries what could be a preliminary sketch of that painting's composition, mixed in with geometric and architectural designs. And from the Albertina in Vienna comes a powerfully resolved drawing on blue paper of an old man who is sometimes identified as St. Peter. Whatever his identity, he is animated[15] by the tense, urgent gravitas[16] of the painting itself.

When French troops invaded Milan in 1499, Leonardo made his way back to Florence. There he whipped up a large-scale drawing titled "Virgin and Child With Saint Anne" and gave himself a one-man show. The drawing—now lost, though later versions on the same theme exist—was rapturously[17] received and resulted in a commission from the city government for the Battle of Anghiari mural, to be painted in the Palazzo della Signoria. Its subject was a Florentine military victory.

---

15. **animated** (AN i MAYT uhd) *adj.* lifelike; lively.
16. **gravitas** (GRAV i TAS´) *n.* dignity; seriousness.
17. **rapturously** (RAP chur uhs lee) *adv.* Enthusiastically.

The assignment was a very big, very public deal; Michelangelo, the local reigning prince of art, was to paint the opposite wall. Once more, Leonardo feverishly poured out ideas on paper, and the studies in the show are fantastic, from an explosive drawing of a horse in motion (several legs, many heads) to a hyperrealistic[18] depiction of a screaming soldier. As for the mural, Leonardo designed a cartoon and expensive scaffolding, then left town, heading back to Milan.

Once there, he did what he had always done: many things simultaneously[19]. He painted; he taught; he studied anatomy and geometry. He designed maps, architectural plans and stage sets. He conducted scientific experiments and recorded his findings in notebooks, writing from right to left and in mirror image, which, as a lefty, he had always done.

And he sketched. Small drawings of grotesque human heads flowed from his hand like telephone pad doodles. His famous "Deluge" pictures date to this time. Imaginary scenes of tidal waves over-whelming minute towns, they are both aquatic studies and apocalyptic[20] visions. In 1516, the French king Francis I, who collected trophy artists as well as art, invited him to live at his court. Leonardo, old at 64, moved to France and died there three years later.

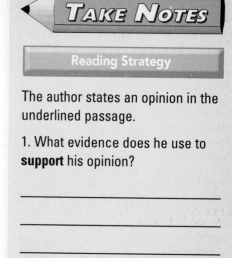

TAKE NOTES

Reading Strategy

The author states an opinion in the underlined passage.

1. What evidence does he use to **support** his opinion?

_____

_____

_____

2. Do you think the support is convincing? Explain your answer.

_____

_____

_____

Reading Check

What unusual method did da Vinci use to record his scientific findings?

_____

_____

---

18. hyperrealistic (HY per REE uh LIS tik) *adj.* excessively lifelike.
19. simultaneously (sy muhl TAY nee us lee) *adv.* at the same time.
20. apocalyptic (uh PAK uh LIP tik) *adj.* pertaining to the end of the world where evil is destroyed and goodness overcomes all.

Read the bracketed paragraph. What does the author like about his favorite pieces in the exhibit?

_____

_____

_____

Reread the last paragraph of the selection. What is the author's conclusion?

_____

_____

_____

_____

He left behind a godlike reputation, worshipful disciples, a scant handful of paintings—about 15 survive—and the 4,000 works on paper that are his primary visual legacy[21]. Some of his drawings are art historical icons; the face of Mary in a study for the painting of "The Virgin and Child With St. Anne," now in the Louvre, is one. He invented this expressive type, with its interior smile and apparitional[22] draftsmanship, and with it a Western ideal of human perfection.

My favorite drawings, though, are of a different kind. They're ones where everything is happening, nonlinearly, all at once, and anything goes: double-sided sheets filled with animals, armaments[23], allegorical[24] scenes, geometrical diagrams, exploding buildings, . . . dissected muscles, wheels and bridges, flowing water, reminder notes, sums, scratches, spots and stains.

In these, for me, the curtain parts that little bit, to reveal an artist who always preferred to dream and draw rather than to do, who remained at some level a venturesome[25] child controlling his world by taking it apart, piece by piece, to see how the whole thing worked. By thinking big, Leonardo became big; illusions sometimes work that way. And the neat thing is that in his company, we get to think big, too.

---

21. **legacy** (LEG uh see) *n.* anything handed down from an ancestor.
22. **apparitional** (AP uh RISH uhn uhl) *adj.* appearing unexpectedly or in a special way.
23. **armaments** (AR muh ments) *n.* guns and military equipment.
24. **allegorical** (AL uh GOR i kuhl) *adj.* containing symbols or emblems.
25. **venturesome** (VEN chuhr suhm) *adj.* adventurous.

THINKING ABOUT FEATURE ARTICLES

1. What three things did da Vinci invent?

_____

_____

_____

2. Review the first page of the article. What does the author think are da Vinci's supreme gifts?

_____

_____

READING STRATEGY

3. What evidence does the author give to **support** the idea that da Vinci preferred dreaming to doing?

_____

_____

_____

4. Does this support convince you of the author's claim? Explain your answer.

_____

_____

TIMED WRITING: DESCRIPTION (25 MINUTES)

Use the information in the article to describe the Met's da Vinci show. Mention the works, the organization, and the qualities of the show.

• Scan the article for those works of da Vinci included in the show. List the titles here.

_____

_____

- Reread the first two pages of the article. How is the show organized?

_____

_____

_____

_____

- How does the author describe the show? How would you describe the qualities of the show?

_____

_____

_____

_____

from Faust: Prologue in Heaven • The First Part of the Tragedy

LITERARY ANALYSIS

Romanticism is a style of writing and art that was popular in the 19th century. Romantics focused on:

- the importance of emotion and intuition over reason and intellect
- the power of creativity and imagination
- the importance of the individual
- a love of nature
- the mysterious and exotic

READING STRATEGY

Drawing inferences means making educated guesses about the meaning of a passage or a selection. Look for these clues in the text to help you draw inferences:

- details about the characters, events, setting (time and place), and mood (feeling you get from a literary work)
- the writer's choice of words in a passage

Use the chart below to help you draw inferences as you read. One example from this selection has been filled in for you.

Passage	What Can Be Inferred	Clues
"I work as the cat does with the mouse."		

from Faust
Prologue in Heaven

Johann Wolfgang von Goethe
Translated by Louis MacNeice

Summary The "Prologue" begins with the three chief angels praising the Lord for creating the world. However, the Devil, known as Mephistopheles (MEF uh STAHF uh LEEZ), does not praise the Lord. Mephistopheles finds fault with mankind, the Lord's most important creation. Mephistopheles makes a bet with the Lord that he can ruin the soul of one of the Lord's servants, Dr. Faust. The Lord believes that Mephistopheles will loose the bet. The Lord gives Mephistopheles permission to try to ruin the soul of Faust.

Note-taking Guide

Use the chart below to describe the main characters, the setting, and the events that happen in this story.

Characters	Setting	What Happens

from Faust
Prologue in Heaven

Johann Wolfgang von Goethe
Translated by Louis MacNeice

The characters in this scene are the Lord, Mephistopheles,[1] and the three chief angels. The angels' names are Raphael, Gabriel, and Michael. The "Prologue," or introduction, takes place in Heaven.

Each of the three angels praises something in nature. Raphael talks about the sun. Gabriel talks about the sea. Michael talks about the raging storms, with their lightning and thunder.

Then Mephistopheles enters. He knows that all the heavenly angels make fun of him. He talks about how man hurts himself on earth.

©   ©   ©

MEPHISTOPHELES: The little god of the
  world, one can't reshade, reshape him;
He is as strange today as that first day you
  made him.
His life would be not so bad, not quite,
Had you not granted him a gleam of
  Heaven's light;
He calls it Reason, uses it not the least

©   ©   ©

Mephistopheles compares man to a grasshopper who thrusts himself around and gets his nose in the dirt.

©   ©   ©

LORD: <u>Mephistopheles, have you no other news?</u>
<u>Do you always come here to accuse?</u>
<u>Is nothing ever right in your eyes on earth?</u>

---

1. Mephistopheles (MEF uh STOF uh leez) *n.* the devil.

Literary Analysis

One important idea of **Romanticism** is the belief in emotion over reason. Underline the words in the bracketed text that support this idea.

Reading Strategy

The underlined text reveals something about the character of Mephistopheles. What **inference** can you draw about his character?

_____

_____

Circle the clues in the underlined text that helped you draw the inference.

Read Fluently

Read aloud the bracketed text. How does Mephistopheles describe conditions on earth?

_____

_____

Reading Strategy

Mephistopheles reveals more about himself in the second bracketed text. What **inference** can you draw about the kind of people that appeal to him?

_____

_____

Circle the words in the bracketed text that helped you make this inference.

Stop to Reflect

Why do you think the Lord agrees to let Mephistopheles try to win Faust's soul?

_____

_____

Stop to Reflect

In his speech on this page, what idea does the Lord express about the nature of man?

_____

_____

MEPHISTOPHELES: No, Lord! I find things
   there as downright bad as ever.
I am sorry for men's days of dread and <u>dearth</u>;
Poor things, my wish to <u>plague</u> 'em isn't
   <u>fervent</u>.

◆   ◆   ◆

Mephistopheles says that he knows Faust, the Lord's servant. He thinks that Faust is very emotional and spiritual. Then the Devil bets that he can win Faust's soul away from the Lord. The Lord gives Mephistopheles permission to try to tempt Faust. The Lord says that Faust may make a mistake, but he will still try to follow the Lord's path.

◆   ◆   ◆

MEPHISTOPHELES: I thank you for that;
   as regards the dead,
The dead have never taken my fancy.
I favor cheeks that are full and rosy-red;
No <u>corpse</u> is welcome to my house;
I work as the cat does with the mouse.

LORD: Very well; you have my permission.
<u>Divert</u> this soul from its <u>primal</u> source
And carry it, if you can seize it,
Down with you upon your course—
And stand ashamed when you must needs
   admit:
A good man with his groping intuitions[2]
Still knows the path that is true and fit.

Vocabulary Development

dearth (DERTH) _n._ famine, a lack of food
plague (PLAYG) _v._ to harm
fervent (FUR vent) _adj._ showing great warmth, earnest
corpse (KORPS) _n._ dead body
divert (dī VERT) _v._ turn around the direction, distract
primal (PRĪ muhl) _adj._ original

2. intuitions (in too ISH inz) _n._ things that are understood without thinking or reasoning.

♦ ♦ ♦

Mephistopheles is certain that he will
win the bet. The Lord explains that he has
never hated the Devil. In fact, he thinks that
the existence of Mephistopheles, who is very
active, prevents man from becoming too
lazy.

At the end of the Prologue, Heaven
closes and Mephistopheles stands alone on
the stage. He tells the audience that he
enjoyed his visit with the Lord who has
always spoken kindly to him.

Reading Check

According to the Lord, what
purpose does the Devil serve?

_____

_____

_____

from Faust: The First Part of the Tragedy

Johann Wolfgang von Goethe
Translated by Louis MacNeice

Summary Faust sits in his dark study, angry about the years he has spent studying. He thinks he has not learned enough about the world. His hopelessness makes him think about taking his own life. Mephistopheles appears and tells Faust to experience life. At first, Faust is not tempted by Mephistopheles. However, Mephistopheles is able to get Faust to agree to a bet. The bet is that Mephistopheles will be Faust's servant if Faust agrees to be Mephistopheles' servant in the afterlife. Faust agrees and signs the contract in blood.

Note-taking Guide

Use the diagram below to help you understand Faust's reason for agreeing to Mephistopheles' bet.

What Faust Says	What Faust Wants	What Faust Does

from Faust: Prologue in Heaven • The First Part of the Tragedy

1. **Infer:** In "Prologue in Heaven," what are Mephistopheles' feelings about human beings?

   _____

   _____

2. **Literary Analysis: Romanticism** is a literary movement that focuses on the imagination, emotion, nature, individuality, and the exotic or mysterious. Find two examples of the mysterious in *Faust*.

   _____

   _____

3. **Literary Analysis:** Use the chart below to write down passages from *Faust* that show key features of Romanticism.

Features of Romanticism	Passage from *Faust*
Emotion	
Intuition	
Individuality	

4. **Reading Strategy:** By **drawing inferences** from lines 1–6 of "The First Part of the Tragedy," name one reason why Faust makes a deal with the Mephistopheles. (Hint: Look for what Faust tells you about his school experiences and how he feels about them.)

   _____

   _____

   _____

   _____

SUPPORT FOR WRITING AND EXTEND YOUR LEARNING

Writing a Film Script

Imagine that you are a movie screenwriter. You have been hired to create a movie version of Goethe's *Faust.* Think about how the original play should be rewritten for a movie. Your script should only focus on the parts of *Faust* that you have read.

Imagine what the scene would look like on a movie screen. List any special effects that you would like to see, such as lighting, sound, and digital effects.

Use the chart below to list the effects and how they will be used.

Special effect	Scene description	How effect will be used

Listening and Speaking: Brief Dialogue

Rehearse and present a **brief dialogue** based on a specific part of the play that you choose. As you rehearse, think about the following:

- What is the tone, mood, and setting of the work?

- What are Faust's and Mephistopheles' strengths and weaknesses?

- Then, write out your ideas for dialogue on the lines below.

I Have Visited Again • The Lorelei • The Lotus Flower

LITERARY ANALYSIS

Lyric poetry is a type of poetry that expresses a speaker's thoughts and feelings. Many early lyric poems were written as songs. Most of these poems tend to be melodic, like songs, and focus on producing a single, unified effect. As you read the poems, use the chart below to record the words and phrases that create a single effect.

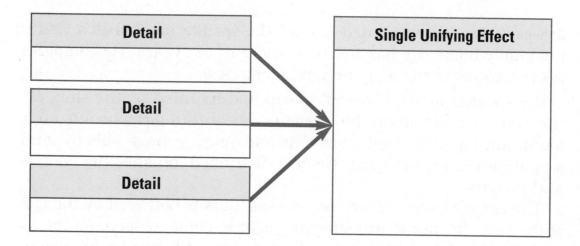

A **symbol** is a person, place, or object that has its own meaning but also has a larger meaning. Lyric poems often use symbols that express emotions. Symbols can also contribute to a poem's single, unifying effect.

READING STRATEGY

Reading between the lines can help you get a deeper understanding of a poem. To read between the lines, do the following:

- Make inferences, or educated guesses, about the meanings of lines or passages.
- Find clues about the characters, setting, mood, and symbols.
- Look at the meanings of specific words, including the title.

I Have Visited Again • The Lorelei • The Lotus Flower

**Alexander Pushkin,
Heinrich Heine**
Translated by D.M. Thomas,
Aaron Kramer,
Edgar Alfred Bowring

Summaries In "I Have Visited Again," the speaker describes a visit to his family home. He has not been there in ten years. He compares his memories to the way the land looks now.

The speaker in "The Lorelei" is sad and haunted by the story of the lorelei. In the story, the lorelei is a beautiful girl who sits on a mountain top. She combs her hair and sings. A boat sails by, and a boatman hears her song. He gets distracted, crashes his boat, and drowns.

"The Lotus Flower" describes how the lotus is bothered by the light of the sun. The flower waits for the night to come to open. As the lotus flower looks at the moon, she cries out with love for the moon.

Note-taking Guide

For each of the poems, use the chart below to record the actions described in the poem. For "I Have Visited Again" focus on the memories of the speaker. For "The Lorelei" focus on the story of the lorelei and the boatman. For "The Lotus Flower" focus on the lotus flower's actions when she sees the moon.

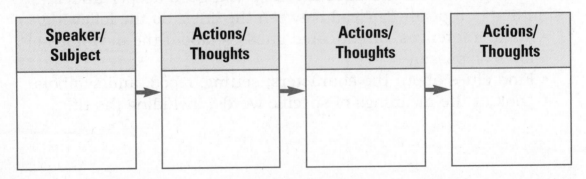

Speaker/ Subject	Actions/ Thoughts	Actions/ Thoughts	Actions/ Thoughts

I Have Visited Again • The Lorelei • The Lotus Flower

1. **Infer:** In "I Have Visited Again," the speaker thinks of "other shores and other waves." What does the speaker mean by "other shores"?

   _____

   _____

   _____

2. **Literary Analysis:** In "The Lorelei," the words *sings, evensong, melody, hears, cry,* and *singing* all refer to sounds. How do these words reflect the original purpose of many **lyric poems**?

   _____

   _____

   _____

3. **Literary Analysis:** Complete the chart shown to analyze the **symbols** in "I Have Visited Again." List people, places, or objects and the words that describe them. In the last column explain what each symbol means.

Person, Place or Object	Words Describing the Image	What the symbol means

4. **Reading Strategy:** By **reading between the lines**, what deeper understanding of the speaker can you find in the fifth stanza of "I Have Visited Again"?

   _____

   _____

   _____

SUPPORT FOR WRITING AND EXTEND YOUR LEARNING

Writing: Analytical Essay

In "I Have Visited Again," the speaker uses images from nature as a way to describe the passing stages of his life. Write an essay explaining how the poet uses nature images to represent the passage of time.

Use the chart below to record details in the poem. Describe the detail as it appears in the "past," "present," and "future." See the sample response as a guide for your own note taking.

Detail	Past	Present	Future
Cottage	It is where he used to live.	It is now neglected. No one lives there.	The cottage will be ruined.
Three pine trees	They used to welcome him when he rode by at night.	They are still there. Their roots are old.	
A thicket of young pines	They were not there when he was a boy.		

Research and Technology: Museum Exhibit

Use the Internet and encyclopedias to look up the term *siren*. Find out about the role sirens played in literature. This information will help you create a **museum exhibit**. Use these questions to guide your research:

- What did sirens usually do when they saw humans?

____

- What usually happened when men saw sirens?

____

- How are the sirens of mythology like the Lorelei?

____

____

Invitation to the Voyage • The Albatross • The Sleeper in the Valley • Ophelia • Autumn Song

LITERARY ANALYSIS

Romantic Poetry is part of a literary movement called Romanticism. Romantic poetry focuses on the following:

- imagination
- emotion
- nature
- individuality
- the exotic

Romantic poetry guides a reader's imagination toward an emotional response. As you read poetry, think about the emotions you feel.

READING STRATEGY

Your job as a reader is to understand a poet's message. Another job is to compare the poet's message with your own life experiences. When you **judge a poet's message,** you decide whether or not you agree or disagree with the poet's ideas. As you read these poems, use a chart like the one shown to identify and judge each poet's message.

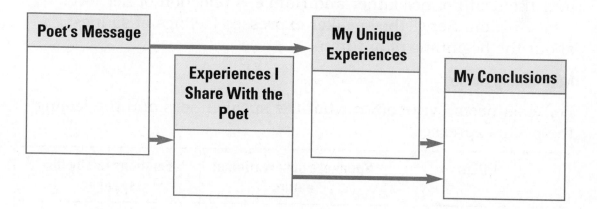

Invitation to the Voyage • The Albatross • The Sleeper in the Valley • Ophelia • Autumn Song

Charles Baudelaire • Arthur Rimbaud • Paul Verlaine

Translated by Richard Wilbur, Richard Howard, William Jay Smith, Daisy Aldan, Louis Simpson

Summaries In "Invitation to the Voyage," the speaker imagines the life he would lead far away.

The speaker in "The Albatross" (AL buh TRAHS) describes the cruel way a bird is treated by sailors.

"The Sleeper in the Valley" describes a dead soldier "sleeping" on the bed of nature.

"Ophelia" (oh FEEL yuh) focuses on a character from Shakespeare's play, *Hamlet*. The poem describes Ophelia as upset over the death of her father and Hamlet's rejection of her love.

In "Autumn Song" the speaker expresses feelings of sadness about the beginning of autumn.

Note-taking Guide

For each poem, write down what the speaker sees and the feeling the poem expresses.

POEM	Speaker's observation of nature	Emotions felt by the speaker
Invitation to the Voyage		
The Albatross		
The Sleeper in the Valley		
Ophelia		
Autumn Song		

Invitation to the Voyage • The Albatross • The Sleeper in the Valley • Ophelia • Autumn Song

1. **Interpret:** In "Invitation to the Voyage," the speaker says the "kind land" has beautiful weather, sweet flowers, and lovely scenery. What idea about the land do these images suggest?

   _____

   _____

2. **Literary Analysis:** For each poem, find details that are typical of **Romantic poetry.** List them in the chart below.

Poem	Imagination	Emotion	Nature	Individuality	The Exotic
Invitation to the Voyage					
The Albatross					
The Sleeper in the Valley					
Ophelia					
Autumn Song					

3. **Reading Strategy:** In "Invitation to the Voyage" the poet wants to escape to a perfect world. **Judge the poet's message** by explaining the possible benefits of this escape.

   _____

   _____

   _____

SUPPORT FOR WRITING AND EXTEND YOUR LEARNING

Writing: Comparison and Contrast Essay

In each of the poems, nature affects both the speakers and the events. Write an essay comparing the role of nature in three of the poems in the grouping.

Choose three poems. Use the chart below to compare the ways nature is described in each poem. Use your notes to help you write your essay.

Treatment of Nature

How Nature is Described in Poem 1	How Nature is Described in Poem 2	How Nature is Described in Poem 3

What is the same about how nature is described in the three poems?

_____

_____

_____

What is different about how nature is described in the three poems?

_____

_____

_____

Listening and Speaking: Comparing Monologues

With a partner, compare Queen Gertrude's **monologue** in *Hamlet* at the end of Act IV, Scene vii with the speaker's in "Ophelia," Section II. First reread both of them. Then, together, complete the chart shown.

Discussion Questions	My Findings	My Partners Findings	Our Conclusion after discussion
Who is the audience for each speaker?			
What is the main message of each speaker?			
How does each speaker feel about Ophelia's death?			

Two Friends • How Much Land Does a Man Need? • A Problem

LITERARY ANALYSIS

Characters in a literary work are either dynamic or static. The behavior and attitudes of a **dynamic character** change as a story, novel, or play progresses. A **static character** remains the same throughout the literary work. Use a chart like the one shown to determine whether a character is dynamic or static.

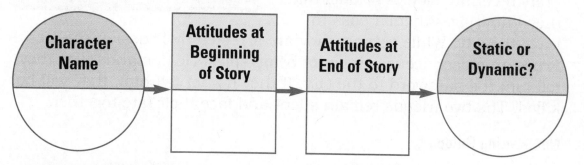

READING STRATEGY

When you **evaluate a character's decision**, you make judgments about the character's choices. Think about a choice a character makes and how it affects future actions. To do this, answer the following questions:

- Is the decision right for the character?
- How does the decision affect other characters?
- Does the decision turn out to be harmful or helpful?
- Would you make a similar decision?

Two Friends
Guy de Maupassant
Translated by Gordon R. Silber

Summary This story takes place in Paris during the Franco-Prussian War (1870-1871). Two friends, Morissot (MO ree soh) and Sauvage (SOH vazh), go fishing in the French countryside. A colonel that they know gives them a pass to leave the city. While fishing, they are arrested by Prussian soldiers. A Prussian officer accuses them of being spies. He demands that they tell him the password to the city. If they do not tell him, they will be killed. The two friends remain silent and face their fate together.

Note-taking Guide

Use the chart to record details from the story.

Setting:

Problem:

Event 1:

Event 2:

Event 3:

Event 4:

Conclusion:

Two Friends
Guy de Maupassant
Translated by Gordon R. Silber

This story takes place in France during the Franco-Prussian War. The war began in July of 1870 and was between France and Prussia, a state in the German empire. The Germans proved to be stronger than the French. In September of 1870, the German army established a blockade around Paris. Paris managed to hold out under a provisional government until January of 1871, during which the citizens lived with famine and a sense of hopelessness. The story begins while Paris is on the verge of surrender.

Mr. Morissot, a watchmaker, unexpectedly meets an old friend, M. Sauvage, on a street in Paris. Before the war, the men often went fishing together at Marante Island outside the city. They miss each other's good company. Now fishing is just a pleasant memory. The friends walk together and then stop in some wine shops to drink.

◆ ◆ ◆

On leaving they felt giddy, muddled, as one does after drinking on an empty stomach. It was mild. A caressing breeze touched their faces.

The warm air completed what the absinthe had begun. M.[1] Sauvage stopped. "Suppose we went?"

"Went where?"

"Fishing, of course."

"But where?"

---

1. M. abbreviation for *Monsieur* (muh SYUR), or "Mister" or "Sir" (French).

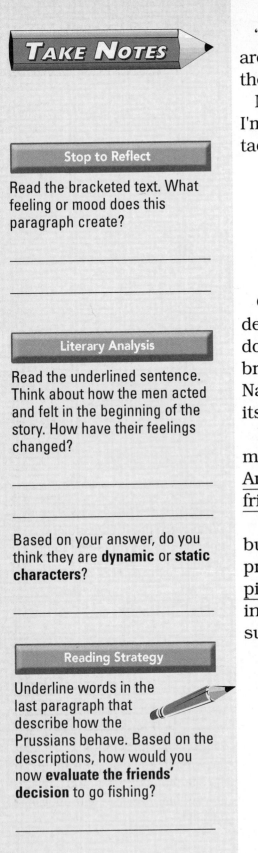

Read the bracketed text. What feeling or mood does this paragraph create?

_____

_____

Read the underlined sentence. Think about how the men acted and felt in the beginning of the story. How have their feelings changed?

_____

_____

Based on your answer, do you think they are **dynamic** or **static characters**?

_____

_____

Underline words in the last paragraph that describe how the Prussians behave. Based on the descriptions, how would you now **evaluate the friends' decision** to go fishing?

_____

_____

_____

"Why, on our island. The French outposts are near Colombes. I know Colonel Dumoulin; they'll let us pass without any trouble."

Morissot trembled with eagerness: "Done! I'm with you." And they went off to get their tackle.

◆ ◆ ◆

An hour later they reach Colonel Dumoulin's house. He gives the friends a pass to leave the city. Soon they travel through an abandoned village outside Paris.

◆ ◆ ◆

Opposite, the village of Argenteuil seemed dead. The heights of Orgemont and Sannois dominated the whole countryside. The broad plain which stretches as far as Nanterre was empty, absolutely empty, with its bare cherry trees and its colorless fields.

Pointing up to the heights, M. Sauvage murmured, "The Prussians are up there!" And a feeling of uneasiness paralyzed the two friends as they faced this deserted region.

"The Prussians!" They had never seen any, but for months they had felt their presence—around Paris, ruining France, pillaging, massacring, starving the country, invisible and all-powerful. And a kind of superstitious terror was superimposed on

Vocabulary Development

outposts (OWT posts) *n.* small military stations, away from the main forces, that are used to guard an area against attack

pillaging (PIL ij ing) *v.* robbing by force, often during a war

massacring (MAS uh ker ing) *v.* killing many helpless people

superimposed (SOO per im POHZD) *v.* placed on top of something else the hatred which they felt for this unknown and victorious people.

Morissot stammered, "Say, suppose we met some of them?"

◆ ◆ ◆

The friends continue their journey. When they think it is safe, they begin to fish happily. Suddenly they hear the loud sound of a nearby cannon. They seem unconcerned by the sound. As they fish, they talk about politics. They agree that men will never be free.

◆ ◆ ◆

But they shuddered in terror when they realized that someone had just come up behind them, and looking around they saw four men standing almost at their elbows, four tall men, armed and bearded, dressed like liveried[2] servants, with flat caps on their heads, pointing rifles at them.

The two fish lines dropped from their hands and floated off down stream.

In a few seconds they were seized, <u>trussed</u> up, carried off, thrown into a rowboat and taken over to the island.

◆ ◆ ◆

The German soldiers take the frightened men to their officer. He speaks to them in French.

◆ ◆ ◆

"As far as I am concerned, you are two spies sent to keep an eye on me. I catch you and I shoot you. You were pretending to fish in order to conceal your business. You have fallen into my hands, so much the worse for you. War is like that.

Vocabulary Development

trussed (TRUST) *v.* tied

---

2. liveried (LIV ur eed) *adj.* uniformed.

TAKE NOTES

Read Fluently

Read aloud the bracketed text. Underline the phrases that describe what happens to the fishermen.

Literary Analysis

Circle the words in the bracketed text that describe the fishermen's feelings in this scene. Based on this description, do you think they are **dynamic** or **static characters**? Explain.

_____

_____

_____

_____

Reading Check

What does the Prussian officer accuse the men of doing?

_____

_____

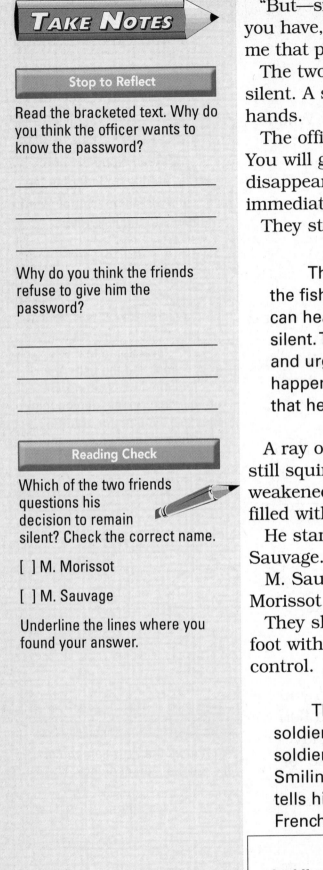

Read the bracketed text. Why do you think the officer wants to know the password?

_____

_____

_____

Why do you think the friends refuse to give him the password?

_____

_____

_____

Which of the two friends questions his decision to remain silent? Check the correct name.

[ ] M. Morissot

[ ] M. Sauvage

Underline the lines where you found your answer.

"But—since you came out past the outposts you have, of course, the password to return. Tell me that password and I will pardon you."

The two friends, side by side, pale, kept silent. A slight nervous trembling shook their hands.

The officer went on: "No one will ever know. You will go back <u>placidly</u>. The secret will disappear with you. If you refuse, it is immediate death. Choose."

They stood motionless, mouths shut.

◆　◆　◆

The Prussian officer threatens to kill the fishermen in five minutes. The friends can hear the cannon fire. Yet they remain silent. The officer pulls each man aside and urges him to speak. Morissot happens to look down at the sack of fish that he and M. Sauvage had caught.

◆　◆　◆

A ray of sunshine made the little heap of still squirming fish gleam. And he almost weakened. In spite of his efforts his eyes filled with tears.

He stammered, "Farewell, Monsieur Sauvage."

M. Sauvage answered, "Farewell, Monsieur Morissot."

They shook hands, trembling from head to foot with a shudder which they could not control.

◆　◆　◆

The Prussian officer orders his soldiers to shoot the fishermen. Then the soldiers throw their bodies into the river. Smiling, the officer calls to his chef. He tells him to fry the fish that the Frenchmen had caught.

Vocabulary Development

placidly (PLAS id lee) *adv.* calmly

How Much Land Does a Man Need?

Leo Tolstoy
Translated by Louise and Aylmer Maude

Summary One day, a peasant named Pakhom (PAHK hohm) decides that his family's life would be easier if they had more land. He travels to visit a group of people called the Bashkirs (BAHSH keerz) to purchase more land. They tell Pakhom he has one day to stake out as much land as he wants. He must return to his starting point before sunset. If he does not make it back in time, he will give up the land and his money.

Note-taking Guide

Use the chart below to fill in details about Pakhom.

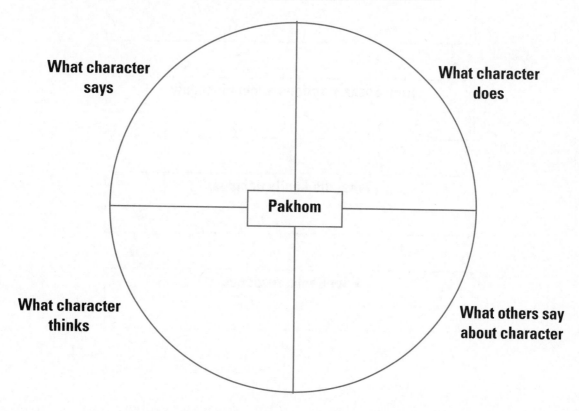

A Problem

Anton Chekhov
Translated by Constance Garnett

Summary In "A Problem," three uncles are trying to decide what to do about their problematic nephew, Sasha (SAH shuh). Sasha has borrowed money and not repaid it. The uncles must decide whether to pay Sasha's debt or let his case go to trial. A kind uncle convinces the family to pay the debt. Although Sasha is relieved, he has not learned his lesson. He now knows that he can manipulate his family when he gets into trouble.

Note-taking Guide

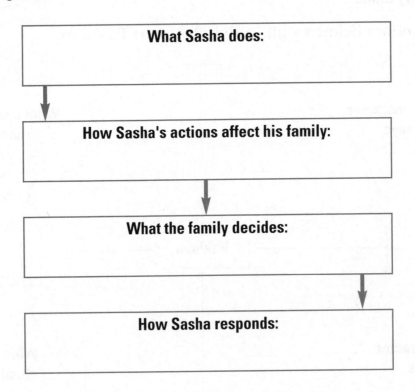

What Sasha does:

How Sasha's actions affect his family:

What the family decides:

How Sasha responds:

Two Friends • How Much Land Does a Man Need? • A Problem

1. **Analyze:** At the end of "How Much Land Does a Man Need?" Pakhom needs only six feet of land for his grave. What is surprising about this ending?

   _____

   _____

2. **Interpret:** At the end of "A Problem," Sasha asks his uncle for a hundred rubles. His uncle is horrified. Why does he react in this way?

   _____

   _____

3. **Literary Analysis:** A **dynamic character** changes. A **static character** stays the same. Are the main characters in "Two Friends" dynamic or static? Use details from the story to support your answer.

   _____

   _____

4. **Reading Strategy:** When you **evaluate characters' decisions,** you decide whether their choices are good or bad. Use the chart below to evaluate the characters' decisions in these three stories.

Character(s):	Decision:	Criteria:	Evaluation:
The two friends		• Is the decision right for the character?	
Pakhom		• How does the decision affect others?	
Sasha		• Would I make a similar decision?	

SUPPORT FOR WRITING AND EXTEND YOUR LEARNING

Writing: Analyzing a Character's Decision

The characters in these stories make important decisions. Write an essay in which you analyze one of these decisions. To prepare, choose a character from one of the stories. Then, answer the questions below.

- What key decision does the character make?

____

- How does that decision affect what happens in the story?

____

____

- What other decision might the character have made?

____

____

- How would that decision have changed the outcome of the story?

____

____

Use your notes as you write your essay.

Listening and Speaking: Monologue

At the end of "A Problem," Sasha makes a bad decision. He asks his uncle Ivan to loan him money. Write a **monologue** in which Sasha speaks to Uncle Ivan five years later. Use the chart below to organize your thoughts.

What has Sasha been doing the last five years?
What has Sasha learned about himself since taking the money from Uncle Ivan?
What kind of relationship does Sasha want to have with Uncle Ivan and the family?

A Doll House, Act One

LITERARY ANALYSIS

Ibsen developed the **modern realistic drama**—a type of play unlike anything audiences had seen before. Modern realistic drama has the following characteristics:

- It is written in language with sentences not in verse.
- It shows characters and situations as they really are.
- It focuses on popular issues and beliefs and often raises questions about those popular beliefs.

Like real life, modern realistic dramas have **conflict**. Conflicts can be either **internal** or **external**. Internal conflicts happen inside the mind of the character, while external conflicts happen between a character and society, nature, another person, God, or fate.

In *A Doll House*, Nora experiences both internal and external conflicts.

READING STRATEGY

A drama is written to be performed. When **reading drama**, picture how the scenes would look on stage. Imagine how the dialogue would sound and how the characters would move. To get the most out of your reading:

- Picture the setting described in the stage directions.
- Imagine voice and tone as you read dialogue.
- Picture the characters' gestures and movements.

As you read, look for details that will help you picture the drama in your mind. Then, use this chart to help you form mental images. An example has been done for you.

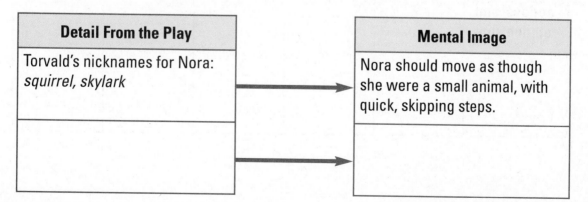

Detail From the Play	Mental Image
Torvald's nicknames for Nora: *squirrel, skylark*	Nora should move as though she were a small animal, with quick, skipping steps.

A Doll House, Act One

Henrik Ibsen
Translated by Rolf Fjelde

Summary Nora appears to be the perfect wife to her husband, Torvald. She seems to be obedient to him. However, Nora is keeping a secret from Torvald. Years ago, Nora borrowed money from Krogstad. She used it to pay for Torvald's treatment when he was ill. Krogstad visits and demands that Nora help him keep his job. Torvald is Krogstad's boss, and Nora would have to ask Torvald not to fire Krogstad. Torvald needs this job to rebuild his reputation. Long ago, he did some foolish things, and it ruined his reputation. If Nora does not agree to help Krogstad, he told Nora he will tell her husband what she did. She forged a signature on the loan paper. Nora refuses to believe that Krogstad would do that. However, she is concerned that her lies will hurt her children.

Note-taking Guide

As you read the play, use the following character guide to help you remember details about each character.

Characters	Nora	Torvald	Dr. Rank	Mrs. Linde	Krogstad
Details about characters, actions, and relationships					

A Doll House, Act One

1. **Draw Conclusions:** What does Torvald's behavior when he questions Noa about the macaroons show you about their relationship?

_____

_____

2. **Literary Analysis:** Review the parts of **modern realistic drama**. Use a chart like the one shown to record details that show *A Doll House* as a modern realistic drama.

Characteristics of modern realistic drama	Details
Ordinary language	
Realistic characters and situations	
Issues and beliefs	

3. **Literary Analysis:** Nora has owed Krogstad money for years. What does Krogstad do that intensifies this **conflict**?

_____

_____

_____

4. **Reading Strategy:** Identify one example from the play that supports each of these statements: Stage directions help illustrate the relationships between characters when **reading a drama**. Stage directions also give hints about how certain lines are said.

_____

_____

_____

Writing: Monologue

Use the following graphic organizer to help you take notes for a **monologue** in which Nora confesses her secrets to Torvald. Record details from the play that show Nora's personality and experiences.

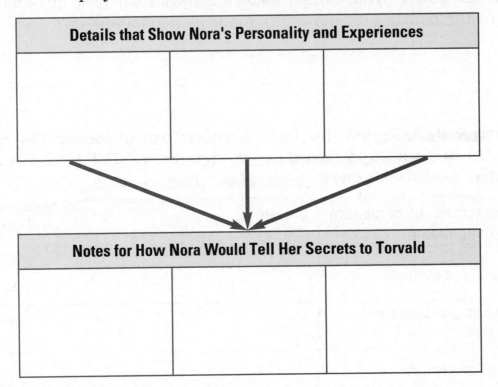

Details that Show Nora's Personality and Experiences		

Notes for How Nora Would Tell Her Secrets to Torvald		

On a separate page, use your notes to write a monologue in which Nora confesses her secrets to Torvald. After rehearsing, present your monologue to the class.

Research and Technology

Answer these questions to help you prepare to make a **rendering of the set** from Act One of *A Doll House*. A *rendering* is a drawing showing how something should look.

1. Which stage directions from Act One give a clear picture of how the set should look?

   _____

   _____

2. What supplies will we need and where can we get them?

   _____

   _____

A Doll House, Act Two

LITERARY ANALYSIS

Characterization is the way a writer shows a character's personality. Characterization is developed through:
- direct statements about a character
- a character's actions, thoughts, or comments
- comments made about the character by other characters.

Characterization in drama also uses stage directions and dialogue. Look for these elements as you read Act Two.

The main character in a drama is called the **protagonist.** The audience often feels sympathy for the protagonist. The **antagonist** is the character or force that opposes the protagonist. In *A Doll House*, Nora is the protagonist. As you read, think about the antagonists whom Nora struggles against.

READING STRATEGY

Inferring beliefs of the period means noting how social, religious, and cultural practices of a time affect characters and the choices they make. As you read:
- Notice how husbands and wives talk to each other.
- Note what women do and what they talk about doing.
- Look for clues about social behaviors and customs.

Use an organizer like the one shown to infer the beliefs of the period as you read Act Two of *A Doll House*.

What a Character Says or Does	What a Character Says or Does	What a Character Says or Does

Inferred Belief of the Period	Inferred Belief of the Period	Inferred Belief of the Period

A Doll House, Act Two

Henrik Ibsen
Translated by Rolf Fjelde

Summary Nora begs Torvald not to fire Krogstad, but Torvald fires him anyway. Nora wants to ask Dr. Rank to give her the money she needs to pay Krogstad. Rank, however, tells her that he is in love with her. Nora cannot ask him after this confession. Krogstad comes to the house with a letter about Nora's secret. When he leaves, he puts it in Torvald's personal mailbox. Nora asks Mrs. Linde to help her get the letter before Torvald can read it. Mrs. Linde agrees, and she goes to Krogstad's house to speak with him. Meanwhile, Nora desperately tries to stop Torvald from opening the mailbox.

Note-taking Guide

As you read, use the following chart to note the events in Act Two of the play.

Time and Place of Act Two:	
Characters in Act Two:	
Event 1:	
Event 2:	
Event 3:	
Event 4:	
Event 5:	
How Act Two ends:	

A Doll House, Act Two

1. **Infer:** Krogstad says that Torvald is the reason Krogstad is getting a bad reputation. What does Krogstad seem to think of Torvald?

_____

_____

2. **Literary Analysis:** Use the chart below to track the **characterization** of Nora. Look for descriptions of her behavior, the comments she makes, and comments made about her by other characters.

Behavior	Comments She Makes	Comments Made by Other Characters

3. **Literary Analysis:** Which details in the play—or in your response to it—reveal that Nora is the **protagonist** of this work?

_____

_____

_____

4. **Reading Strategy:** Mrs. Linde, Anne-Marie, and Nora are qualified to do household-related work. What can you **infer about beliefs of the period** regarding educating women?

_____

_____

_____

SUPPORT FOR WRITING AND EXTEND YOUR LEARNING

Writing: Letter

Put yourself in Krogstad's place and write the **letter** that he mailed to Torvald. Complete the chart below to better understand Krogstad's point of view before you begin to write.

Krogstad's Experience with Nora	Krogstad's Experience with Helmer	Krogstad's Reasons for Writing the Letter

Listening and Speaking: Radio Play Script

Use the following chart to help you prepare the **script of a radio play** based on a scene from Act Two. Before you begin drafting your script, take notes on the language that is appropriate for each character.

Character	Kind of Language for This Character
Nora	
Mrs. Linde	
Helmer (Torvald)	
Dr. Rank	
Krogstad	

A Doll House, Act Three

LITERARY ANALYSIS

A **theme** is a central message about life that is revealed by a literary work. In a drama, a theme may be stated directly or it may be made known through what the characters say and do. A play like *A Doll House* may have more than one theme:

- Real love is not based on beauty or social status.
- A relationship is based on trust, and respect.
- Every person has the right to live as he or she chooses.

To help readers recognize important themes, Ibsen uses **foreshadowing**. When a writer uses foreshadowing, he or she hints at things to come. As you read, note how foreshadowing keeps you guessing.

READING STRATEGY

Dramatic tension is the suspense that an audience feels while watching a play. To **recognize dramatic tension**, pay attention to the moments that you feel suspense and nervousness during the play. Then, ask questions such as these:

- Why are these characters in conflict with one another?
- What will the protagonist lose if he or she is unsuccessful?

Record moments of conflict or mystery in the chart shown. For each one, write a question that expresses the suspense or lack of knowledge that you feel in that moment.

Moment of Conflict or Mystery	Moment of Conflict or Mystery	Moment of Conflict or Mystery
Mrs. Linde asks Krogstad to speak with her about Nora's debt.		

Question	Question	Question
Will Mrs. Linde reveal Nora's desperation?		

A Doll House, Act Three

Henrik Ibsen
Translated by Rolf Fjelde

Summary Mrs. Linde and Krogstad discuss their past. Although Krogstad suspects Mrs. Linde wants him to reclaim the letter from Torvald, Mrs. Linde does not ask. She tells Krogstad that Torvald must read the letter and discover Nora's secret. She believes the Helmers must learn the truth about each other. Krogstad and Mrs. Linde decide to get married. When Nora and Torvald return from the costume party, Torvald reads Krogstad's letter. Torvald tells Nora that she has ruined his life. Then, Torvald receives another letter from Krogstad. Torvald is happy that Krogstad has forgiven the debt and he forgives Nora her mistake. Nora, however, has the realization that her husband does not really love her, and only thinks of her as a doll. She then tells him that she is leaving him.

Note-taking Guide

Use the following guide to trace the events in Act Three of the play.

Event 1:	
Event 2:	
Event 3:	
Event 4:	
Event 5:	
Event 6:	
Event 7:	
Event 8:	

A Doll House, Act Three

1. **Speculate:** Nora tells Torvald that she will not accept any help from him. Why do you think Nora refuses his help?

   _____

   _____

2. **Literary Analysis:** One **theme** of *A Doll House* is how to have to a successful relationship. Use the chart shown to give three examples of dialogue from Act Three that support this theme.

Character	Dialogue	Keys to a Successful Relationship
Character	**Dialogue**	**Keys to a Successful Relationship**
Character	**Dialogue**	**Keys to a Successful Relationship**

3. **Literary Analysis:** Mrs. Linde says to Krogstad, "Anyone who's sold herself for somebody else once isn't going to do it again." In what way does this comment **foreshadow** Nora's decision to leave Torvald?

   _____

   _____

   _____

4. **Reading Strategy:** The scene when Torvald reads Krogstad's letter is the moment with the most **dramatic tension?** Which conflicts are resolved when the dramatic tension breaks?

   _____

   _____

   _____

Writing: Persuasive Essay

Write a **persuasive essay** in which you argue for or against Nora's decision to leave Torvald. To help you begin, use the following graphic organizer to list the pros and cons of Nora's decision.

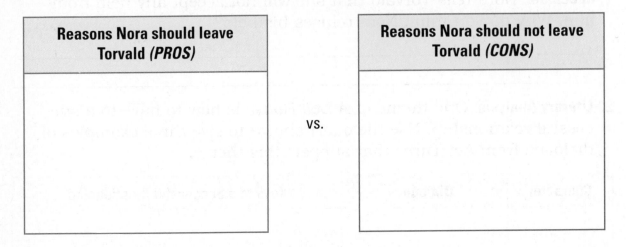

Reasons Nora should leave Torvald (*PROS*)	Reasons Nora should not leave Torvald (*CONS*)

vs.

Research and Technology: Costume Design Display

Choose one character and one scene from *A Doll House* and develop a **costume design display.** Use the chart below to help you organize your information for your sketch.

Character	Description of Costume (and how it fits into the time period)	Colors or Patterns to use	Accessories (hat, shoes, cane, tie, handbag, and so on)
Nora			
Mrs. Linde			
Helmer (Torvald)			
Dr. Rank			
Krogstad			

CRITICAL REVIEWS

About Critical Reviews

A **critical review** analyzes and evaluates a product, an artistic performance, or even the behavior of a person or group. Critical reviews usually contain strong opinions. In a review, the word *critical* can mean either a positive or a negative judgment. Most critical reviews contain the following:

- a brief summary
- a carefully thought-out and clearly stated opinion
- supporting evidence

Because the purpose of a critical review is often to persuade, expect to find strong arguments and powerful language.

Reading Strategy

Opinions can vary greatly from person to person. When you read a review, it's important to be objective, or open to different views. Therefore, you should read more than one critical review on a subject in order to arrive at the "big picture" of what is being reviewed. To **compare and contrast critical reviews,** do the following:

- Compare the reviews to find out where critics share the same point of view.
- Contrast the reviews to find points where the critics disagree.

As critics, the writers of the following critical reviews saw the same performance of Ibsen's A *Doll's House*. However, they did not agree on all parts of the performance.

BUILD UNDERSTANDING

Knowing these terms will help you understand these critical reviews.

Norway (NOR way) *n.* a country in northern Europe in the western part of the Scandinavian peninsula

production (proh DUK shuhn) *n.* something that is produced, such as a play or movie

performance (per FORM uhns) *n.* the enactment of a musical or dramatic role in front of an audience

CurtainUp Review: A Doll's House

by Judd Hollander & Sue Feinberg

From the moment she steps onto the stage of the Belasco Theater, Janet McTeer delivers a riveting[1] performance as Nora Helmer, the heroine of Henrik Ibsen's *A Doll's House*, currently playing at the Belasco Theatre.

Set in a small Norwegian town during Christmas 1879 (and inspired by actual events), the play tells the story of a young wife (McTeer) and mother who's still pretty much a child herself. This time out, however, the 118-year-old work has been given a 1990s feel. McTeer's Nora is a whirling dervish,[2] full of life and laughter, a woman who would be more at home on the stage of an English Music Hall than with her husband Torvald (Owen Teale) and three children. (Her idea of a perfect life is having "pots and pots and pots of money.")

After years of struggle, the couple has finally achieved a measure of financial security, thanks to Torvald's new job as a bank manager. But then a ghost from Nora's past appears in the form of Nils Krogstad (Peter Gowen). Several years earlier, Nora secretly borrowed money for a trip to a warmer climate to allow her desperately ill husband to recover. In order to guarantee the loan, she forged a signature on a contract. Krogstad wants his money back and Nora, not able to give it, is terrified that Torvald will learn the truth.

1.riveting (RIV it ing) *adj.* holding firmly.
2.edervish (DUR vish) *n.* a person known for using howls and whirls in religious practices.

Reading Critical Reviews

A **critical review** always includes a brief summary of the reviewer's topic. In the first paragraph, underline the summary of thesubject of the review.

Stop to Reflect

What kind of person is the character Nora Helmer?

_____

_____

_____

Reading Check

Read the bracketed passage.

How did Nora help her husband?

_____

_____

_____

Who is Nils Krogstad?

_____

_____

Why is Nora frightened?

_____

_____

_____

As events unfold, Nora slowly comes to realize that the "perfect" life she has led is nothing but a fairy tale. Her life has been that of a *doll* to be pampered and protected, first by her father and then by her husband. But even as she's forced to face reality, she tries to do the *right* thing, only to realize that what she loves the most is the biggest lie of all.

Ibsen's work caused quite a shock when it first premiered in 1879 and was heralded as one of the first modern, post-Shakespeare "women's plays." McTeer takes the role of Ibsen's *doll wife* and brilliantly makes it her own. Her Nora runs the gamut[3] of emotions from fear to rage to loathing to desperation. Even her demeanor and manner alter and she seems to age before our eyes, gaining not experience or wisdom, but the understanding that these are the qualities she must find. Just before the show ends, there's a scene where she mocks her former "sing-song" persona. That Nora is light-years removed from the one we first met only three hours or, according to the play's time frame, three days before.

While McTeer is the play's linchpin[4], she does not have the toughest role in the piece. That honor goes to Owen Teale. His Torvald at first glance seems the stereotypical nineteenth-century husband, a man with a keen sense of

Reading Critical Reviews

A **critical review** should include a carefully thought out and clearly stated opinion. In the bracketed passage, underline the critics' opinion of McTeer's performance.

Read Fluently

Read the underlined passage aloud.

Who do the critics think has the hardest role in the play?

_____

_____

3. **gamut** (GAM uht) *n.* entire range.
4. **linchpin** (LINCH pin) *n.* something that holds different parts together.

propriety who knows that a man is ruler of his home. He unquestionably loves Nora, and Teale lets us see and feel the passion beneath the propriety of the character—as well as a mean streak that makes him dangerous if crossed.

Many of Teale's lines, which would not have raised an eyebrow in 1879 Norway, drew roars of contemptuous laughter from the 1997 audience. Yet when his whole world comes crashing down and he's forced (after much prodding) to confront the lie his life has become, he makes a subtle, almost unnoticed, transformation. Slowly he begins to understand his wife's pain and the role he has played in letting it continue. When he says to Nora <u>"I have the strength in me to become another man,"</u> we're seeing a soul laid bare in a way that's totally convincing.

Director Anthony Page keeps the pace moving during the more active scenes, and he and the actors managed to hold the audience's interest even during the slow sections, which consist of lengthy, two-person conversations with very little action (though they do provide vital plot information).

The script, taken from a literal translation of the work, could probably have been cut by a half-hour. However, the cast and producers seemed more interested in presenting a definitive version of the Ibsen work rather than adapting it to suit a 90s audience. And in this, they have succeeded admirably. Despite its wordiness, the play gradually draws you into its emotional web and delivers a knockout punch of a payoff.

Quibbles[5] about slow-pacing aside, *A Doll's House* is an intense and compelling journey through the human spirit and well worth the trip.

---

5. **quibbles** (KWIB uhlz) *n.* minor objections.

Stop to Reflect

Read the underlined text. Why do you think the reviewers chose to include this quote?

_____

_____

_____

Reading Critical Reviews

A thorough **critical review** covers all the different aspects of the thing that is being reviewed. What elements of this production are covered in the bracketed section?

_____

_____

_____

A Lot of Baggage for Nora to Carry

After a History of Misinterpretation, Ibsen's Leave-Taking Heroine Finally Gets Her Due

By Lloyd Rose
Washington Post Staff Writer

As Nora in the London-produced *A Doll's House* now playing on Broadway, the tall, rangy Janet McTeer is as gawkily graceful as a young swan. This Nora is a six-foot bundle of adorability—and she knows it. Everything in her movement and manner—especially her hoarse, self-conscious giggle—says to the men in her life, "Aren't I silly, aren't I scatterbrained, aren't I helpless, don't you adore me?" And they do.

A Doll's House, the story of a pampered bourgeois[6] wife who rebelliously leaves her domineering husband, has a problematic reputation. . . . At least one reviewer felt constrained to point out that the New York production is more than "a feminist screed[7]." Henrik Ibsen . . . has been getting bopped with accusations of feminism since the play's debut in 1880. When Nora realized her life was a lie and walked out on her husband and children, nineteenth-century audiences were scandalized.

---

6. **bourgeois** (bor ZHWAH) *adj.* middle-class.
7. **screed** (SKREED) *n.* a long, tiresome speech or piece of writing.

Reading Strategy

How does the opinion stated in the opening paragraph **compare** to the opinion of Janet McTeer in the previous review?

_____

_____

_____

Read Fluently

Read the second paragraph of the review aloud. What did Nora do to shock 19th century audiences?

_____

_____

_____

Reading Critical Reviews

The critic gives an **opinion** of the show in the bracketed passage. What does he think of this performance?

_____

_____

_____

Stop to Reflect

After reading this review, would you be interested in seeing *A Doll's House*? Why or why not?

_____

_____

_____

McTeer and director Anthony Page bring this production very close to what I've always thought is the essential truth of *A Doll's House*. . . . McTeer's Nora doesn't realize so much that Torvald is a cad (Owen Teale's honorable, grounded performance makes that impossible anyway) as that she has constructed a fantasy about his being a hero. The mistake is hers, for being a grown woman who believes in a fairy tale.

This discovery doesn't put Nora in a lecturing mood. She's staggered, a little dazed, as if she'd been punched in the head by reality.

As McTeer plays it, the last speech isn't superior and scolding; she doesn't even don her coat until toward the end. Her Nora is tentative, feeling her way through the revelations that have been forced upon her, realizing what she has done. As a result, the character is fascinating, surprising, disturbing, instead of being all dreary and moral and right.

This production doesn't go quite as far as it could—Nora still scores some too-easy points over Torvald—but it goes a long, brave way. In London, McTeer won an Olivier Award for her performance, beating out such powerhouse talents as Diana Rigg and Vanessa Redgrave, and you certainly see why. She's not as luminous[8] as Redgrave. She's not as witty and fierce as Rigg. But she is certainly, as Ralph Richardson used to

---

8. **luminous** (LOO muh nís) *adj.* shining.

A Doll's House

By Henrik Ibsen
A New Version by Frank McGuiness

Reviewed by David Spencer

The first thing you have to understand about this so-called revival of *A Doll's House*—which comes to Broadway by way of London—is that it's not a revival at all. It follows the general outline of Ibsen's famous drama about a woman's coming of age—it contains the same characters and the same events—but it's essentially a new play by Frank ("Someone Who'll Watch over Me") McGuiness. Note his credit: not "translation by" but "a new version by." It's a credit I note with particular emphasis because I have one such on my own resumé. . . . So as you read all the paeans[9] to Janet McTeer's performance as a devastating "new" Nora, keep in mind that a new Nora is precisely, *literally*, what's on offer. And it starts not with the actress, but with the script—whose spin on Ibsen is both compelling and subversive.[10]

<u>That [Janet McTeer] is vivacious, sensual, charismatic, explosive—everything you want a "star" to be—is undeniable. Her Nora trembles with suppressed giggles, bursts with surprise, teases mercilessly, touches, hugs, whispers conspiratorially, revels in her own outrageousness. In the play's first act, this electrifies the audience—palpably.</u> At first, it all but overwhelms Owen Teale's performance as her husband Torvald (a portrayal of a vigorously

---

9. **paeans** (PEE ahns) *n.* songs of praise.
10. **subversive** (sub VER siv) *adj.* seeking to overthrow or destroy.

TAKE NOTES

Stop to Reflect

Read the first paragraph of this review. How would you summarize Spencer's opinion of this production of *A Doll's House*?

_____

_____

_____

Reading Critical Reviews

In a **critical review**, the writer uses powerful language to make his or her point. Circle the examples of powerful language in the underlined passage.

insecure martinet[11] wannabe) . . . but it creates a buzz of excitement and discovery.

It's not a buzz that sustains, though. Because after intermission, with Acts Two and Three (performed in one stretch), the vivacity turns to a jittery desperation and finally to out-and-out hysteria. It seems like a perfectly logical progression: once the tight rein on Nora's sense of stability is released by the threat of blackmail and ruination, her energy would fly out of control, she would find herself without moorings.[12] But in the playing, it is merely relentless.

Happily, in Acts Two and Three, with the shock of the new Nora no longer a novelty, we do get to concentrate on the others in the ensemble—and they are fine within the parameters of the script.

They don't, however, bring the audience closer to the play. Yes, with this *Doll's House* being so different, so modern of intent, it is endlessly fascinating—but it's a fascination experienced from a distance. You are always aware of the revisionist take on things, always pausing to *note* the controversial new choices, to *compare* them to Ibsen's original . . . rather than just experiencing them on a visceral[13] level.

I don't mean to condemn this production—or, for that matter, Ms. McTeer. McGuiness' revisionist take is a fine and noble experiment, and his Nora is clearly a magnificent actress. I just feel as if—in the final analysis, in the grand karmic sweep of the universe—this *A Doll's House* is not the be-all, end-all revelation the hype would have you believe, but rather an intermediary step.

---

11. **martinet** (MART´n et) *n.* someone who maintains strict discipline.
12. **moorings** (MOOR ings) *n.* lines or anchors that keep ships tied to a dock.
13. **visceral** (VIS er uhl) *adj.* instinctive or emotional.

Compared to the "CurtainUp Review" and the review by Lloyd Rose, do you think the producers of *A Doll's House* would be happy with Spencer's review? Explain.

_____

_____

_____

Critical reviews provide evidence, or support, for their opinions. Do you think Spencer provides enough support for his opinion of this production? Explain.

_____

_____

_____

© Pearson Education, Inc., publishing as Pearson Prentice Hall.

THINKING ABOUT THE CRITICAL REVIEWS

1. What words or phrases from these reviews would be effective in an advertisement for this production of *A Doll's House*? Why?

_____

_____

_____

_____

READING STRATEGY

2. Which critic might disagree with the awarding of the Best Revival Tony Award to this production of *A Doll's House*? Why?

_____

_____

_____

_____

_____

3. What opinion of this production do David Spencer and Lloyd Rose share?

_____

_____

_____

_____

_____

TIMED WRITING: EVALUATION (30 minutes)

Write a **critical review** of a movie or television show that you have seen recently. When you evaluate a movie or television show, it is important to think about the different elements of that performance. For each element in the chart below, note whether you thought it was well done. For each element, include a reason for your opinion and an example.

Element	Opinion	Reason	Example
Acting			
Costumes			
Script			
Set			

The Metamorphosis

LITERARY ANALYSIS

Around the year 1900, writers began turning away from the style, form, and subjects of earlier literature in favor of new ways of writing. This movement, called **Modernism**, included many smaller movements in literature. Most Modernist works share certain qualities:

- They try to capture the truth about modern life.
- They express a sense of feeling separate from other people.
- They leave readers to make up their own minds.

The first paragraph of this story drops you into a world in which something impossible has happened. "The Metamorphosis" places something imaginary in a real setting. This makes the story an example of literature of the fantastic. The **literature of the fantastic** is a kind of writing that mixes imagination with reality.

READING STRATEGY

"The Metamorphosis" is not the story of Franz Kafka's life. But **applying the author's biography**—making connections to Kafka's life—can shed light on the story's meaning. Applying the author's biography means connecting the story to the writer's life. Use a diagram like the one shown to record facts from Kafka's life that shed light on "The Metamorphosis."

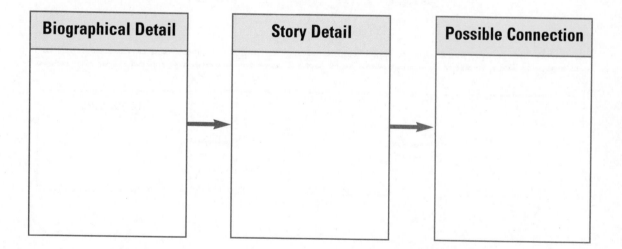

Biographical Detail	Story Detail	Possible Connection

The Metamorphosis

Franz Kafka
Translated by Stanley Corngold

Summary One morning, Gregor Samsa discovers that he has become a beetle. Gregor thinks he is dreaming. However, his family and his boss are shocked and horrified by his new appearance. Gregor's father forces him to remain in his bedroom. In Part II, Gregor behaves more like an insect. His sister, Grete, cares for him even though she is disgusted by his appearance. Grete and her mother rearrange the furniture in his room. This furniture is Gregor's last link to his human self. Upset, he scares his mother and his father beats him. In Part III, the family has learned to accept Gregor's new condition. However, they neglect him. They are busy working to support themselves. Gregor later dies alone in his bedroom. His family is left to start over.

Note-taking Guide

As you read, use this chart to trace the series of events in the story.

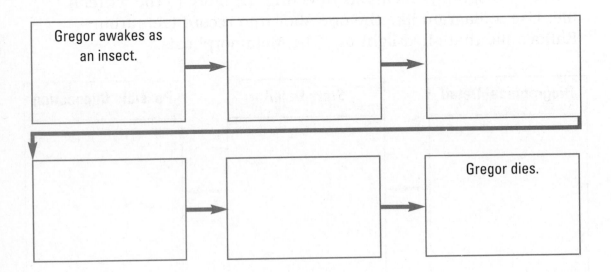

The Metamorphosis

1. **Compare and Contrast**: In what ways does Grete change as a result of Gregor becoming an insect?

   _____

   _____

   _____

2. **Literary Analysis: Modernism** showed the realities and uncertainties of modern life. Using the chart below, write two details from Part I of "The Metamorphosis" that show everyday realities in modern life.

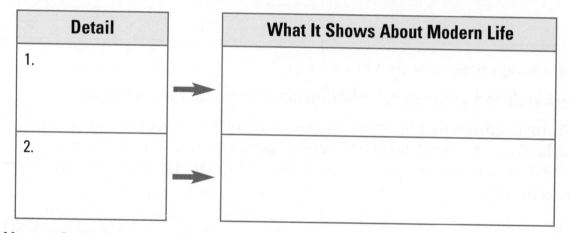

Detail		What It Shows About Modern Life
1.	→	
2.	→	

3. **Literary Analysis**: In what ways is the opening scene an example of literature of the fantastic?

   _____

   _____

4. **Reading Strategy: Apply the author's biography** by reading about Franz Kafka's life on SE page 1064. How are Kafka's feelings toward his own family similar to Gregor Samsa's feelings in the story? Support your answer with details from the story

   _____

   _____

   _____

Writing: Essay Responding to a Critical Perspective

Your **response** to Vladimir Nabokov's criticism will argue either for or against Nabokov's statement about "The Metamorphosis." For example, you might disagree with Nabokov's view that Gregor has a "sweet" nature. If so, you should find examples in the story in which Gregor behaves bitterly or angrily. Use the following chart to list Nabokov's judgments, your opinion of these judgments, and the reasons you either agree or disagree with these judgments.

Nabokov's View	Do I Agree or Disagree?	Reasons

Use these notes to write your essay.

Research and Technology: Multimedia Classroom Presentation

Your **multimedia classroom presentation** will compare Modernist works from different forms of art. To prepare, use the chart below to record details about specific examples of Modernist art works for your presentation.

Topic	Example	Artist	Year
Visual Arts			
Music			
Drama			
Architecture			

SCIENTIFIC TEXTS

About Scientific Texts

Scientific texts contain knowledge acquired through testing and observing. These texts include detailed information about different branches of science, such as biology, chemistry, geology, and physics. Scientific texts usually contain the following kinds of information:

- facts about a variety of science topics
- hypotheses (hy PAHTH uh seez), or theories, that explain scientific facts
- descriptions of experiments that scientists have conducted to prove their hypotheses
- diagrams, called figures, of relevant scientific details

Reading Strategy

Analyzing text features will help you learn and remember new information from your textbooks. As you read a textbook, find and study the following features:

- headings of chapters and sections
- visuals, such as charts, graphs, diagrams, and photographs
- the first paragraph of each section
- the lesson or chapter summary and review questions
- text printed in bold (dark) or italic (slanted) type

Use this chart to help you analyze the text features.

Text Feature	How It Is Used	How It Helps Me Learn

Build Understanding

Knowing these terms will help you read this scientific text.

stimuli (STIM yoo ly) *n.* things that stir or rouse plants or animals to action

molt (MOLT) *v.* to shed skin in preparation for new growth

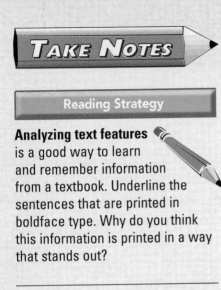
Analyzing text features is a good way to learn and remember information from a textbook. Underline the sentences that are printed in boldface type. Why do you think this information is printed in a way that stands out?

_____

_____

_____

Read the bracketed section aloud. How are an insects eyes different from a human's? List two differences below.

1. _____

_____

2. _____

_____

What Is an Insect?

Like all arthropods, insects have a segmented body, an exoskeleton, and jointed appendages. They also have several features that are specific to insects. **Insects have a body divided into three parts—head, thorax, and abdomen. Three pairs of legs are attached to the thorax.** The beetle in **Figure 28–15** exhibits these characteristics. In many insects such as ants, the body parts are clearly separated from each other by narrow connections. In other insects, such as grass-hoppers, the divisions between the three body parts are not as sharply defined. A typical insect also has a pair of antennae and a pair of compound eyes on the head, two pairs of wings on the thorax, and tracheal tubes that are used for respiration.

The essential life functions in insects are carried out in basically the same ways as they are in other arthropods. However, insects have a variety of interesting adaptations that deserve a closer look.

✔CHECKPOINT **What are the names of the three parts of an insect's body?**

Responses to Stimuli Insects use a multitude of sense organs to respond to stimuli. Compound eyes are made of many lenses that detect minute changes in color and movement. The brain assembles this information into a single, detailed image. Compound eyes produce an image that is less detailed than what we see. However, eyes with multiple lenses are far better at detecting movement—one reason it is so hard to swat a fly!

Insects have chemical receptors for taste and smell on their mouthparts, as might be expected, and also on their antennae and legs. When a fly steps in a drop of water, it knows immediately whether the water contains salt or sugar. Insects also have sensory hairs that detect slight movements in the surrounding air or water.

As objects move toward insects, the insects can feel the movement of the displaced air or water and respond appropriately. Many insects also have well-developed ears that hear sounds far above the human range. These organs are located in what we would consider odd places—behind the legs in grasshoppers, for example.

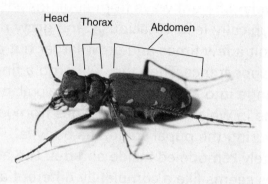

Figure 28–15 Insects have a body divided into three parts—head, thorax, and abdomen. Three pairs of legs are attached to the thorax. In addition to these features, this green tiger beetle has other characteristics of a typical insect—wings, antennae, compound eyes, and tracheal tubes for respiration.

Metamorphosis 🔑 **The growth and development of insects usually involve metamorphosis, which is a process of changing shape and form. Insects undergo either incomplete metamorphosis or complete metamorphosis.** Both complete and incomplete metamorphosis are shown in **Figure 28–18.** The immature forms of insects that undergo gradual or **incomplete metamorphosis,** such as the chinch bug, look very much like the adults. These immature forms are called **nymphs** (NIMFS). Nymphs lack functional sexual organs and other adult structures, such as wings. As they molt several times and grow, the nymphs gradually acquire adult structures. This type of

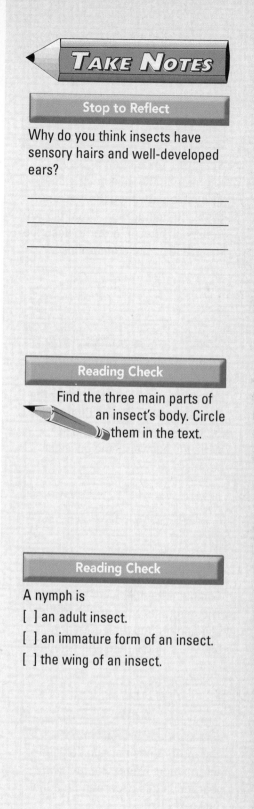

TAKE NOTES

Stop to Reflect

Why do you think insects have sensory hairs and well-developed ears?

_____

_____

_____

Reading Check

Find the three main parts of an insect's body. Circle them in the text.

Reading Check

A nymph is
[ ] an adult insect.
[ ] an immature form of an insect.
[ ] the wing of an insect.

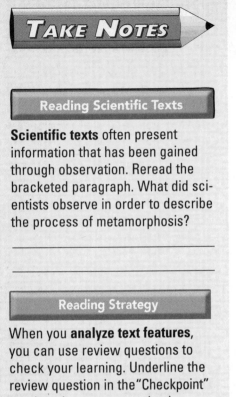

TAKE NOTES

Reading Scientific Texts

Scientific texts often present information that has been gained through observation. Reread the bracketed paragraph. What did scientists observe in order to describe the process of metamorphosis?

_____

_____

Reading Strategy

When you **analyze text features**, you can use review questions to check your learning. Underline the review question in the "Checkpoint" section about metamorphosis. Write the answer to the question here

_____

_____

Reading Check

Complete the following sentence: The diagrams in Figure 28-18 help you understand the difference between incomplete and complete.

_____

Reading Informational Materials

Scientific texts contain detailed information. Name one fact you learned in this excerpt from a biology text.

_____

_____

What text feature helped you remember that fact?

_____

development is characterized by a similar appearance throughout all stages of the life cycle.

Many insects, such as bees, moths, and beetles, undergo a more dramatic change in body form during a process called **complete metamorphosis**. These animals hatch into larvae that look and act nothing like their parents. They also feed in completely different ways from adult insects. The larvae typically feed voraciously and grow rapidly. They molt a few times and grow larger but change little in appearance. Then they undergo a final molt and change into a **pupa** (PYOO-puh; plural: pupae)— the stage in which an insect changes from larva to adult. During the pupal stage, the body is completely remodeled inside and out. The adult that emerges seems like a completely different animal. Unlike the larva, the adult typically can fly and is specialized for reproduction. **Figure 28–18** shows the complete metamorphosis of a ladybug beetle.

✓**CHECKPOINT** **What is a pupa?**

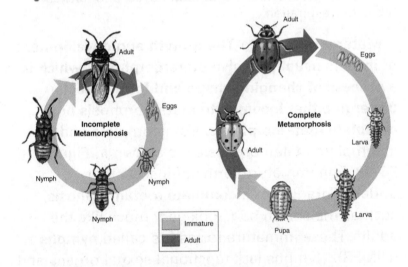

Figure 28–18 The growth and development of insects usually involve metamorphosis, which is a process of changing shape and form. Insects undergo incomplete metamorphosis or complete metamorphosis. The chinch bug (left) undergoes incomplete metamorphosis, and the developing nymphs look similar to the adult. The ladybug (right) undergoes complete metamorphosis, and during the early stages the developing larva and pupa look completely different from the adult.

THINKING ABOUT THE SCIENTIFIC TEXTS

1. How do insects sense movement?

_____

2. Which type of eye would be better for driving a car: an insect's or a human's? Explain.

_____

READING STRATEGY

3. List three types of **text features** in the text and explain how they help the reader to understand insects.

_____

4. Use Figure 28-18 on page 302 to understand the two types of metamorphosis. Then, explain how the drawing shows the similarities and differences between the two types.

_____

_____

TIMED WRITING: EVALUATION (15 minutes)

Sections of text in a textbook are often divided according to the topic they cover. Often, a heading at the beginning of the section identifies the main idea of the section. In the chart below, note the main ideas of the three sections of the scientific text. Record two important details from each section. Then, write a paragraph summarizing the main ideas of this scientific text.

Main Idea of Section	Details
	• •
	• •
	• •

The Bracelet

LITERARY ANALYSIS

An **epiphany** is a sudden flash of understanding that a person has about himself or herself, another person, or life itself. This thought may be positive or negative. In older stories, a series of events usually leads to the solution of a conflict. However, in many modern stories, events lead to an epiphany. This epiphany often affects the conflict without solving it. As you read, use the chart to identify details that suggest an epiphany Madame Augelier experiences. Then, decide whether the conflict is solved or simply changed.

Details Leading to Epiphany	Statement Expressing Epiphany

READING STRATEGY

When you **draw conclusions,** you reach decisions based on evidence. For example, if someone comes inside shaking a wet umbrella, you might draw the conclusion that it is raining. When reading, draw conclusions by using your knowledge and experiences to reach decisions. In "The Bracelet," draw conclusions about Madame Augelier's life and character.

The Bracelet

Colette
Translated by Matthew Ward

Summary Madame Augelier is a wealthy, fifty-year-old woman. As the story begins, she is looking at a diamond bracelet, an anniversary present from her husband. She thinks back to past anniversaries and other gifts. This makes her feel restless and unhappy. Then she remembers a bracelet she loved, a beautiful blue glass bracelet she received as a child. She searches shops and flea markets and finally finds such a bracelet. Madame Augelier thought that finding the bracelet would make her feel happy. What she ends up feeling, however, is a surprise, even to her.

Note-taking Guide

Use the diagram below to record Madame Augelier's feelings and the reasons for those feelings. The first row is filled in for you.

Feelings	Reasons for Madame Augelier's Feelings
unhappiness	As she looks at her new diamond bracelet, she ses the wrinkles on her wrist.

Read Fluently

Read aloud the direct quotation in the bracketed text. Use the tone of voice and expression you think Madame Augelier would use.

Reading Check

What "other bracelet" is Madame Augelier looking at as the story begins?

_____

_____

Underline the words in the bracketed text that describe the other bracelet.

Reading Strategy

When you **draw conclusions**, you make decisions about characters and situations. What conclusion can you draw about Madame Augelier's feelings about getting older?

_____

_____

_____

_____

_____

The Bracelet

Colette
Translated by Matthew Ward

Madame Augelier sits in her home. She counts the twenty-nine diamonds on a bracelet her husband has given her for their anniversary. She puts it on and admires how the diamonds sparkle. But Madame Augelier is looking more closely at the wrinkles on her wrist. She thinks of her husband and recalls all of the past anniversary gifts he has given her over the years. She wonders what he will give her next. In her mind, Madame Augelier refers to her husband as "poor Francois." She feels guilty because she thinks that she does not love him enough.

◆　◆　◆

Madame Augelier raised her hand, tucked her little finger under, extended her wrist to erase the bracelet of wrinkles, and repeated intently, "It's so pretty . . . the diamonds are so white . . . I'm so pleased . . ." Then she let her hand fall back down and admitted to herself that she was already tired of her new bracelet.

◆　◆　◆

Madame Augelier continues to tell herself that she is grateful for what she has. But as she tries on some of her many pieces of jewelry, she still feels dissatisfied.

◆　◆　◆

"I don't know what's wrong with me. I'm not feeling all that well. Being fifty is a bore, basically . . ."

◆　◆　◆

Madame Augelier starts to feel sick and restless. She then questions whether a diamond is such a pretty object. She begins to wonder what else would please her.

Madame Augelier <u>craved</u> a visual pleasure which would involve the sense of taste as well; the unexpected sight of a lemon, the unbearable squeaking of the knife cutting it in half, makes the mouth water with desire . . .

◆ ◆ ◆

She suddenly realizes that she does not want a lemon and that the pleasure she is seeking is one from forty years ago. She recalls a certain blue glass bracelet that she had as a child. Having that bracelet brought her the wonderful nameless pleasure that she is looking for.

As she recalls the blue glass bracelet, she remembers that it was unusual and beautiful. She also recalls how delighted she felt as she looked at the fascinating colors and shapes it reflected. When she returns to reality and loses the image of the bracelet, she does not feel good.

◆ ◆ ◆

But the next day she began searching, from antique shops to flea markets, from flea markets to crystal shops, for a glass bracelet, a certain color of blue. <u>She put the passion of a collector, the precaution, the dissimulation[1] of a lunatic into her search.</u>

◆ ◆ ◆

Literary Analysis

An **epiphany** is a sudden realization or insight. What sudden realization does Madame Angelier have?

_____

_____

Underline the words that show what she suddenly remembers.

Reading Check

Madame Augelier searches for a blue glass bracelet. In the underlined sentence, circle three words that describe her search.

Vocabulary Development

craved (KRAYVD) *v.* longed for; wanted desperately

---

1. **dissimulation** (di SIM yoo LAY shun) *n.* the hiding of one's feelings or motives.

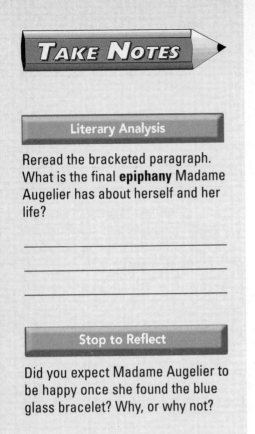

Literary Analysis

Reread the bracketed paragraph. What is the final **epiphany** Madame Augelier has about herself and her life?

_____

_____

_____

Stop to Reflect

Did you expect Madame Augelier to be happy once she found the blue glass bracelet? Why, or why not?

_____

_____

_____

At last, she finds the special bracelet and buys it for a few coins. But when Madame Augelier brings the bracelet home and looks at it, she sees only a round piece of blue glass. Although she recognizes it, the bracelet does not evoke the sense of wonder that she recalls from her childhood.

Resigned, Madame Augelier thus came to know how old she really was and measured the infinite plain over which there wandered, beyond her reach, a being <u>detached</u> from her forever, a stranger, turned away from her, rebellious and free even from the <u>bidding</u> of memory: a little ten-year-old girl wearing on her wrist a bracelet of blue glass.

Vocabulary Development

detached (dee TACHT) *adj.* separate; standing alone
bidding (BID ing) *n.* command; order

The Bracelet

1. **Analyze:** Madame Augelier describes the gifts her husband has given her. How do these descriptions show her feelings toward life and marriage?

   _____

   _____

2. **Literary Analysis:** What is Madame Augelier's reaction to the **epiphany,** or deep and sudden thought, she experiences at the end of the story?

   _____

   _____

3. **Literary Analysis:** Does Madame Augelier's epiphany make you feel sorry for her? Why or why not?

   _____

   _____

4. **Reading Strategy:** Use the chart below to identify details that help you to **draw the conclusion** that Madame Augelier is unhappy.

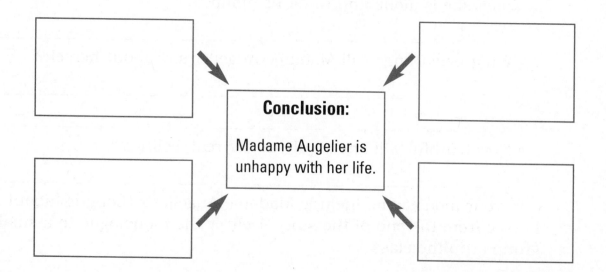

Conclusion:

Madame Augelier is unhappy with her life.

SUPPORT FOR WRITING AND EXTEND YOUR LEARNING

Writing: Analytical Essay

Fill in the chart below. Look for words or phrases that create pictures in your mind. As you look for these images, connect them to the theme—or main idea—of the story.

- Find images.
- Explain how the image connects to the theme. The first image and connection is filled in for you.
- Use the examples in this chart to support your statement of the theme in your essay.

Image	Connection to the Theme
bracelet of wrinkles	Madame Augelier is rich but unhappy because she thinks she is old.

Listening and Speaking: Monologue

Write a **monologue**, a speech given entirely by one person, based on the character of Madame Augelier in "The Bracelet." To prepare, answer the following questions:

- Will Madame Augelier speak to the audience or will she speak as if she is alone and thinking aloud?

_____

- What new things will Madame Augelier say about herself?

_____

- How truthful will she be about her real feelings?

_____

In your monologue, include Madame Augelier's thoughts about herself from the end of the story. Deliver the monologue to a small group or to the class.

War

LITERARY ANALYSIS

The **setting** of a story is the time and place in which it occurs. Some settings provide only a background for the action. Other settings have a direct effect on the characters and plot.

Characterization is the art of creating characters. There are two types of characterization:

- **Direct characterization:** The writer simply tells the reader what a character is like.

- **Indirect characterization:** The reader learns about a character through descriptions of the character's appearance, words, and actions, and what other characters say.

READING STRATEGY

When you **compare and contrast characters**, you look for similarities and differences between characters. In "War," for example, the author introduces characters who have similar problems but who react in very different ways.

Details about the "red-faced" man appear in the chart below. Compare and contrast this character with another character by filling out the chart as you read.

	Appearance	Words	Behavior and/or Emotions
Character 1	Red-faced, fat	"Do we give life to our children for our own benefit?"	Angry
Character 2			

War

Luigi Pirandello
Translated by Samuel Putnam

Summary In the story "War," a group of passengers travel on a train through Italy during wartime. Several of the passengers have sons who have been called upon to fight for their country. The story shows the parents' fears for their sons' safety. As the passengers argue over whose situation is worse, a fat, red-faced man expresses disgust. He states that his son died in the war and that they should be proud that their sons are fighting for something they believe in. His disgust, however, may be hiding his true feelings.

Note-taking Guide

Use the chart below to note details of the story.

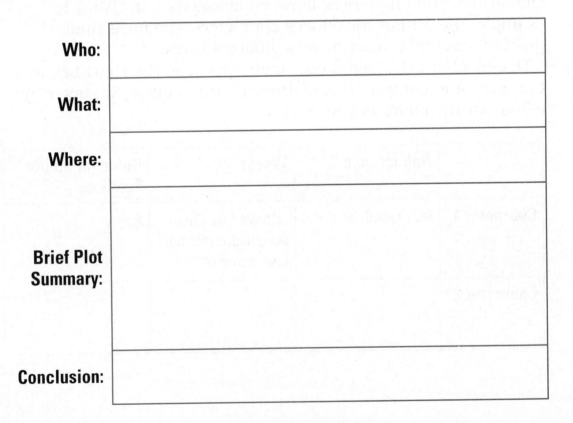

Who:	
What:	
Where:	
Brief Plot Summary:	
Conclusion:	

War

Luigi Pirandello
Translated by Samuel Putnam

The story begins on a local train between small towns in Italy. The passengers have been traveling throughout the night.

♦ ♦ ♦

At dawn, in a stuffy and smoky second-class carriage in which five people had already spent the night, a bulky woman in deep mourning,[1] was hoisted in—almost like a shapeless bundle. Behind her—puffing and moaning, followed her husband—a tiny man, thin and weakly, his face death-white, his eyes small and bright and looking shy and uneasy.

♦ ♦ ♦

The husband tells the other passengers that they should pity his poor wife. He explains that their only son is due to leave for war in three days. They are traveling to say goodbye to him.

The woman is unhappily twisting in her big coat. Sometimes she growls with sadness. She feels sure that no one else could understand her sadness. The other passengers look at her and one speaks to her.

♦ ♦ ♦

"You should thank God that your son is only leaving now for the front. Mine has been sent there the first day of the war. He has already come back twice wounded and been sent back again to the front."

"What about me? I have two sons and three nephews at the front," said another passenger.

1. **in deep mourning** wearing dark clothing as a symbol of sorrow or grieving

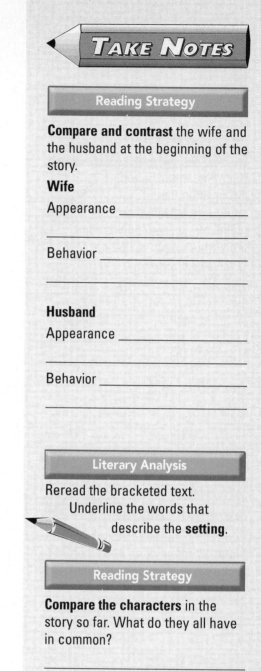

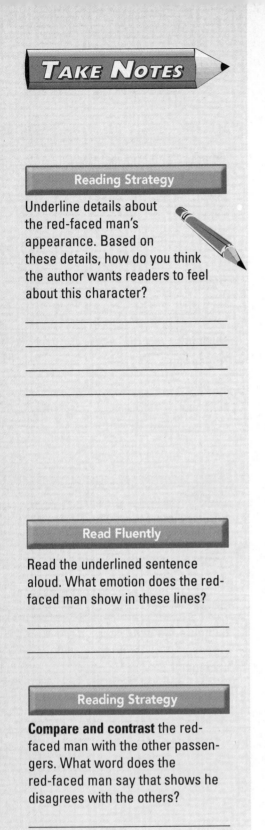

Underline details about the red-faced man's appearance. Based on these details, how do you think the author wants readers to feel about this character?

_____

_____

_____

_____

Read the underlined sentence aloud. What emotion does the red-faced man show in these lines?

_____

_____

Compare and contrast the red-faced man with the other passengers. What word does the red-faced man say that shows he disagrees with the others?

_____

_____

The passengers continue to compare their situations. They argue about whether it is harder to lose a son if you have only one, or if it is harder when you are the parent of more than one. One passenger argues that he gives his love to all his children equally, so that he suffers equally for his two sons. If one son dies, he must continue to live for the other. Therefore, he argues, it is worse to have two sons.

◆　◆　◆

"Nonsense," interrupted another traveler, a fat, red-faced man with bloodshot eyes of the palest grey.

◆　◆　◆

The traveler had bulging eyes, and he seemed to carry great anger inside him. He spoke forcefully again.

◆　◆　◆

"Nonsense. Do we give life to our children for our own benefit?"

◆　◆　◆

The red-faced man argues that their children have their own lives. He says that children have many interests at age 20. And he maintains that the others in this train car would also have gone to war at age twenty, even if their parents had said no. The other passengers seem to agree.

The red-faced traveler says that it is natural for their children at age twenty to love their country more than their parents.

◆　◆　◆

"If Country exists, if Country is a natural necessity like bread, of which each of us must eat in order not to die of hunger, somebody must go to defend it. And our sons go, when they are twenty, and they don't want tears, because if they die, they die inflamed and happy (I am speaking, of course, of decent boys). Now, if one dies young and happy, without having the ugly sides of life, the boredom of it, the pettiness, the bitterness of disillusion . . . what more can we ask for him? Everyone should stop crying: everyone should laugh, as I do . . .

◆　◆　◆

This is why, he explains, he does not wear mourning clothes.

The other passengers agree.

The wife, who has been trying to control her sorrow, is amazed. As she listens, she feels that the red-faced man's words have helped her more than the words of her friends or her husband. She understands that other people have faced their children's death bravely. She realizes that she must be able to accept her son's possible death. She is happy to hear the other passengers congratulate the red-faced man for speaking with such calmness about his son's death.

The woman suddenly turned to the red-faced man. She spoke as if she had not heard him talking. Then she asked him a question.

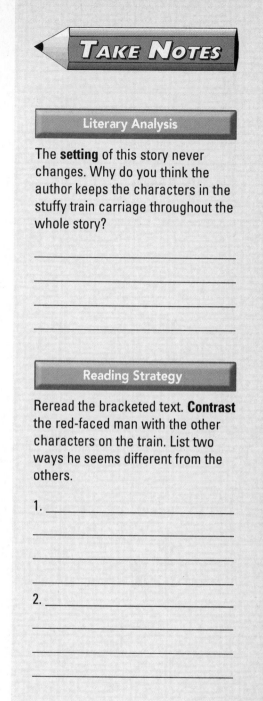

TAKE NOTES

Literary Analysis

The **setting** of this story never changes. Why do you think the author keeps the characters in the stuffy train carriage throughout the whole story?

_____

_____

_____

_____

Reading Strategy

Reread the bracketed text. **Contrast** the red-faced man with the other characters on the train. List two ways he seems different from the others.

1. _____

_____

_____

2. _____

_____

_____

_____

Circle the question that makes the red-faced man realize that his son is really dead.

"Then . . . is your son really dead?"

. . . He looked and looked at her, almost as if only then—at that silly, <u>incongruous</u> question—he had suddenly realized at last that his son was really dead . . . gone for ever . . . for ever. His face contracted, became horribly distorted, then he snatched in haste a handkerchief from his pocket and, to the amazement of everyone, broke into <u>harrowing</u>, heart-rending, uncontrollable sobs.

Vocabulary Development

incongruous (in KAHNG groo us) *adj.* not suitable or appropriate; not fitting a situation

harrowing (HAR oh ing) *adj.* disturbing; frightening

War

1. **Assess:** Can any one person on the train win the argument? Why or why not?

   _____

   _____

   _____

2. **Literary Analysis:** Use the chart below to analyze the **setting** of "War." Name two details about the time and two details about the place in which the story is set.

Time	Place
1.	1.
2.	2.

3. **Literary Analysis:** How does the setting affect the attitudes of the characters in the story?

   _____

   _____

4. **Literary Analysis:** List two examples of **direct characterization** and two examples of **indirect characterization** in the story.

   _____

   _____

5. **Reading Strategy:** Compare and contrast the characters by examining Pirandello's descriptions of the mother and the fat man. How do these descriptions suggest similarities and differences between the two characters?

   _____

   _____

   _____

SUPPORT FOR WRITING AND EXTEND YOUR LEARNING

Writing: Newspaper Article

Newspaper articles begin with a *lead*, a strong first paragraph that introduces the subject in an interesting way. Sometimes the first sentence of a lead asks a question. Other times, a lead might include an interesting quotation. Finally, a lead might start with a bold statement. On the lines below, write a sample first sentence for each type of lead. Use the strongest one to begin your newspaper article about the passengers on the train.

1. **Question:**

_____

_____

2. **Quotation:**

_____

_____

3. **Exclamation:**

_____

_____

Research and Technology: Multimedia Report

Media are ways that people communicate. A **multimedia report** uses several different ways to share information. To prepare a multimedia report about a World War I soldier's experience, visit the library. Look at books, diaries, films, and photographs. Decide what media would be best for presenting the information you gather from your research. On the chart below, write down the information you would share using each of the different media.

Media	Types of Information
Individual Handouts	
Large Visual Aids	
Oral Presentations	

The Guitar • Ithaka • Fear • The Prayer • Green

LITERARY ANALYSIS

Lyric poems show the views and feelings of a single speaker. Unlike narrative poems, lyric poems do not tell complete stories. Instead, they reveal a moment of insight—an **epiphany**, or sudden awareness. The poet Dante Gabriel Rossetti called one type of lyric poem a "moment's monument." Because of this stress on the moment, lyric poems leave out details that a narrative would supply. As you read each poem, look for moments of insight.

A **metaphor** is a comparison between two things that would ordinarily seem different. In the example below, García Lorca compares the sound of a guitar to a moaning cry, and he then characterizes the sky as a kind of building:

Now begins <u>the cry</u> / <u>Of the guitar,</u> /

Breaking <u>the vaults</u> / <u>Of dawn.</u>

Most metaphors are brief. But an **extended metaphor** flows throughout the poem. Several comparisons may be made along the way, creating a larger meaning. Some of the poems in this grouping contain extended metaphors. As you read, compare the use of metaphors and extended metaphors in the poems.

READING STRATEGY

Most poems are made up of stanzas. *Stanzas* are groupings of lines separated from other groupings by blank lines. Like a paragraph in a short story or essay, a stanza usually expresses one main idea. To help you understand a poem, **read stanzas as units of meaning** in the same way that you read paragraphs. Pause after each stanza to think about what the poet is saying. Use this chart to record statements expressing these ideas.

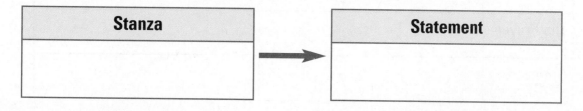

Stanza		Statement
	→	

The Guitar • Ithaka • Fear • The Prayer • Green

Federico García Lorca • Constantine Cavafy • Gabriela Mistral • Juan Ramón Jiménez

Translated by Elizabeth du Gué Trapier • Edmund Keeley and Philip Sherrard • Doris Dars • John A. Crowe • J. B. Trend

Summary In "The Guitar," Lorca uses the sound of a guitar to describe a person's feelings of longing and sadness. In "Ithaka," the speaker uses the story of Odysseus' journey to encourage the reader to live a life of adventure and discovery. "Fear" is a poem that describes a mother's fear of separation from her daughter. She imagines her daughter as a bird, a princess, and a queen. The mother also pictures how her daughter could be taken away in each situation. In "The Prayer," the speaker begs God to watch over her beloved, who is now dead. "Green" describes a woman who will always have a place in the speaker's heart.

Note-taking Guide

Use this chart to describe and compare the feelings created by the images in each of the five lyric poems.

Poem	Images	Feelings
The Guitar		
Ithaka		
Fear		
The Prayer		
Green		

The Guitar • Ithaka • Fear • The Prayer • Green

1. **Analyze:** Which **lyric poem** uses images to create a sad feeling? Explain.

   _____

   _____

2. **Literary Analysis:** Describe an **epiphany**, or sudden insight, from one of the five poems.

   _____

   _____

3. **Literary Analysis:** Use this chart to examine the meaning of a metaphor from each poem.

Poem	Metaphor	Two Things Compared	Meaning

4. **Reading Strategy:** Read stanzas as units of meaning by writing a one-sentence summary of the main idea for each of the first four stanzas of "The Prayer."

   _____

   _____

   _____

Writing: Interpretive Essay

Decide how the phrase "poems of love dedicated to death" applies to the two Mistral poems you read. Fill in a chart like the one shown to help you plan and organize your **interpretive essay**.

	Fear	**The Prayer**
Examples or images of love		
Examples or images of death		

Listening and Speaking: Oral Interpretation

Answer the following questions to help you prepare your **oral interpretation:**

- Which words or phrases from the poem most caught your attention?

_____

_____

- What feelings do these words or phrases communicate?

_____

_____

_____

- What body movements and changes in voice will you use to capture these feelings for your audience?

_____

_____

_____

The Artist

LITERARY ANALYSIS

Conflict is the struggle between opposing forces. Most plots have a central conflict that drives them. While there are many types of literary conflict, they can be divided into two large categories:

- *Internal conflict* takes place within the mind of a character. It involves a struggle with ideas, beliefs, attitudes, or emotions.
- *External conflict* takes place between a character and an outside force, such as another person, society, nature, fate, or God.

As you read, use the chart shown to examine the conflicts in the story and to label them as either internal or external.

Conflicts	
External 1.	Internal 1.
2.	2.

Characters are the people or animals who take part in the action of a literary work. Like a real person, **round characters** are complex, displaying both good and bad qualities. By comparison, **flat characters** are simple, usually showing only a single part of their personalities.

READING STRATEGY

A **cause** is an event, an action, or a feeling that produces a result. An **effect** is the result that is produced. Sometimes, words like *because, so,* and *therefore* indicate causes and effects. However, fiction writers often do not show connections between causes and effects in an obvious way. As you read this story, figure out the cause and effect connections between events and each character's feelings, thoughts, and actions.

The Artist

Rabindranath Tagore
Translated by Mary Lago, Tarun Gupta, and Amiya Chakravarty

Summary Satyabati's husband allows her to pursue her passion for art. After he dies, Satyabati's brother-in-law, Govinda, takes responsibility for the family. Govinda thinks that money is the most important thing in the world. He wants to raise Satyabati's son, Chunilal, to think the same way. However, Satyabati encourages Chunilal to develop his artistic talent. One day, Govinda catches Chunilal drawing a picture. He tears Chunilal's picture to pieces. Satyabati must decide if she should stay silent out of respect for Govinda or make a stand for her son.

Note-taking Guide

Use the plot diagram shown to fill in the major events of the story. Be sure to identify the main conflict and the climax, or high point, of the story.

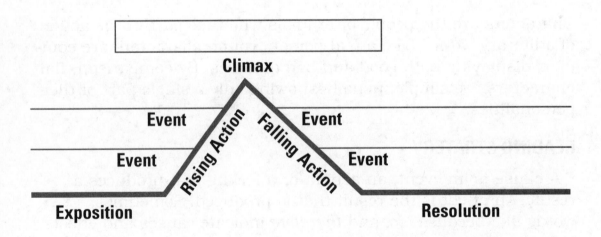

The Artist

1. **Compare and Contrast:** Compare and contrast Mukunda's attitude toward money and art with Govinda's attitude.

   _____

   _____

   _____

2. **Literary Analysis:** What internal **conflicts** does Satyabati experience as a result of her external conflict with Govinda?

   _____

   _____

3. **Reading Strategy:** Use the chart shown to **identify causes and effects** in this story, beginning with Mukunda's death.

Mukunda's Death		
Effect	**Effect**	**Effect**

4. **Reading Strategy:** What are some possible effects of Satyabati's decision to move away with Chunilal at the end of the story?

   _____

   _____

   _____

SUPPORT FOR WRITING AND EXTEND YOUR LEARNING

Writing: Newspaper Editorial

Write an **editorial** in the voice of Satyabati to argue that society should reject Govinda's worship of money in favor of other values. Begin by finding details that illustrate the importance of Satyabati's values and show the damage resulting from Govinda's love of money. Use the chart below to organize the information from the story.

Effects of Satyabati's Values	Effects of Govinda's Values

Listening and Speaking: Themed Reading

Find two or three poems by Tagore that share a similar theme. Then, present a **themed reading**. Use the chart to help you organize your reading and decide what parts of the poems to stress.

Title	Central Images	Important Phrases
1.		
2.		
3.		

The Handsomest Drowned Man in the World

LITERARY ANALYSIS

Magical realism is a literary style that emerged in Latin America. It mixes reality and fantasy to create a rich sense of life. For example, "The Handsomest Drowned Man in the World" begins with a frightening event that could really happen. A dead body washes up on a beach. Soon, the author begins to describe the body in a way that makes sense only in a myth or fairy tale.

Magical realist tales often use **archetypes**. Archetypes are symbols that call up deep responses in people of many cultures. For example, in "The Handsomest Drowned Man in the World," the archetype of the sea plays an important role. As you read, notice other archetypes that the author uses. Note the ways in which each adds to the magical feeling of the story.

READING STRATEGY

When you **hypothesize**, you make guesses based on what you know. You might also propose ideas based on clues in a text. New details in the text then prove your hypothesis true or false. As you read this story, use the chart below to hypothesize.

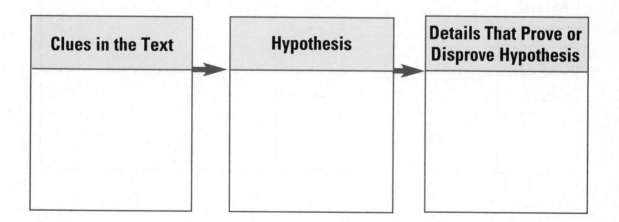

Clues in the Text	Hypothesis	Details That Prove or Disprove Hypothesis

The Handsomest Drowned Man in the World

Gabriel García Márquez
translated by Gregory Rabassa

Summary A drowned man washes ashore near a small village. He is the tallest, handsomest man that the townspeople have ever seen. The women think about the kind of man he probably was when he was alive. They think that he was shy and that his name was Esteban. Although Esteban is a stranger, the women pity him and begin to think of him as one of their own. The villagers hold a large funeral for him. Esteban's beauty and the story that the villagers invent about him inspire them to live more beautiful lives in honor of his memory.

Note-taking Guide

Both the women and the men of the village change their views about Esteban over time. Use the chart shown to record how their responses to Esteban change.

	Women's View of Esteban	Men's View of Esteban
At First		
Later		

The Handsomest Drowned Man in the World

1. **Interpret:** How do the men first react to the women's fuss over the body? Explain.

   _____

   _____

   _____

2. **Literary Analysis:** Which details in the story support the **archetype** of the sea as the source of life?

   _____

   _____

3. **Literary Analysis:** Use the chart below to write down details from the story that are true to life and those that are not.

	Realistic Details	Fantastic Details
Characters		
Setting		
Events		

4. **Reading Strategy:** State one **hypothesis** you formed as you began to read the story. Did the events prove or disprove your hypothesis? Explain.

   _____

   _____

SUPPORT FOR WRITING AND EXTEND YOUR LEARNING

Writing: Essay Tracing the Development of a Character

Write an essay in which you describe how the drowned man changes from a mysterious thing to a fully realized character. Prepare to write by completing the sequence chart below. Number each event listed in the chart to establish the proper sequence of events.

Event	Numerical Order
The drowned man gets a family.	
The drowned man is clothed.	
The women name the drowned man Esteban.	
The men recognize the beauty of the drowned man.	
The women recognize the beauty of the drowned man.	

Research and Technology: Collage

Using old magazines or the Internet, collect both large and small images that remind you of the emotions and details in "The Handsomest Drowned Man in the World." Then, create a **collage** that represents Esteban's story. Use the chart to help you match images to emotions and details from the story. Also, keep track of the sources for your images.

Image	Source	Emotion or Detail
1.		
2.		
3.		
4.		

"A Walk to the Jetty" *from* Annie John

LITERARY ANALYSIS

Most stories are told from either a first-person or third-person **point of view**.

- *First-person point of view*: the narrator is part of the story, uses the word *I*, and shares his or her own thoughts and feelings.

- *Third-person point of view*: the narrator is not part of the action and does not use *I*. Thoughts and feelings are shared through a character or characters in the story.

"A Walk to the Jetty" is told from the first-person point of view. The first-person point of view often uses **flashback**—the telling of an event from the past. Flashbacks may be dreams, memories, stories, or shifts in time. As you read, identify the details that spark Annie John's flashbacks.

READING STRATEGY

As Annie walks to the jetty, buildings and sights trigger her memories. In order to understand her experience, it is helpful to **understand spatial relationships**. Spatial relationships are the closeness of people, buildings, and other features to one another in a certain space. To get a clearer picture of Annie John's walk, use the chart below to note four landmarks she passes.

Landmark 1	Landmark 2
Miss Dulcie's house	
Landmark 3	**Landmark 4**

"A Walk to the Jetty"
from *Annie John*

Jamaica Kincaid

Summary "A Walk to the Jetty" is about a daughter's feelings of being apart from her mother. Annie John and her parents are walking to the jetty, or pier. The ship in which Annie will sail to England is docked there. While she walks, Annie passes familiar places. She remembers the events that happened at these places. As she prepares to board the boat, Annie is unsure whether she is happy or sad to leave her home and family.

Note-taking Guide

Choose any character from the story and use this character wheel to write down what you learn about him or her as you read.

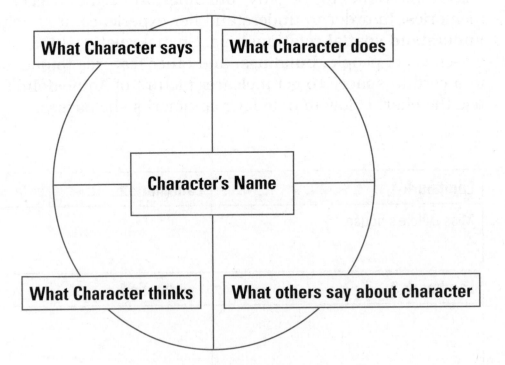

What Character says

What Character does

Character's Name

What Character thinks

What others say about character

"A Walk to the Jetty" from *Annie John*

1. **Analyze:** Why does Annie John remember her old fear of slipping between the boards of the jetty as she prepares to leave the island?

_____

_____

2. **Literary Analysis:** Why might using the first-person **point of view** make you feel more for the narrator than would another point of view?

_____

_____

3. **Literary Analysis:** Each flashback in this story is triggered as Annie John passes a familiar place. Use the chart below to analyze four of her flashbacks.

Place	Triggered Memory	What We Learn

4. **Reading Strategy:** Describe the ways in which the **spatial relationships** between Annie John and her parents change as they start their walk, travel on the launch, board the ship, and say goodbye.

_____

_____

_____

_____

SUPPORT FOR WRITING AND EXTEND YOUR LEARNING

Writing: A Reminiscence

Before beginning your story, think of interesting details you might include in your reminiscence. Start by writing down sounds, sights, smells, or other strong memories.

_____

_____

_____

Now rewrite some of these details, adding descriptive words to make the images more powerful for your reader.

_____

_____

_____

Use these descriptions to add life to your reminiscence.

Research and Technology: Map

Using details from the text, create a **map** showing Annie's walk to the jetty. Include landmarks, illustrations, and other references to help make your map a colorful representation of Kincaid's narrative. Prepare to make your map by completing this chart.

	Landmark 1	Landmark 2	Landmark 3	Landmark 4
Name of place				
Memory connected with place				
Emotions or feelings narrator has for place				

The Guest

LITERARY ANALYSIS

Existentialism is a way of looking at life that teaches the importance of making your own choices. The different forms of Existentialism share these traits:

- Our lives matter because of our own actions, not because we are part of a greater plan.

- The universe does not care about us one way or another.

- The individual has total freedom to choose and to act.

- Human life is valuable; freedom is an end in itself.

As you read, look for details that show Existentialist ideas. The **setting** of a story is the time and place of the action. In many stories, the setting is only part of the background. Sometimes, the setting adds meaning. In "The Guest," the landscape reflects the **theme**—the story's central message. As you read, think about how the setting and theme are intertwined.

READING STRATEGY

Cultural attitudes are the customs, values, and beliefs that are held by people living in a separate place and time. You can **infer cultural attitudes** by looking at the details of the dialogue, actions, and descriptions. Use this chart to find details and to **infer** the cultural attitudes they show.

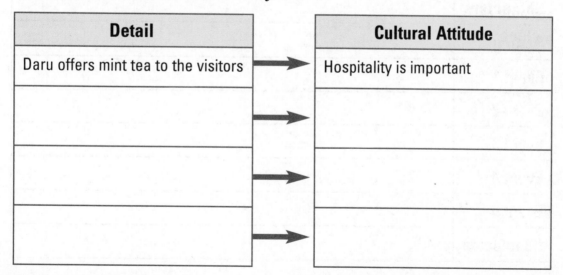

Detail		Cultural Attitude
Daru offers mint tea to the visitors	→	Hospitality is important
	→	
	→	
	→	

The Guest

Albert Camus
Translated by Justin O'Brien

Summary Daru is a French school-teacher. Balducci, the policeman, orders Daru to bring an Arab prisoner to the police station a day's walk away. The prisoner is accused of murdering his cousin. Daru does not want to bring the prisoner, but he has no choice. While they are walking toward the prison, Daru stops and gives the Arab some food and money and tells him to make a choice. The Arab can either follow the road that leads to the prison, or he can follow the road that would lead him to freedom. The Arab becomes confused by Daru's actions. Daru turns his back on the prisoner and begins the walk back to the schoolhouse. When he looks back, he sees that the Arab chooses to walk to the prison. Daru arrives back at the schoolhouse and sees something written on the blackboard. The message accuses him of handing over the Arab to the police and says that he will "pay" for what he has done.

Note-taking Guide

Use the chart below to list the details of the story.

Characters	
Setting	
Event 1	
Event 2	
Event 3	
Event 4	
Event 5	
Conclusion	

The Guest

1. **Analyze:** Balducci demands that Daru bring the prisoner to the police. Why do you think Daru refuses?

   _____

   _____

   _____

2. **Literary Analysis:** Daru shows the Arab two paths and leaves him to make his own choice. How does this action reflect **Existentialism**?

   _____

   _____

   _____

3. **Literary Analysis:** Use this chart to write down details about the climate, the landscape, and the cultural conflicts that connect the **setting** and **theme** in this story.

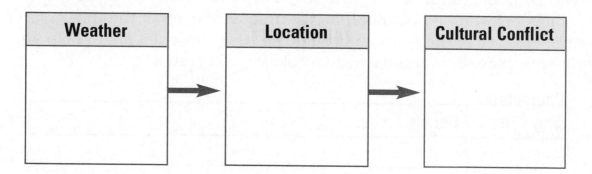

4. **Reading Strategy:** What cultural attitudes can you **infer** from the message the Arab's supporters leave on Daru's blackboard? Explain.

   _____

   _____

SUPPORT FOR WRITING AND EXTEND YOUR LEARNING

Writing: Essay Evaluating Fiction as an Expression of Philosophy

Write an essay in which you discuss the ways in which Daru's situation, thoughts, and actions in "The Guest" do or do not show an Existentialist point of view (refer to the bulleted list on the Build Skills page). Use the chart below to list details that describe Daru's circumstances, actions, thoughts, and statements. Then, explain how the detail does or does not reflect Existentialist views. An example has been provided.

Detail	Connections to Theme
Daru's Situation: Daru is isolated and alone.	Human beings are alone in an indifferent universe.
Daru's Thoughts:	
Daru's Actions:	

LISTENING AND SPEAKING: Dramatic Performance

With a small group, rewrite and perform "The Guest" as a **play**. Use the chart below to list details that are unique to each of the three characters, Daru, the Arab, and Balducci. Use those details to help you write your play. In addition, write a role for a narrator.

Character	Details
Daru	
The Arab	
Balducci	
The Narrator	

from Survival in Auschwitz • *from* Night • When in early summer...

LITERARY ANALYSIS

An **autobiography** is a nonfiction work in which a person tells his or her own life story. People write autobiographies for many reasons. For example, a famous person might write an autobiography because people want to know about his or her life. A person who has seen or been involved in an important historic event, however, might write an autobiography to provide insight into this event.

When you read an autobiography, think about details and the meaning those details convey. As you read, fill in the chart below to show how the authors use details in his autobiography to convey meaning about the Holocaust.

	Details	Meaning
Survival in Auschwitz		
Night		
When in early summer . . .		

READING STRATEGY

Many books, such as these autobiographies by Primo Levi and Elie Wiesel, are written about historical events. To understand these events fully, **connect to historical context**. To do this, link the work to important events and ideas in history.

As you read, pay careful attention to the background information at the beginning of the selection. Connect this information to events and images in the selection.

from Survival in Auschwitz

Primo Levi
Translated by Stuart Woolf

Summary In this excerpt from *Survival in Auschwitz*, Primo Levi describes his arrival at Auschwitz. Auschwitz was a Nazi concentration camp where millions of people were killed. Levi and the other Jewish prisoners are placed in a large empty room. They are all hungry and thirsty. There is a faucet in the room, but the water is undrinkable. The prisoners are mocked by the German officers. They are ordered to strip naked and left standing for hours. Levi realizes that the men are in a kind of hell. Eventually, everything is taken from them: their clothing, their families, their jobs, and even their names. In the end the only thing that makes each man unique is a number tattooed on his left arm.

Note-taking Guide

As you read, fill in the chart below to record the autobiographer (Who), the time period (When), the setting (Where), the event described (What), and why it happened (Why).

	Survival in Auschwitz
Who	
When	
Where	
What	
Why	

from Survival in Auschwitz: On the Bottom

Primo Levi
Translated by Stuart Woolf

The Holocaust was the systematic persecution and murder of millions of Jews and others deemed unfit by Germany's Nazi party. The Nazis came to power in Germany in 1933. During World War II (1939–1945), Nazi forces rounded up Jews throughout German-occupied lands and shot them or shipped them to concentration camps. There, the prisoners were worked or starved to death or killed, often by poison gas. In this excerpt, Primo Levi describes his arrival at the complex of the three camps at Auschwitz, in Poland.

After a short truck ride, the author and the other prisoners arrive at the camp. They see a sign in German above a door. The sign says "Work gives freedom." Then the group enters a large, poorly heated, empty room. They have had nothing to drink for several days. However, they cannot drink the foul water from a tap in the room.

©   ©   ©

<u>This is hell. Today, in our times, hell must be like this.</u> A huge, empty room: we are tired, standing on our feet, with a tap which drips while we cannot drink the water, and we wait for something which will certainly be terrible, and nothing happens and

---

Literary Analysis

Read the underlined text. Why do you think the author includes these words in his **autobiography**?

_____

_____

_____

Reading Check

What are the conditions of the room where the author and the other prisoners have been placed?

_____

_____

_____

To **connect a work to its historical context**, link details in the text to actual events that occurred during the time the work was written. You can learn more about actual events by reading footnotes.

1. Who is the German who enters the room and speaks to the prisoners?

_____

_____

2. How does knowing the historical context add to your understanding of the author's experience?

_____

_____

Read the bracketed text aloud. How would you describe the German officer's attitude toward the prisoners?

_____

_____

_____

nothing continues to happen. What can one think about? One cannot think anymore, it is like being already dead. Someone sits down on the ground. The time passes drop by drop.

We are not dead. The door is opened and an SS[1] man enters, smoking. He looks at us slowly and asks, "*Wer kann Deutsch?*"[2] One of us whom I have never seen, named Flesch, moves forward; he will be our interpreter. This SS man makes a long calm speech; the interpreter translates.

The men have to undress and take off their shoes. They do not know what will happen to their things, such as watches and important papers. Another German enters the room. He tells the prisoners to put their shoes in a corner. They obey him. There seems to be nothing else for them to do.

The outside door opens, a freezing wind enters and we are naked and cover ourselves up with our arms. The wind blows and slams the door; the German reopens it and stands watching with interest how we <u>writhe</u> to hide from the wind, one behind the other. Then he leaves and closes it.

Vocabulary Development

writhe (RYTH) *v.* to move the body with a twisting, turning motion

---

1. **SS** Schutzstaffel (SHOOTZ shtahf ul), a Nazi secret police organization.
2. **Wer kann Deutsch** (ver kan doych) German for "Who knows German?"

Now the second act begins. Four men with razors, soapbrushes and clippers burst in; they have trousers and jackets with stripes, with a number sewn on the front; perhaps they are the same sort as those others of this evening (this evening or yesterday evening?); but these are robust and flourishing. We ask many questions but they catch hold of us and in a moment we find ourselves shaved and sheared.

◆ ◆ ◆

Then the group is locked in a shower room. They do not know what is happening. The prisoners are forced to stay in the shower room without clothes.

One of the men is worried about the women prisoners. He has a wife and daughter. Primo Levi tells the man that he believes they will see the women again. However, he really believes that the prisoners will be killed.

The German officer returns, and he tells the prisoners to be quiet. The prisoners have many questions for the German officer. However, the translator in their group does not translate their questions into German. He knows that it is useless. The German leaves. Then someone else enters the room. He is a prisoner in the camp. The man speaks to the group in Italian.

◆ ◆ ◆

Reading Check

What happens to the men during the "second act" of their arrival at the camp?

_____

_____

_____

Stop to Reflect

In the bracketed passage, underline the details describing the four men with razors. What role do you think they play in the camp?

_____

_____

Reading Check

Read the bracketed passage. Then answer the questions below.

1. Where are the prisoners being held?

_____

_____

2. What type of place is it?

_____

_____

3. How many prisoners are there?

_____

_____

4. What do the prisoners do?

_____

_____

_____

Stop to Reflect

How do you think the prisoners feel as they wait for the shower?

_____

_____

_____

_____

Literary Analysis

In the underlined text of this **autobiography,** what insight or truth about life in the camp does Levi give readers?

_____

_____

_____

We are at Monowitz, near Auschwitz, in Upper Silesia, a region inhabited by both Poles and Germans. This camp is a work-camp, in German one says, *Arbeitslager,*[3] all the prisoners (there are about ten thousand) work in a factory which produces a type of rubber called Buna, so that the camp itself is called Buna.

We will be given shoes and clothes—no, not our own—other shoes, other clothes, like his. We are naked now because we are waiting for the shower and the disinfection . . .

©   ©   ©

The man says that he is a Hungarian doctor and the dentist for the camp. He explains that he is in the camp because he is a criminal. The prisoners ask him a lot of questions. He does not answer all of them. He tells the prisoners that they will see the women soon. The doctor makes the prisoners think that life in the camp isn't that bad. Then he leaves. Many of the men believe what he said but the author does not.

Then a bell rings. The camp awakens. The men are given a short, boiling hot shower. People throw some prison clothes at them. They must run naked into the icy snow with these rags in their hands. In the next hut they get dressed. At this point, the men realize how terrible their situation is.

©   ©   ©

It is not possible to sink lower than this; no human condition is more miserable than this, nor could it conceivably be so. Nothing belongs to us anymore; they have taken away our clothes, our shoes, even our hair; if we

_____

3. Arbeitslager (AHR byits LAHG er) *n.* "work camp."

speak, they will not listen to us, and if they listen, they will not understand. They will even take away our name: and if we want to keep it, we will have to find in ourselves the strength to do so, to manage somehow so that behind the name something of us, of us as we were, still remains.

◎   ◎   ◎

The author says that even the smallest habits and possessions become a part of human beings. He says that those who are deprived of their loved ones and their possessions will become hollow, suffering people who forget dignity. Being stripped of everything in his life has made the author better understand the term "extermination camp" and the phrase "to lie on the bottom."

◎   ◎   ◎

Häftling.[4] I have learnt that I am a Häftling. My number is 174517; we have been <u>baptized</u>, we will carry the <u>tattoo</u> on our left arm until we die.

◎   ◎   ◎

The author explains that, one by one, he and the other men were tattooed with a number. Prisoners had to show their numbers in order to get bread and soup. They had to learn what the number sounded like in German. For several days, the author looked for the time on his wristwatch, but instead he would find the tattoo of the blue identification number.

Vocabulary Development

baptized (BAP tyzhd) *v.* admitted into a Christian church by means of a religious ceremony

tattoo (ta TOO) *n.* a permanent colored pattern or design mark on the skin

---

4. *Häftling* (HEFT ling.) *n.* German for "prisoner."

Reading Strategy

Read the bracketed passage. Circle the text that explains what the author learns. With your understanding of the **historical context** of the Holocaust, what can you tell about the future of most of the prisoners?

_____

_____

_____

Stop to Reflect

Why do you think the Nazis assigned an identification number to each prisoner?

_____

_____

_____

Literary Analysis

Why do you think Levi writes about how the prisoners were tattooed in such detail in his **autobiography**?

_____

_____

_____

from Night

Elie Wiesel
Translated by Stella Rodway

When in early summer . . .

Nelly Sachs
Translated by Ruth and
Matthew Mead

Summaries The excerpt from Elie Wiesel's *Night* takes place at the end of World War II. As the Allied armies approached, the Germans forced their prisoners on "death marches." Elie Wiesel and his father were sent on such a journey. Wiesel's father arrived at their destination sick and weak. In the weeks that followed, Wiesel wanted to care for his father, but he also wanted to survive. He felt deep sadness seeing his father ill. However, he also felt anger and shame that his father seemed unwilling to fight for himself.

The speaker in **"When in early summer . . ."** begins by describing the beauty of summer and the promise of dreams. Then, the dreams are interrupted by dark memories. A voice accuses the world, the sun, and the moon of not remembering the Holocaust.

Note-taking Guide

In *Night*, Elie Wiesel reveals conflicting feelings he had toward his sick father. In the chart, record examples from the selection that show each feeling.

Feeling	Example from Selection
Caring and concern	
Anger and shame	

from Survival in Auschwitz • from Night • When in early summer...

1. **Analyze Cause and Effect:** Although he loves his father, Wiesel feels numb when his father finally dies. What has caused this change in Wiesel?

_____

_____

_____

2. **Literary Analysis:** Use the chart below to record details from Levi's **autobiography** that you found powerful. Tell why you think Levi included that detail. The first set of boxes is filled in for you.

Detail	Purpose
"...with a tap which drips while we cannot drink water, and we wait for something which will certainly be terrible..."	To show how helpless, fearful, and thirsty the prisoners are. All they can think about is water.

3. **Reading Strategy:** Reread the information on the Preview page for *Night*. Explain how **connecting to the historical context** helps you understand the ending of Wiesel's autiobiograpy.

_____

_____

_____

SUPPORT FOR WRITING AND EXTEND YOUR LEARNING

Writing: Persuasive Essay

Write a persuasive essay telling why teachers should use either Levi's or Wiesel's memoir's or Sach's poem to help teach students about the Holocaust. Explain your choice, giving reasons that will convince the teachers at your school.

- First, choose the selection you would like to include.

  _____

  _____

- Did you choose your selection because of its emotional power or its historical insights?

  _____

  _____

  _____

  _____

  _____

- List three reasons why your selection should be included in a unit about the Holocaust.

  _____

  _____

  _____

  _____

  _____

Listening and Speaking: Group Discussion

Use the chart below to compare and contrast Levi's and Wiesel's memoirs. Discuss your ideas with a small group.

	Levi	Wiesel
Most important event described		
Use of conversation in selection		
Images that describe the camp		
Images that describe himself		
Images that describe the other prisoners		

MAGAZINE ARTICLES

About Magazine Articles

A magazine article is an important source of information. Magazine articles provide news, information, and entertainment. Topics in specialty magazines reach readers with specific interests, such as tennis, skateboarding, or cooking. Readers can also find magazines that are written for their age group.

Reading Strategy

People have many reasons or purposes for reading. Readers may pick up a newspaper to learn about something that has happened, and they may read a short story for entertainment.

To **establish a purpose** for reading a magazine article:

- Scan the title and the first few paragraphs to identify the topic.
- Decide what you want to learn or understand as you read.

   Then, focus on that specific concept, idea, or goal.

- As you read, complete the chart below with details related to your reading purpose.

Title _____   Subject _____

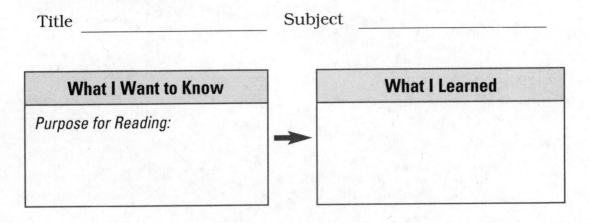

What I Want to Know	**What I Learned**
Purpose for Reading:	

Build Understanding

Knowing these words will help you to understand this article.

Exodus n. the flight of the Israelites from enslavement in Egypt

Passover n. the celebration of the Exodus from Egypt

THE HOLOCAUST HAGGADAH

Selections from the Rare Book, Manuscript, and Special Collections Library

Zygfryd and Helene Wolloch of New York commissioned a Passover Haggadah in 1981 in memory of their parents, who died in the Holocaust. What began as a personal tribute was soon recognized as an unparalleled contribution to Jewish art and history. The Rare Book, Manuscript, and Special Collections Library at Duke owns an original portfolio of the limited published edition of the Wollochs' Pessach Haggadah in Memory of the Holocaust.

The Haggadah (plural, Haggadot) is the Jewish book of ritual used at Passover Seders in the celebration of the Exodus from Egypt. Religious scholar Cecil Roth has referred to the Haggadah, comparing it to other books in the Jewish tradition, as one of the most amenable to adaptation and artistic

expression. The "Holocaust Haggadah," as the Wollochs' Haggadah is commonly called, illustrated by David Wander with calligraphy by Yonah Weinreb, makes the point beautifully.

Wander and Weinreb juxtapose the themes of the Exodus and the Holocaust by emphasizing the shared histories of slavery, destruction, and redemption. Wander's art is powerful in its simplicity and directness. He depicts crematoria, burning books, and the Star of David alongside the traditional Hebrew text of the Haggadah. He also includes brilliant borders, flowers, and the Israeli flag to symbolize the eventual freedom of the Jewish people. His drawings are devoid of human figures, signifying the absence of those who perished during the Holocaust.

Reading Magazine Articles

✏ Read the title. Underline the definition of *Haggadah* in the text. What does *Haggadah* mean?

_____

_____

Reading Strategy

List one **purpose** a person might have for reading this article.

_____

_____

Stop to Reflect

Why is a special version of the Haggadah an appropriate way to honor and memorialize those killed in the Holocaust?

_____

_____

Reading Check

✏ Underline the image Wander uses to symbolize the eventual freedom of the Jewish people. Why are human figures absent from Wander's drawings?

_____

_____

_____

Reading Strategy

Reread the section that discusses the details of the content and printing of the book itself. Who might be interested in this sort of specific information? Why?

_____

_____

Reading Check

Where would you go to see a copy of Duke's Holocaust Haggadah?

_____

_____

Underline the text that contains your answer.

Stop to Reflect

Why do you think the Holocaust Haggadah is an important addition to Duke's Haggadah Collection?

_____

_____

Reading Informational Materials

This article was written for Duke University graduates. How might this article be changed if it were written for a popular magazine?

_____

_____

Two of Wander's drawings are particularly striking and well-known. One, a concentration-camp uniform placed within a passage reading, "In each generation one is obligated to regard himself as though he personally left Egypt." In the second image, four books illustrate the portion of the Haggadah text in which four children question the leader of the Seder. For the wise child, Judaism is an open book to be studied; for the wicked child the book is on fire; for the simple child the book is open but blank; and for the fourth child, who does not yet know to ask about the Exodus, the book is closed.

The Wollochs exhibited their Holocaust Haggadah at the Milton J. Weill Art Gallery at the 92nd Street Y in New York, where it received such wide public attention that they agreed to its publication in a limited edition to benefit the International Society for Yad Vashem. Herbert Goldman's Art Gallery in Haifa, Israel, was the publisher, and David Wander himself prepared the plates and oversaw the printing of his artwork at the Burston Graphic Center in Jerusalem.

Each hand-printed portfolio consists of twelve full-page prints signed and numbered by the artist, thirty-one illuminated pages, and thirteen black-and-white pages. A total of 290 Haggadot were produced: 250 were numbered 1 to 250; and 31 were numbered I to XXXI. Duke's copy is number 70 of 250. Nine artists' proofs were reserved for the publisher, the artists, and their colleagues.

Duke's Holocaust Haggadah is one of many impressive Haggadot within the Special Collections Library's extensive Abram and Frances Pascher Kanof Collection of Jewish Art, Archeology, and Symbolism. According to Eric Meyers, Bernice and Morton Lerner Professor of religion, Duke's Haggadah Collection, containing originals and facsimiles representing more than 1,000 years of Jewish experience, is a rich resource for students and scholars of Jewish history. Meyers says that the Duke Center for Judaic Studies intends to publish an online catalog of the collection, as well as a booklet highlighting selected holdings.

Pessach Haggadah in Memory of the Holocaust
Original portfolio, 1981
Illustrated by David Wander
Calligraphy by Yonah Weinreb
Hand printed on Velin Cuvé Rives,250-gram paper

Thinking About the Magazine Article

1. What question might a person unfamiliar with Jewish history and tradition have after reading the title of the article?

   _____

2. What themes and images do the illustrators of the Holocaust Haggadah use to strengthen their work?

   _____

Reading Strategy: Setting a Purpose

3. What purpose for reading is most appropriate for the article?

   _____

4. Why might someone interested in history read this article?

   _____

   _____

Timed Writing: Evaluation (25 minutes)

Evaluate the author's statement that "What began as a personal tribute was soon recognized as an unequalled gift to Jewish art and history."

- In the box below, list at least three details from the article that support the author's statement.
- Draft a thesis statement in which you state whether you think the article supports the author's statement effectively.

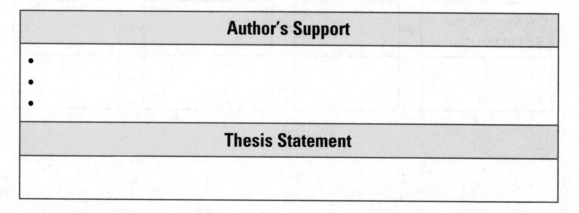

Author's Support
•
•
•
Thesis Statement

A Song on the End of the World • The End and the Beginning

LITERARY ANALYSIS

Irony occurs when writers create a difference between what they state and what they mean. It also occurs when there is a difference between what you expect and what actually happens.

- **Situational Irony** is a difference between what happens and what you think is going to happen.

- **Verbal Irony** is a difference between the words used to describe something and the reality.

Look for examples of both verbal irony and situational irony as you read these poems.

READING STRATEGY

A **writer's philosophy** is the writer's way of looking at the world. For example, in "A Song on the End of the World," Miłosz shows that ordinary life is precious.

You can find the writer's philosophy by looking for the details that point to a common meaning. Use this graphic organizer to chart the details, the meanings they suggest, and the philosophy of each poem.

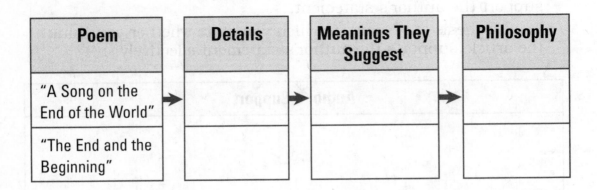

Poem	Details	Meanings They Suggest	Philosophy
"A Song on the End of the World"			
"The End and the Beginning"			

A Song on the End of the World

by Czesław Miłosz

The End and the Beginning

by Wisława Szymborska

Summaries In "A Song on the End of the World," the speaker describes the end of the world. It happens on an ordinary day. Animals and people are going about their regular business. They do not seem to know what is happening. Some people are disappointed. They expected the world to end in a more dramatic way. One man does understand that the world is ending, but he is too busy working in his garden to tell other people.

In "The End and the Beginning," the speaker describes what people do when a war ends. They pick up their lives and begin again. Their recovery is physical and mental. They clean up the destruction. Then, people start to forget about the war. They begin to live their ordinary lives.

Note-taking Guide

As you read, use this chart to identify the main idea of each poem.

Poem	Main Idea
"A Song on the End of the World"	
"The End and the Beginning"	

A Song on the End of the World • The End and the Beginning

1. **Infer:** In the last stanza of "A Song on the End of the World," the old man is binding his tomatoes. Why do you think he does this if he believes that the world is ending?

_____

_____

2. **Literary Analysis:** Use this chart to list one example of **verbal irony** and one example of **situational irony** from each poem.

Poem	Verbal Irony Example	Situational Irony Example
"A Song on the End of the World"		
"The End and the Beginning"		

3. **Reading Strategy:** What **statement of his philosophy** does Miłosz make about the value of an ordinary day? Explain.

_____

_____

4. **Reading Strategy:** What statement of her philosophy does Szymborska make about our ability to learn from the past? Explain.

_____

_____

SUPPORT FOR WRITING AND EXTEND YOUR LEARNING

Writing: Narrative About a Quiet Hero

The old man in Miłosz's poem is a kind of hero. He devotes himself to ordinary work in his garden even in the middle of danger. Choose someone you know, or make up a character, who shows this kind of devotion. Write an account of that person. In your account, show why he or she deserves your admiration.

Prewriting: Use this chart to brainstorm for precise verbs and adjectives that you can use to show the quiet heroism of your character.

Details of Your Account	Verbs or Adjectives That Could be Used

Use these verbs and adjectives as you draft your account.

Research and Technology: Set of Maps

In their poems, Miłosz and Szymborska respond to Poland's difficult history. Create two **maps.** Use the maps to show how Poland's boundaries shifted in the twentieth century.

• Start your research with the year 1920.

• Clearly indicate which nations ruled Poland.

• Show the birthplace or main city of residence of each poet.

Freedom to Breathe • *from* Nobel Lecture • Visit

LITERARY ANALYSIS

The **speaker** of a work is the character who "says" the words. There are different types of speakers. A speaker may be

- a fictional character who tells the story.

- a character who is similar to the writer.

- a writer speaking as himself or herself.

- a general voice, as in an essay.

For example, in "Visit," the speaker has a personal voice. The speaker also uses details from the poet's life. Therefore, the speaker is the poet speaking as himself.

READING STRATEGY

The **speaker's attitude** is what the speaker feels about ideas and events. The details of the work can help you to infer the speaker's attitude. Use this chart to list details that are clues to the speaker's attitude.

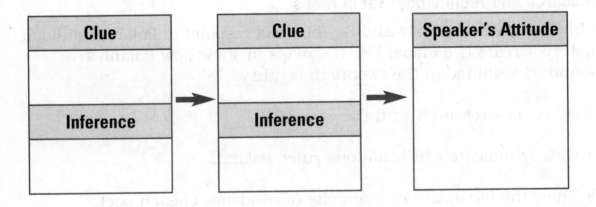

Clue		Clue		Speaker's Attitude
	→		→	
Inference		**Inference**		

Freedom to Breathe • Visit

Alexander Solzhenitsyn • Yevgeny Yevtushenko

Translated by Michael Glenny • Robin Milner-Gulland and Peter Levi, S.J.

Summaries In the essay "**Freedom to Breathe,**" the author uses the image of breathing to explain the importance of freedom. He could not breathe this freely when he was in a prison camp. He explains that a person needs to be free to survive. "**Visit**" describes the speaker's return to his hometown. He remembers how ordinary his life was. He understands how little he has done in his life, but he knows that he can do more in the future.

Note-taking Guide

The speakers in each of these two works experience a change. Use the chart below to list three details of how each speaker was before. Then, list details that show how each one has changed.

Title of Work	Details of Speaker Before	Details of Speaker's Change
"Freedom to Breathe"		
"Visit"		

from Nobel Lecture

Alexander Solzhenitsyn
Translated by F. D. Reeve

Summary In this excerpt, Solzhenitsyn shows how important literature and writers are to society. People can use literature to understand themselves and the world around them. Writers have the duty to show the truth in their writing.

Note-taking Guide

In Solzhenitsyn's Nobel speech, he describes his attitude toward world literature. In the chart below, identify five key words and phrases he used to describe world literature.

1. _____

2. _____

3. _____

4. _____

5. _____

Freedom to Breathe • *from* Nobel Lecture • Visit

1. **Evaluate:** Do you agree that the "freedom to breathe" is a basic necessity? Explain.

_____

_____

_____

2. **Literary Analysis:** Explain whether the **speaker** in each work uses a personal voice, a public voice, or a mixed voice.

_____

_____

_____

3. **Literary Analysis:** Compare the shift in the speaker's role in "Freedom to Breathe" and in "Visit." Analyze the details by using this chart.

Speaker's Role		Meaning of Events	
Beginning	**End**	**Beginning**	**End**

4. **Reading Strategy:** What is the **speaker's attitude** toward city life in "Freedom to Breathe"? Give details to support your answer.

_____

_____

_____

SUPPORT FOR WRITING AND EXTEND YOUR LEARNING

Writing: Persuasive Speech

Write an essay in which you support or oppose Solzhenitsyn's ideas about the power of words. Use the following guide to outline your essay.

Summary of Solzhenitsyn's idea of truth:

_____

_____

_____

Your statement agreeing or disagreeing:

_____

_____

Your reasons supporting your statement:

_____

_____

As you draft your speech, use precise words to add force.

Listening and Speaking: Oral Description

Present an **oral description** of a place you love. Brainstorm for words that appeal to the senses. List them in the chart below. Include the most effective words and phrases in your description.

Favorite Place: _____

Sense	Descriptive words
Sight	
Sound	
Taste	
Smell	
Touch	

Half a Day

LITERARY ANALYSIS

Surrealism

Surrealism is the use of realistic, or real-life, events, characters, and objects to create a dreamlike world in literature. By connecting realistic elements in strange new ways, events take place that are not what the reader expects.

As you read "Half a Day," use the chart below to identify realistic events and the ways in which they become surrealistic or dreamlike.

Realistic Detail	Dreamlike Effect
Tall new buildings line the street near school.	The boy has been in school for only half a day. New buildings have been constructed in that time.

READING STRATEGY

Determining the Author's Purpose

When you **determine the author's purpose**, you figure out the author's reason for writing. To do this, think about the author's choice of details as you read. For example, details that are amusing are meant to entertain the reader.

In the passage below from "Half a Day," the author's purpose is to convey the wonderful experience the narrator has in school.

"I never imagined school would have this rich variety."

As you read "Half a Day," consider the effect that the story is meant to have on the reader.

Half a Day

Naguib Mahfouz
Translated by
Denys Johnson-Davies

Summary A young Egyptian boy fearfully begins his first day of school. At school, he makes new friends, plays new games, and learns about the world. Gradually, he overcomes his fears and learns to enjoy the many opportunities school has to offer. At the end of the school day, the boy expects to find his father waiting for him. When he leaves school, however, the boy cannot recognize the busy, dirty city that surrounds him. The world he returns to after half a day is very different from the one he woke up to that morning.

Note-taking Guide

Use the chart below to record the main events in the story.

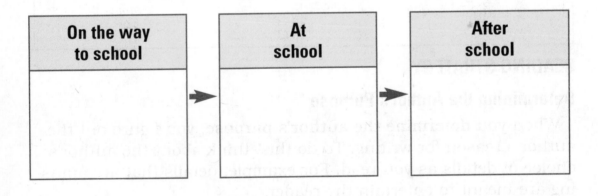

On the way to school	At school	After school

Half a Day

Naguib Mahfouz
Translated by Denys Johnson-Davies

A young boy walked to his first day of school with his father. The boy felt proud of his new clothes, but, he also felt scared of leaving his mother and father. At the school gate, his father promised to wait for him at the end of the school day.

The gate closed and some children began to cry. A woman and a group of men arranged the students into groups in the school courtyard.

◆ ◆ ◆

"This is your new home," said the woman. "Here too there are mothers and fathers. Here there is everything that is enjoyable and <u>beneficial</u> to knowledge and religion. Dry your tears and face life joyfully."

◆ ◆ ◆

Soon the narrator made friends with the other students. He believed that there was nothing to be afraid of in his school.

◆ ◆ ◆

I had never imagined school would have this rich variety. We played all sorts of different games: swings, the vaulting horse, ball games. In the music room we chanted our first songs. We also had our first introduction to language. We saw a globe of the Earth, which revolved and showed the various continents and countries. We started learning the numbers.

◆ ◆ ◆

Vocabulary Development

beneficial (ben uh FISH ul] *adj.* having a good effect; helpful

---

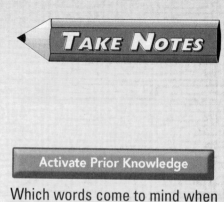

TAKE NOTES

Activate Prior Knowledge

Which words come to mind when you think about going to school for the first time?

_____

_____

Reading Strategy

In the first bracketed passage, the author tries to show that school can be a positive experience. Circle the details that support this **purpose**.

Read Fluently

Read aloud the second bracketed passage. What are three things that the narrator learns at school?

1. _____

2. _____

3. _____

Underline the words in the bracketed text that describe how the lady sometimes treats the students. How do you think the narrator feels about her? Explain.

_____

_____

_____

The underlined **surrealistic** details show the passing of time while the narrator is in school. What is surreal, or dreamlike, about the way time passes at the school?

_____

_____

_____

The students studied religion in school. They also ate well-prepared food and took a short nap during the day. However, they did more than play and enjoy themselves. There were difficulties at school too.

◆　◆　◆

Rivalries could bring about pain and hatred or give rise to fighting. And while the lady would sometimes smile, she would often <u>scowl</u> and scold. Even more frequently she would resort to physical punishment. In addition, <u>the time for changing one's mind was over and gone and there was no question of ever returning to paradise[1] of home. Nothing lay ahead of us but exertion, struggle, and perseverance.</u>

◆　◆　◆

In spite of these problems, the students tried to find happiness.

At the end of the school day a bell rang. The young boy said goodbye to his friends. Then he walked through the front gate of the school. He waited for his father, but his father never came. The boy decided to return home by himself.

On the way home, he met a middle-aged man whom he knew. They hadn't seen one another in a long time. The boy talked briefly with the man. Then they shook hands. The boy walked on by himself.

◆　◆　◆

Vocabulary Development

scowl (SKOWL) *n.* a look of anger
perseverance (per suh VEER ens) *n.* persistence

---

1. **paradise** (PAR uh dis) *n.* a place of great beauty and happiness.

I proceeded a few steps, then came to a startled halt.... Where was the street lined with gardens? Where had it disappeared to? When did all these vehicles invade it? And when did all these <u>hordes</u> of humanity come to rest upon its surface?

How did these hills of <u>refuse</u> come to cover its sides? And where were the fields that bordered it?

◆　◆　◆

The strange sights and sounds in the busy streets surprised the young boy. Magicians practiced their tricks. A circus band marched by him. He heard the loud siren of a fire engine. He felt very confused. He did not understand how all of this could suddenly appear after half a day. He hoped that his father would explain what had happened.

To reach his home, he had to cross a very busy street. However, the number of cars in the street made it difficult to cross right away. He began to get angry at the long wait.

◆　◆　◆

I stood there a long time, until the young lad employed at the ironing shop on the corner came up to me. He stretched out his arm and said gallantly, "Grandpa, let me take you across."

Vocabulary Development

hordes (HORDZ) *n.* large groups
refuse (REF yoos) *n.* anything thrown away, such as garbage

Stop to Reflect

Read the bracketed passage. What happened while the narrator was in school?

_____

_____

_____

Reading Check

What are three things the narrator notices about the world outside the school gates?

1. _____

2. _____

3. _____

Reading Check

In the second bracketed text, circle the description of the person who speaks to the narrator. By what name does this person call the narrator?

_____

_____

_____

Literary Analysis

What **surrealistic** event has taken place while the narrator was in school?

_____

_____

_____

Half a Day

1. **Hypothesize:** After school, the narrator meets a middle-aged man outside the gate. Who do think this person could be? Explain.

   _____

   _____

2. **Analyze:** A young man calls the narrator "Grandpa" at the end of the story. What has happened to the narrator? Give two details that support your answer.

   _____

   _____

   _____

3. **Literary Analysis: Surrealism** uses realistic objects and events but makes them seem like a dream. When do the events in this story start to seem like a dream? Explain.

   _____

   _____

   _____

4. **Reading Strategy:** Use the chart below to list three details that give clues about the **author's purpose**. Explain what each detail tells you about the author's purpose. The first row is done for you.

Detail	Author's Purpose
"There was no question of ever returning to the paradise of home. . . "	The author is letting the reader know that the boy will never find the home he left that morning.

SUPPORT FOR WRITING AND EXTEND YOUR LEARNING

Writing: Surrealistic Descriptive Essay

Mahfouz writes about ordinary life as if it were a dream. Write a **description** about an ordinary object or an event as it might appear in a dream. Choose a common object or event as your topic. Use the chart below to list ordinary and dreamlike details about it.

Object or event: _____	
Ordinary details	**Dreamlike details**

Use these details as your write your essay.

Listening and Speaking: Discussion Panel

In Mahfouz's story, the boy goes through change. Form a **discussion panel** with your classmates to talk about the effects of change. Prepare by amswering these questions:

- Do you think most young children like change? Explain.

  _____

  _____

- Do you think most adults like change? Explain.

  _____

  _____

- How do you feel about change in your life?

  _____

  _____

Pride • The Diameter of the Bomb • From the Book of Esther I Filtered the Sediment

LITERARY ANALYSIS

Imagery is used to create feelings and pictures in the reader's mind. An **image** is a word picture. Poets often use imagery to develop **figurative language**, or language that is not meant to be taken as a fact. **Figures of speech** include

- **metaphor**—one thing is spoken of as if it were something else

- **simile**—one thing is compared to another using *like* or *as*

- **personification**—a nonhuman subject is given human characteristics

Notice the poet's use of **figurative language** in the three poems.

READING STRATEGY

To **evaluate a writer's message,** find the work's main idea. Then, think about whether the main idea makes sense and whether there is enough detail to support it.

As you read, use this chart to evaluate the writers' messages.

Pride	The Diameter of the Bomb	From the Book of Esther I Filtered the Sediment
Message	Message	Message
↓	↓	↓
Support	Support	Support
↓	↓	↓
Evaluation	Evaluation	Evaluation

Pride

Dahlia Ravikovitch

translated by Chana Bloch and Ariel Bloch

The Diameter of the Bomb
•From the Book of Esther I Filtered the Sediment

Yehuda Amichai

translated by Chana Bloch and Stephen Mitchell

Summaries "Pride" uses the image of rocks to describe how something that seems strong can suddenly crumble. The rocks in this poem break at the touch of a little seal. In a similar way, a small event may reveal a deep wound in a person.

"**The Diameter of the Bomb**" states that a bomb's size must be measured by the amount of human suffering it causes.

In "**From the Book of Esther I Filtered the Sediment**," the speaker explains that he has taken out the parts of the Bible that he finds useless. The parts he removes deal with human feelings.

Note-taking Guide

In the chart, record the main idea of each poem. Then, write words from the poem that support the main idea.

	Main Idea	Support
Pride		
The Diameter of the Bomb		
From the Book of Esther I Filtered the Sediment		

Pride • The Diameter of the Bomb • From the Book of Esther I Filtered the Sediment

1. **Analyze:** How does the last line of "Pride" help you understand the poem's deeper meaning? _____

    _____

2. **Interpret:** What does the growth of the circle suggest about human suffering in "The Diameter of the Bomb"? _____

    _____

3. **Apply:** What advice would you give the speaker of "From the Book of Esther I Filtered the Sediment"? _____

    _____

4. **Literary Analysis:** In the chart, identify three **images** in "Pride." Explain to which of the five senses each image appeals.

Image	Sight, Sound, Smell, Touch, or Taste?
1.	
2.	
3.	

5. **Reading Strategy:** In which poem is the **writer's message** best supported? Explain.

    _____

    _____

SUPPORT FOR WRITING AND EXTEND YOUR LEARNING

Writing: Poem with a Strong Central Image

Write a poem with a strong central image that conveys a message about life. Follow the examples of Ravikovitch and Amichai. Make sure that your poem is focused, with each detail supporting your central image.

Use this chart to get started. In the center, identify your central image. Then, note the meaning of the image. Finally, list powerful adjectives you will use to describe the image.

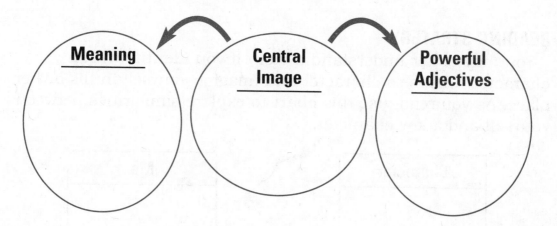

Meaning

Central Image

Powerful Adjectives

Listening and Speaking: Oral Interpretation

Answer these questions to prepare for an **oral interpretation** of "From the Book of Esther I Filtered the Sediment."

- What is the speaker's attitude toward life?

  _____

- How does the speaker feel about his attitude?

  _____

- What tone of voice will help you express the speaker's feelings?

  _____

Comrades • Marriage is a Private Affair

LITERARY ANALYSIS

In literature, **atmosphere** is the emotional quality of the world the author creates. It is also called **mood**. Atmosphere is created through descriptions. It often reflects the emotions of characters. For example, in "Marriage is a Private Affair," a cloudy sky is like the pain in an old man's heart. As you read these stories, try to identify the atmosphere in each one.

READING STRATEGY

You may better understand a story if you **identify with a character**. Choose a character and imagine yourself in his or her place. As you read, use this chart to explore similarities between yourself and a key character.

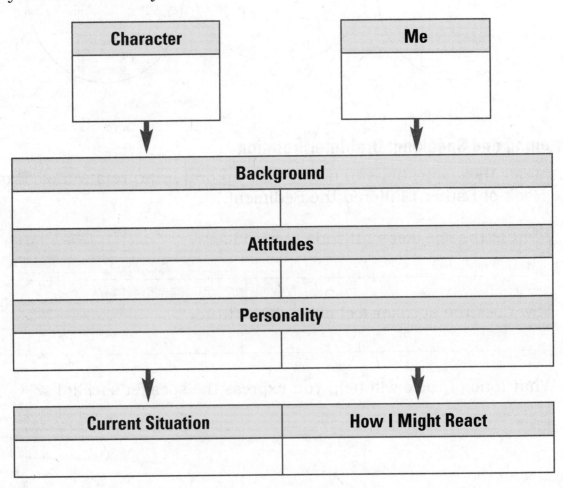

Comrades

Nadine Gordimer

Summary "Comrades" tells the story of Mrs. Telford. She is a white, middle-class woman who is actively engaged in the struggle against apartheid. Apartheid was the legal separation of the races in the country of South Africa. After a political rally, Mrs. Telford offers food to three young black men. While they are in her home, she is confronted with the reality of their lives. She realizes that she can not truly understand their lives as they suffer under the unjust apartheid system.

Note-taking Guide

Use this chart to take notes on the characters in the story.

Mrs. Hattie Telford	The Three Boys
What we know about her:	What we know about them:
What she does:	What they do:
How she feels:	What we learn about them:
What Hattie and the boys have in common:	

Marriage is a Private Affair

Chinua Achebe

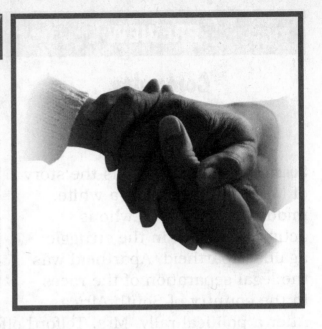

Summary "Marriage is a Private Affair" is about the conflict between traditional values and personal ones. Nnaemeka (n NEE muh kuh) decides to marry Nene (NAY NAY), even though she comes from a different tribe. Nnaemeka's decision angers his father, Okeke (oh KAY kay). Okeke wants him to follow tradition and marry a woman who has been chosen for him. Nnaemeka refuses. Okeke ignores his son for eight years. One day, a surprising letter arrives that makes Okeke begin to reconsider his views.

Note-taking Guide

Use the chart below to record the main ideas from the story.

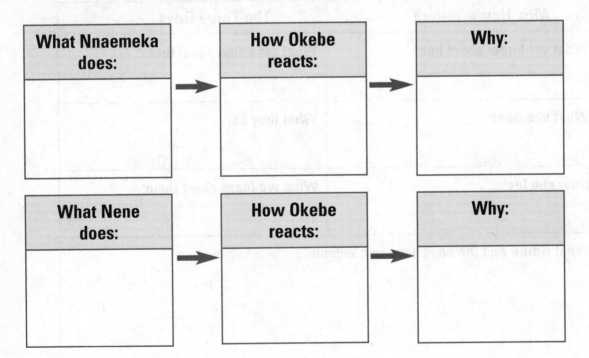

What Nnaemeka does:		How Okebe reacts:		Why:
	→		→	

What Nene does:		How Okebe reacts:		Why:
	→		→	

Comrades • Marriage is a Private Affair

1. **Evaluate:** Nnaemeka and Okeke have different beliefs about choosing a wife. Does the author prefer one set of beliefs over the other? Explain.

_____

_____

_____

2. **Literary Analysis: Atmosphere** is the emotional quality of the world the author creates. How would you describe the atmosphere in the first paragraph of "Comrades"?

_____

_____

3. **Literary Analysis:** Use this chart to write down descriptive details that contribute to the atmosphere in the first paragraph of "Comrades."

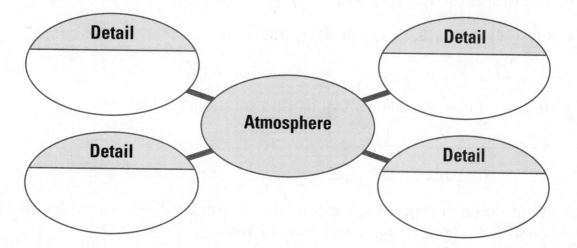

4. **Reading Strategy:** To **identify with a character,** try to experience events through his or her eyes. With which character in each story do you most strongly identify? Explain.

_____

_____

SUPPORT FOR WRITING AND EXTEND YOUR LEARNING

Writing: Manual on How to Change a Story's Atmosphere

Nadine Gordimer uses descriptive details to create an atmosphere in "Comrades." Using her story as an example, write a manual for young authors on how to create different types of atmospheres in a story. Fill in the chart below to help you write practice sheets for your manual.

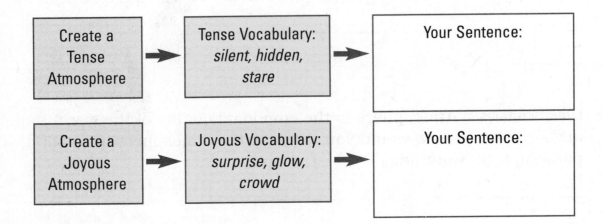

| Create a Tense Atmosphere | → | Tense Vocabulary: *silent, hidden, stare* | → | Your Sentence: |
| Create a Joyous Atmosphere | → | Joyous Vocabulary: *surprise, glow, crowd* | → | Your Sentence: |

Listening and Speaking: Dramatization

In a **dramatization**, people act out a scene or scenes from a story. Choose a scene from "Comrades" and prepare a dramatization. Prepare by answering these questions:

- What characters are involved in the scene?

_____

- How do these characters feel at that moment?

_____

- What could you do to show how the characters feel? Consider using scenery, body language, and tone of voice.

_____

_____

Use your notes to prepare your dramatization.

Thoughts of Hanoi • All • Also All • Assembly Line

LITERARY ANALYSIS

Political poetry connects the speaker's private feelings to what is going on in society. In the poem, the speaker responds to political events or talks about political situations.

As you read these poems, think about the way each poet discusses the effects of political events on people's lives. People react to the suffering caused by war and politics in different ways.

As you read, compare each speaker's feelings toward both the suffering and the hope for the future.

READING STRATEGY

Political poems will carry deeper meaning for you if you **connect to the historical context** that they reflect. Use this chart to list a detail from each poem and the historical background from which the detail arises.

Detail	Detail	Detail	Detail

How It Relates to Historical Context	How It Relates to Historical Context	How It Relates to Historical Context	How It Relates to Historical Context

Thoughts of Hanoi
Nguyen Thi Vinh
translated by Nguyen Ngoc Bich with
Burton Raffel and W.S. Merwin

All
Bei Dao
translated by Donald Finkel and
Xueliang Chen

Also All • Assembly Line
Shu Ting
translated by Donald Finkel and Jinsheng Yi • Carolyn Kizer

Summary In "Thoughts of Hanoi," the speaker, who is in South Vietnam, dreams about Hanoi. He is worried that he will meet his friend on the battlefield and that they will be forced to fight each other. "All" describes what it is like to live in a society where there is little freedom. The government controls many aspects of people's lives. This control makes people feel sad and hopeless. In "Also All," Shu Ting writes a hopeful, determined response to the sad and hopeless situation described in "All." In "Assembly Line," Ting uses the image of the assembly line to show the harm caused to people who are forced to live a tightly controlled life.

Note-taking Guide

The poets in each poem write about the effects of war on people's lives. In the chart below, list one image that shows the effect of war in each poem.

Title	Image and Effect
Thoughts of Hanoi	
All	
Also All	
Assembly Line	

1. **Interpret:** What details in the first three lines of "Thoughts of Hanoi" suggest a foreboding or ominous mood?

_____

_____

2. **Infer:** In "Also All," the line "No, not all is as you say." is repeated once. Why does the speaker repeat this line and to whom is she speaking?

_____

_____

3. **Analyze:** In "Assembly Line," the speaker notices several natural objects. How are the people and the natural objects alike?

_____

_____

4. **Literary Analysis: Political poetry** is poetry written in response to political events. Use this chart to identify personal and political details in each poem.

	Thoughts of Hanoi	All	Also All	Assembly Line
Personal Details				
Political Details				

5. **Reading Strategy:** Choose a single line from "All" or "Also All" that you think best **connects** you **to the historical context** of China's repressive rule. Explain your choice.

_____

_____

SUPPORT FOR WRITING AND EXTEND YOUR LEARNING

Writing: Literary Analysis

Write a literary analysis of one of the poems in this group. In your literary analysis, explore how elements of the poem work together to support its overall theme.

Prewriting: Choose a poem for your analysis and reread it carefully. Use the lines below to jot five details that seem especially powerful and important. Then, note how these details support the poem's theme.

Title: _____

Detail One _____

Detail Two _____

Detail Three _____

Detail Four _____

Detail Five _____

Support for Theme

_____

_____

Research and Technology: Multimedia Report

With a small group, prepare a **multimedia report** on the events that occurred at Tiananmen Square in 1989. Use books, magazines, and the Internet to gather information.

Do an Internet search and answer the following questions:

1. What does the word "Tiananmen" mean?

_____

2. Where is Tiananmen Square located in the city of Beijing? Print out a map for your multimedia report.

_____

3. Who were the groups that were in conflict?

_____

PART 2: TURBO VOCABULARY

The exercises and tools presented here are designed to help you increase your vocabulary. Review the instruction and complete the exercises to build your vocabulary knowledge. Throughout the year, you can apply these skills and strategies to improve your reading, writing, speaking, and listening vocabulary.

Prefixes V2

Word Roots V4

Suffixes V6

Learning About Etymologies V8

How to Use a Dictionary.................................... V12

Academic Words.. V14

Word Attack Skills: Phonics and Word Patterns V16

Denotation and Connotation V18

Vocabulary and the SAT® V20

Communication Guide: Diction and Etiquette V24

Words in Other Subjects V28

Build Vocabulary: Flash Cards........................... V29

Build Vocabulary: Fold-a-List............................ V33

Commonly Misspelled Words V37

PREFIXES

The following list contains common prefixes with meanings and examples. On the blank lines, write other words you know that begin with the same prefixes. Write the meanings of the new words.

Prefix	Meaning	Example and Meaning	Your Words	Meanings
Anglo-Saxon *fore-*	before	*forestall:* to prevent ahead of time		
Greek *eu-*	good; well	*eulogy:* to speak well of, especially upon death		
Greek *hypo-*	under; less than	*hypothermia:* below normal body temperature		
Greek *mono-*	alone; one	*monopoly:* possession or control by one person or company		
Greek *pro-*	before in place or time; forward	*prologue:* an introduction to a poem, play, or novel		
Latin *ab-*	away; from	*abhor:* to shudder from or to find disgusting		
Latin *ante-*	before	*antebellum:* before the war		
Latin *anti-*	opposed to	*antipathy:* strong dislike		

Prefix	Meaning	Example and Meaning	Your Words	Meanings
Latin con-	with; together	*conduit:* a channel or pipe that joins two things together		
Latin dis-	apart; not	*disgrace:* loss of respect and honor		
Latin en-	to put into or cover; to cause to be	*enrapture:* to put into a state of rapture or ecstasy		
Latin in-	not	*informal:* not formal; casual		
Latin mal-	bad	*malady:* a disease or sickness		
Latin re-	again; back	*restore:* to repair or bring back		
Latin sub-	under; down	*submerge:* to place under water		

The following list contains common word roots with meanings and examples. On the blank lines, write other words you know that have the same roots. Write the meanings of the new words.

Root	Meaning	Example and Meaning	Your Words	Meanings
Greek -path-	feeling; suffering	*apathy:* the feeling of not being interested or not caring		
Latin -cred-	to believe	*incredible:* unbelievable		
Latin -domin-	rule; master	*dominate:* to rule or control		
Latin -firm-	strengthen; strong	*confirm:* to establish or make firm		
Latin -ject-	to throw	*trajectory:* the path of something thrown through space		
Latin -jur-	to swear an oath	*jury:* a group of people sworn to hear evidence and make a decision based on that evidence		
Latin -lustr-	light; shine	*lackluster:* lacking brightness		
Latin -patr-	father	*patriotic:* loyal to one's homeland		

Root	Meaning	Example and Meaning	Your Words	Meanings
Latin -pel-	to push into motion or drive	*impelled:* pushed forward		
Latin -port-	carry; move	*deport:* to expel or move people from a country		
Latin -sacr-	sacred or holy	*sacrifice:* the act of giving up something of value		
Latin -temp-	time	*tempo:* refers to rate of speed		
Latin -tort-	twist	*distort:* to twist out of shape		
Latin -trem-	tremble	*tremor:* a trembling or shaking		
Latin -vert-	turn	*inverted:* turned upside down		
Latin -voc-	speak; say	*vocal:* spoken		

SUFFIXES

The following list contains common suffixes with meanings and examples. On the blank lines, write other words you know that have the same suffixes. Write the meanings of the new words.

Suffix	Meaning	Example and Meaning	Your Words	Meanings
Anglo-Saxon -fold	a specific number of times or ways	tenfold: ten times		
Anglo-Saxon -ful	full of	helpful: willing to help		
Anglo-Saxon -hood	state or quality of	neighborhood: the state of being neighbors		
Anglo-Saxon -less	without	useless: without use		
Anglo-Saxon -ness	the state of being	togetherness: the state of being together		
Anglo-Saxon -some	tending toward being	lonesome: tending to be lonely		
Greek -ate	forms verbs	rejuvenate: to make feel young again		
Greek -ic	forms adjectives	characteristic: distinctive; typical		

Suffix	Meaning	Example and Meaning	Your Words	Meanings
Greek -itis	disease; inflammation	*meningitis:* inflammation of the meninges		
Greek -logy	the science or study of	*psychology:* the study of the mind		
Latin -able/-ible	capable of being	*respectable:* capable of being respected		
Latin -ence	quality of; state of being	*munificence:* the state of being munificent, or generous		
Latin -ity	quality or state of	*authenticity:* state of being authentic, or real		
Latin -ment	turns a verb into a noun	*agreement:* state of agreeing		
Latin -ous	having; full of	*joyous:* full of joy		
Latin -tion	forms nouns that indicate the state of something	*definition:* a statement of what a thing is		

LEARNING ABOUT ETYMOLOGIES

Etymology is the history of a word. It shows where the word came from, or its **origin**. It also shows how it got its present meaning and spelling. Understanding word origins, or etymology, can help you understand and remember the meanings of words you add to your vocabulary.

A good dictionary will tell you the etymology of a word. The word's etymology usually appears in brackets, parentheses, or slashes near the beginning or the end of the dictionary entry. Part of the etymology is the language from which the word comes.

Abbreviations for Languages	
Abbreviation	**Language**
OE	Old English
ME	Middle English
F	French
Gr	Greek
L	Latin

You can find these abbreviations and more in a dictionary's key to abbreviations.

Words from other languages

The English that you speak today began in about the year 500. Tribes from Europe settled in Britain. These tribes, called the Angles, the Saxons, and the Jutes, spoke a Germanic language. Later, when the Vikings attacked Britain, their language added words from Danish and Norse. Then, when Christian missionaries came to Britain, they added words from Latin. The resulting language is called Old English, and it looks very different from modern English.

For example, to say "Listen!" in Old English, you would have said "Hwaet!"

The Normans conquered Britain in 1066. They spoke Old French, and the addition of this language changed Old English dramatically. The resulting language, called Middle English, looks much more like modern English, but the spellings of words are very different.

For example, the word *knight* in Middle English was spelled *knyght*, and the word *time* was spelled *tyme*.

During the Renaissance, interest in classical cultures added Greek and Latin words to English. At this time, English started to look more like the English you know. This language, called Modern English, is the language we still speak.

Modern English continues to add words from other languages. As immigrants have moved to the United States, they have added new words to the language.

For example, the word *boycott* comes from Ireland and the word *burrito* comes from Mexico.

Note-taking Using a dictionary, identify the language from which each of the following words came into English. Also identify the word's original and current meaning.

Word	Original language	Original meaning	Current meaning
comb			
costume			
guess			
mile			
panther			

Words that change meaning over time

English is a living language. It grows by giving new meanings to existing words and by incorporating words that have changed their meaning over time and through usage.

For example, the word *dear* used to mean "expensive."

Note-taking Using a dictionary, identify the original meaning and the current meaning of each of the following words.

	original meaning	current meaning
1. havoc	_____	_____
2. magazine	_____	_____

Words that have been invented, or *coined*, to serve new purposes.

New products or discoveries need new words.

For example, the words *paperback* and *quiz* are coined words.

Note-taking Identify one word that has been coined in each of the following categories.

Category	Coined word
sports	
technology	
transportation	
space travel	
medicine	

Words that are combinations of words or shortened versions of longer words

New words can be added to the language by combining words or by shortening words.

For example, the word *greenback* is a combination of the words *green* and *back*, and the word *flu* is a shortened version of the word *influenza*.

Note-taking Generate a word to fill in the blanks in each of the following sentences correctly. Your word should be a combination of two words or a shortened version of a longer word.

Jerome served one of our favorite dinners, spaghetti and _____.

Many years ago, people might take an omnibus to work, but today they would call that vehicle a _____.

We took the most direct route to Aunt Anna's house, which meant driving forty miles on the _____.

We thought we could get to shelter before the storm started, but we did not quite make it. A few _____ dampened our jackets.

HOW TO USE A DICTIONARY

A dictionary lists words in alphabetical order. Look at this sample dictionary entry. Notice the types of information about a word it gives.

Example of a Dictionary Entry

dictionary (dik´ shə ner´ ē) n., pl. –aries
[ML *dictionarium* < LL *dictio*) 1 a book of
alphabetically listed words in a language,
with definitions, etymologies, pronunciations,
and other information 2 a book of alphabetically
listed words in a language with their equivalents
in another language [a Spanish-English
dictionary]

Answer the questions based on the dictionary entry.

1. What is the correct spelling?_____

2. How do you form the plural? _____

3. What language does the word come from? _____

4. How many definitions are there? _____

5. What example is given? _____

Here are some abbreviations you will find in dictionary entries.

Pronunciation Symbols	Parts of Speech	Origins of Words
´ means emphasize this syllable as you say the word	adj. = adjective	Fr = French
¯ means pronounce vowel with a long sound, such as -*ay*- for a and -*ee*- for e	adv. = adverb	Ger = German
ə means a sound like -*uh*-	n. = noun	L = classical Latin
o͞o means the sound of *u* in *cute*	v. = verb	ME = Middle English OE = Old English

As you read, look up new words in a dictionary. Enter information about the words on this chart.

My Words

New Word	Pronunciation	Part of Speech	Origin	Meanings and Sample Sentence

ACADEMIC WORDS

Academic (A kuh DEM ik) words are words you use often in your schoolwork. Knowing what these words mean will help you think and write better.

On the next two pages, you will find a list of these words. You will also see how to pronounce each word and what it means. On the lines below each word, write sentences from your reading in which the word appears. Then, using your own words, explain what the sentence means.

apply (uh PLY) tell how you use information in a specific situation

_____

_____

_____

clarify (KLA ri FY) make something more understandable

_____

_____

_____

conclude (KUHN klood) use reasoning to reach a decision or opinion

_____

_____

_____

define (dee FYN) tell the qualities that make something what it is

_____

_____

_____

demonstrate (DEM uhn STRAYT) use examples to prove a point

_____

_____

evaluate (ee VAL yoo AYT) determine the value or importance of something

_____

_____

_____

identify (y DEN ti FY) name or show you recognize something

_____

_____

_____

label (LAY bel) attach the correct name to something

_____

_____

_____

predict (pree DIKT) tell what will happen based on details you know

_____

_____

_____

recall (ri KAWL) tell details that you remember

_____

_____

_____

When you are reading, you will find many unfamiliar words. Here are some tools that you can use to help you read unfamiliar words.

PHONICS

Phonics is the science or study of sound. When you learn to read, you learn to associate certain sounds with certain letters or letter combinations. You know most of the sounds that letters can represent in English. When letters are combined, however, it is not always so easy to know what sound is represented. In English, there are some rules and patterns that will help you determine how to pronounce a word. This chart shows you some of the common **vowel digraphs**, which are combinations like *ea* and *oa*. Two vowels together are called vowel digraphs. Usually, vowel digraphs represent the long sound of the first vowel.

Vowel Digraphs	Examples of Usual Sounds	Exceptions
ee and *ea*	steep, each, treat, sea	head, sweat, dread
ai and *ay*	plain, paid, may, betray	aisle
oa, ow, and *oe*	soak, slow, doe	
ie, igh, and *y*	lie, night, delight, my	myth

As you read, sometimes the only way to know how to pronounce a word with an *ea* spelling is to see if the word makes sense in the sentence. Look at this example:

The water pipes were made of *lead*.

First, try out the long sound "ee." Ask yourself if it sounds right. It does not. Then try the short sound "e." You will find that the short sound is correct in that sentence.

Now try this example.

Where you *lead*, I will follow.

WORD PATTERNS

Recognizing different vowel-consonant patterns will help you read longer words. In the following section, the **V** stands for "vowel" and the **C** stands for "consonant."

Single-syllable Words

CV–go: In two letter words with a consonant followed by a vowel, the vowel is usually long. For example, the word *go* is pronounced with a long "o" sound.

In a single syllable word, a vowel followed only by a single consonant is usually short.

CVC-got: If you add a consonant to the word *go*, such as the *t* in *got*, the vowel sound is a short *o*. Say the words *go* and *got* aloud and notice the difference in pronunciation.

Multi-syllable Words

In words of more than one syllable, notice the letters that follow a vowel.

VCC–robber: A single vowel followed by two consonants is usually short.

VCV–begin: A single vowel followed by a single consonant is usually long.

VCe–beside: An extension of the VCV pattern is vowel-consonant-silent *e*. In these words, the vowel is long and the *e* is not pronounced.

When you see a word with the VCV pattern, try the long vowel sound first. If the word does not make sense, try the short sound. Pronounce the words *model, camel,* and *closet.* First, try the long vowel sound. That does not sound correct, so try the short vowel sound. The short vowel sound is correct in those words.

Remember that patterns help you get started on figuring out a word. You will sometimes need to try a different sound or find the word in a dictionary.

As you read and find unfamiliar words, look the pronunciations up in a dictionary. Write the words in this chart in the correct column, to help you notice patterns and remember pronunciations.

Syllables	Example	New Words	Vowel Sound
CV	go		long
CVC	got		short
VCC	robber		short
VCV	begin open		long long
VCe	beside		long

DENOTATION AND CONNOTATION

The words you read and use have different types of meaning.
- The **denotation** [DEE noh TAY shuhn] of a word is its dictionary meaning or its exact meaning.
- The **connotation** [KAHN oh TAY shuhn] of a word is the ideas or feeling usually associated with the word. A word with *positive* connotations produces good feelings and reactions in readers and listeners. A word with *negative* connotations produces bad or unpleasant feelings and reactions. Some words are *neutral* because they do not tap our emotions at all.

The following words have a similar denotation. They all name places where people live.

house, apartment, shack, castle, home

However each word has different connotations, listed below.

house: a place where one family lives. Some connotations may be open spaces, a yard, and family. (neutral connotations)

apartment: a place where a family lives among many other families. Some connotations may be city life, crowded, and neighborhood. (neutral connotation)

shack: run-down, small (negative connotation)

castle: large, royalty, elegant (positive connotation)

home: warmth, family, security (positive connotation)

A. The words *slim, skinny* and *thin* have a similar denotation: "having little fat on your body; not fat." Write a sentence for each word that makes its connotation clear.

slim: attractively thin (positive connotation) _____

_____

skinny: very thin, especially in a way that is unattractive (negative connotation) _____

_____

thin: having little fat on your body (neutral connotation) _____

_____

B. For each word pair, explain the different connotations of each word.

1. unaware/ignorant _____

2. crowded/swarmed _____

3. uninvited/unexpected _____

4. cheap/inexpensive _____

5. dictator/ruler _____

C. Use this chart to take note of word groups and the connotations they suggest. Complete the examples by supplying words with a similar denotation to fill in the blanks. Over time, keep notes on words you read or hear that have strong negative or positive connotations. Complete each section for each word so that you have a list of words to choose from when you are looking for a particular connotation, or when you want a netural word that avoids emotional associations.

Neutral	Positive	Negative
ask	appeal request	demand beg insist
tell	advise	snitch
group	team	clique crowd
attempt		
laugh	guffaw chuckle	snort

D. The words in the following chart also all have a similar denotation. Fill in the missing connotation for each word. Then, use each word in a sentence that makes the connotation of the word clear.

Word	Connotation
walk	
trudge	
saunter	
Shared Denotation: to move on foot	

Write sentences using each of the words in the chart.

_____

_____

_____

FAQS ABOUT THE SAT®

What is the SAT®?

- The SAT® is a national test intended to predict how well you will do with college-level material.

What does the SAT® test?

- The SAT® tests vocabulary, math, and reasoning skills in three sections:
  - Critical Reading: two 25-minute sections and one 20-minute section
  - Math: two 25-minute sections and one 20-minute section
  - Writing: one 35-minute multiple-choice section and one 25-minute essay

Why should you take the SAT®?

- Many colleges and universities require you to submit your SAT® scores when you apply. They use your scores, along with other information about your ability and your achievements, to evaluate you for admission.

How can studying vocabulary help improve your SAT® scores?

- The Critical Reading section of the SAT® asks two types of questions that evaluate your vocabulary.
  - Sentence Completions ask you to fill in one or more blanks in a sentence with the correct word or words. To fill in the blanks correctly, you need to know the meaning of the words offered as answers.
  - Vocabulary in Context questions in Passage-based Reading ask you to determine what a word means based on its context in a reading passage.
- With a strong vocabulary and good strategies for using context clues, you will improve the likelihood that you will score well on the SAT®.

Using Context Clues on the SAT®

When you do not know the meaning of a word, nearby words or phrases can help you. These words or phrases are called *context clues*.

Guidelines for Using Context Clues

1. Read the sentence or paragraph, concentrating on the unfamiliar word.
2. Look for clues in the surrounding words.
3. Guess the possible meaning of the unfamiliar word.
4. Substitute your guess for the word.
5. When you are reviewing for a test, you can check the word's meaning in a dictionary.

Types of Context Clues

Here are the most common types of context clues:

• formal definitions that give the meaning of the unfamiliar word

• familiar words that you may know that give hints to the unfamiliar word's meaning

• comparisons or contrasts that present ideas or concepts either clearly similar or clearly opposite to the unfamiliar word

• synonyms, or words with the same meaning as the unfamiliar word

• antonyms, or words with a meaning opposite to that of the unfamiliar word

• key words used to clarify a word's meaning

Note-taking List several new words that you have learned recently by figuring out their meanings in context. Then, explain how you used context to decide what the word meant.

New Word	How You Used Context to Understand the Word

Sample SAT® Questions

Here are examples of the kinds of questions you will find on the SAT®. Read the samples carefully. Then, do the Practice exercises that follow.

Sample Sentence Completion Question:

Directions: The sentence that follows has one blank indicating that something has been omitted. Beneath the sentence are five words or sets of words labeled **A** through **E**. Choose the word or set of words that, when inserted in the sentence, best fits the meaning of the sentence as a whole.

1. Though he is _____, his nephew still invites him to Thanksgiving dinner every year.

A cheerful

B entertaining

C misanthropic

D agile

E healthy

The correct answer is *C*. The uncle is *misanthropic*. You can use the context clues "though" and "invites him" to infer that the uncle has some negative quality. Next, you can apply your knowledge of the prefix *mis-* to determine that *misanthropic*, like *mistake* and *misfortune*, is a word indicating something negative. Eliminate the other answer choices, which indicate positive or neutral qualities in this context.

Sample Vocabulary in Context Question:

Directions: Read the following sentence. Then, read the question that follows it. Decide which is the best answer to the question.

Martin Luther King, Jr., whose methods motivated many to demand equal rights in a peaceful manner, was an <u>inspiration</u> to all.

1. In this sentence, the word *inspiration* means—

   A politician

   B motivation to a high level of activity

   C the process of inhaling

   D figurehead

The correct answer is *B*. Both *B* and *C* are correct definitions of the word *inspiration*, but the only meaning that applies in the context of the sentence is "motivation to a high level of activity."

Practice for SAT® Questions

Practice Read the following passage. Then, read each question that follows the passage. Decide which is the best answer to each question.

Many people are becoming Internet <u>savvy</u>, exhibiting their skills at mastering the Web. The Internet is also becoming a more <u>reliable</u> source of factual information. A <u>Web-surfer</u> can find information provided by <u>reputable</u> sources, such as government organizations and universities.

1. In this passage, the word *savvy* means—

   A incompetent

   B competent

   C users

   D nonusers

2. The word *reliable* in this passage means—

   A existing

   B available

   C dependable

   D relevant

3. In this passage, the term *Web-surfer* means—

A someone who uses the Internet

B a person who uses a surfboard

C a person who know a great deal about technology

D a student

4. The word *reputable* in this passage means—

A an approved Internet provider

B well-known and of good reputation

C purely academic

D costly

Practice Each sentence that follows has one or two blanks indicating that something has been omitted. Beneath the sentence are five words or sets of words labeled A through E. Choose the word or set of words that, when inserted in the sentence, best fits the meaning of the sentence as a whole.

1. "I wish I had a longer _____ between performances," complained the pianist. "My fingers need a rest."

A post-mortem   C prelude   E solo

B circumlocution   D interval

2. Instead of revolving around the sun in a circle, this asteroid has a(n) _____ orbit.

A rapid   C interplanetary   E regular

B eccentric   D circular

3. He was the first historian to translate the _____ on the stone.

A impulsion   C excavation   E inscription

B aversion   D circumspection

4. To correct your spelling error, simply _____ the i and the e.

A translate   C transcend   E integrate

B transpose   D interpolate

5. Spilling soda all over myself just when the movie got to the good part was a(n) _____ event.

A fortunate   C tenacious   E constructive

B premature   D infelicitous

COMMUNICATION GUIDE: DICTION AND ETIQUETTE

Diction

Diction is a writer's or a speaker's word choice. The vocabulary, the vividness of the language, and the appropriateness of the words all contribute to diction, which is part of a writing or speaking **style**.

- Hey, buddy! What's up?
- Hi, how're you doing?
- Hello, how are you?
- Good morning. How are you?

These four phrases all function as greetings. You would use each one, however, in very different situations. This word choice is called *diction*, and for different situations, you use different *levels of diction*.

Note-taking Here are some examples of levels of diction. Fill in the blanks with the opposite level of diction.

Level of Diction	Formal	Informal
Example	Good afternoon. Welcome to the meeting.	
Level of Diction	Ornate	Plain
Example		I need more coffee.
Level of Diction	Abstract	Concrete
Example		The mayor has asked for volunteers to pick up litter along the river next Saturday.
Level of Diction	Technical	Ordinary
Example	My brother is employed as a computer system design manager.	
Level of Diction	Sophisticated	Down-to-Earth
Example	Thank you very much. I appreciate your help.	
Level of Diction	Old-fashioned	Modern/Slangy
Example	Yes, it is I. Shall we sample the bill of fare?	

With close friends and family, most of your conversations will probably be informal, down-to-earth, even slangy. In school or in elegant surroundings, or among people you do not know well or people who are much older than you, you will probably choose language that is more formal. Sometimes the distinctions can be subtle, so try to take your cues from others and adjust your diction accordingly.

Note-taking Complete the following activities.

1. Make a list of words and phrases that would be appropriate for you to use as you escort a visiting school board member on a tour of your school.

_____

_____

_____

_____

2. Make a second list of words and phrases that you might use as you escort your teenage cousin on a tour of your school.

_____

_____

_____

_____

3. Study the following pairs of phrases. Then, identify one phrase in each pair as formal and the other as informal.

	Phrase	Formal / Informal	Phrase	Formal / Informal
1.	Hello, it's nice to meet you.		How do you do?	
2.	What is your opinion, Professor Hughes?		What do you think, Pat?	
3.	Please accept my deepest sympathy.		That's too bad.	
4.	Sorry. I didn't hear you.		I beg your pardon. Please repeat the question	
5.	I don't get it.		I do not quite understand.	

4. List several common phrases. Then, identify whether each phrase is formal or informal, and give its formal or informal opposite.

	Phrase	Formal / Informal	Phrase	Formal / Informal
1.				
2.				
3.				
4.				
5.				

Etiquette: Using the Vocabulary of Politeness

No matter how many words you know, the way you use those words will impact how your friends, your family, your teachers, and all the people in your life react to you. For almost every interaction you have, choosing a vocabulary of politeness will help you avoid conflicts and communicate your ideas, thoughts, and feelings effectively to others.

When in doubt, always choose the polite word or phrase.

Formal or Informal?

Polite vocabulary does not have to be formal. In fact, the definition of the word *polite* is "behaving or speaking in a way that is correct for the social situation." People often think that *etiquette*, which consists of rules for polite behavior, applies only in formal situations. All interactions with other people, though, should follow the etiquette that is appropriate for the situation.

Etiquette for Classroom Discussions

Use the following sentences starters to help you express yourself clearly and politely in classroom discussions.

To Express an Opinion

- I think that _____.
- I believe that _____.
- It seems to me that _____.
- In my opinion, _____.

To Agree

- I agree with _____ that _____.
- I see what you mean.
- That's an interesting idea.
- My idea is similar to _____'s idea.
- I hadn't thought of that.

To Disagree

- I don't completely agree with _____ because _____.
- My opinion is different from yours.
- My idea is slightly different from yours.
- I see it a different way.

To Report the Ideas of a Group

- We agreed that _____.
- We concluded that _____.
- We had a similar idea.
- We had a different approach.

To Predict or Infer

- I predict that _____.
- Based on _____, I infer that _____.
- I hypothesize that _____.

To Paraphrase

- So you are saying that _____.
- In other words, you think _____.
- What I hear you saying is _____.

To Offer a Suggestion

- Maybe we could _____.
- What if we _____.
- Here's something we might try.

To Ask for Clarification

- Could you explain that another way?
- I have a question about that.
- Can you give me another example of that?

To Ask for a Response

- What do you think?
- Do you agree?
- What answer did you get?

Practice With a partner, discuss an issue about which you disagree. At the end of five minutes, list five or more polite words or phrases that you used to communicate your conflicting opinions.

_____

_____

WORDS IN OTHER SUBJECTS

Use this page to write down academic words you come across in other subjects, such as social studies or science. When you are reading your textbooks, you may find words that you need to learn. Following the example, write down the word, the part of speech, and an explanation of the word. You may want to write an example sentence to help you remember the word.

dissolve *verb* to make something solid become part of a liquid by putting it in a liquid and mixing it

The sugar *dissolved* in the hot tea.

_____

_____

_____

_____

_____

_____

_____

_____

_____

_____

_____

_____

_____

_____

_____

_____

_____

_____

_____

_____

_____

_____

_____

_____

_____

VOCABULARY FLASH CARDS

Use these flash cards to study words you want to remember. The words on this page come from Unit 1. Cut along the dotted lines on pages V31 through V32 to create your own flash cards or use index cards. Write the word on the front of the card. On the back, write the word's part of speech and definition. Then, write a sentence that shows the meaning of the word.

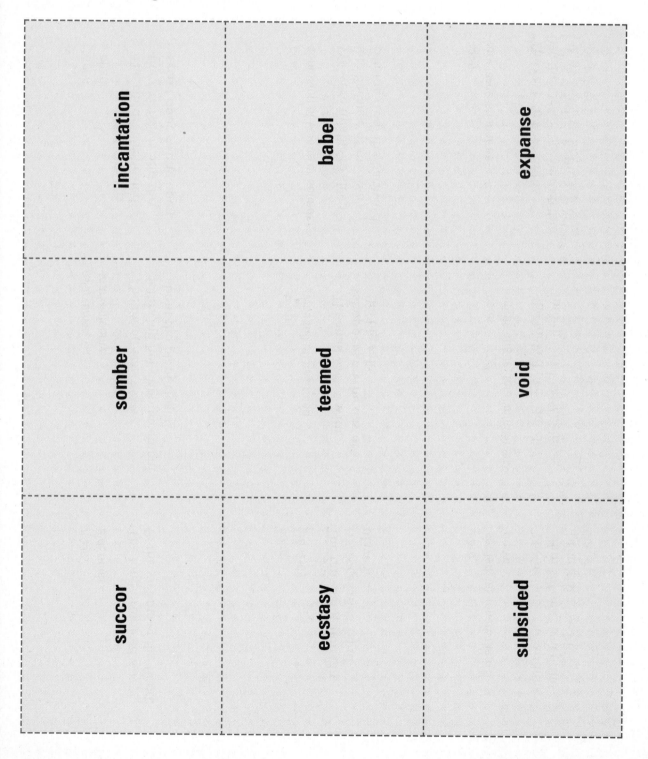

incantation	babel	expanse
somber	teemed	void
succor	ecstasy	subsided

noun chant The children repeated the *incantation* and the secret door swung open.	*adjective* dark; gloomy The mood was *somber* following her announcement about the plant closing.	*noun* aid, relief The king promised *succor* to the victims of the flood.
noun confusion of voices or sounds We were unable to sleep late because of the *babel* coming from the barnyard.	*verb* was full of; swarmed The mall *teemed* with shoppers on the day of the big sale.	*noun* great joy The fans sang along in *ecstasy* as their band played.
noun very large open area The vast *expanse* of the Pacific Ocean became visible as we climbed to the top of the tower.	*noun* empty space; total emptiness She looked over the cliff into the dark *void* below.	*verb* settled; lessened; died down The noise in the auditorium *subsided* when the principal raised his hand.

VOCABULARY FLASH CARDS

Use these flash cards to study words you want to remember. Cut along the dotted lines on pages V31 through V32 to create your own flash cards or use index cards. Write the word on the front of the card. On the back, write the word's part of speech and definition. Then, write a sentence that shows the meaning of the word.

VOCABULARY FLASH CARDS

Cut these flash cards out and use them to remember and study the vocabulary words. Use pages V2 to V31 to create your flash cards. On a different card, write the word on the card. On the back, write the word's part of speech and its definition. Then, write a sentence in a different color. Refer to the card.

VOCABULARY FOLD-A-LIST

Use a fold-a-list to study the definitions of words. The words on this page come from Unit 1. Write the definition for each word on the lines. Fold the paper along the dotted line to check your definition. Create your own fold-a-lists on pages V35 through V36.

glean _____

_____

reapers _____

_____

redeem _____

_____

avenger _____

_____

precepts _____

_____

lucid _____

_____

steadfast _____

_____

incurred _____

_____

affliction _____

_____

recompense _____

_____

Fold In ◄

VOCABULARY FOLD-A-LIST

Write the word that matches the definition on each line.
Fold the paper along the dotted line to check your work.

collect grain left by reapers _____

those who gather a
crop by cutting _____

buy back; fulfill a promise _____

one who takes revenge _____

rules of conduct _____

clear: apparent _____

firm; not changing _____

brought about through
one's own actions _____

something that causes
pain or distress _____

payment of what is
owed: reward _____

Fold In ←

VOCABULARY FOLD-A-LIST

Write the words you want to study on this side of the page. Write the definitions on the back. Then, test yourself. Fold the paper along the dotted line to check your answers.

Word: _____

_____

Word: _____

_____

Word: _____

_____

Word: _____

_____

Word: _____

_____

Word: _____

_____

Word: _____

_____

Word: _____

_____

Word: _____

_____

Word: _____

_____

Fold In ◄

VOCABULARY FOLD-A-LIST

Write the word that matches the definition on each line.
Fold the paper along the dotted line to check your work.

Definition: ______________________________

____

Definition: ______________________________

____

Definition: ______________________________

____

Definition: ______________________________

____

Definition: ______________________________

____

Definition: ______________________________

____

Definition: ______________________________

____

Definition: ______________________________

____

Definition: ______________________________

____

Definition: ______________________________

Fold In ←

COMMONLY MISSPELLED WORDS

The list on these pages presents words that cause problems for many people. Some of these words are spelled according to set rules, but others follow no specific rules. As you review this list, check to see how many of the words give you trouble in your own writing. Then, add your own commonly misspelled words on the lines that follow.

abbreviate	auxiliary	census	deficient
absence	awkward	certain	definitely
absolutely	bandage	changeable	delinquent
abundance	banquet	characteristic	dependent
accelerate	bargain	chauffeur	descendant
accidentally	barrel	chief	description
accumulate	battery	clothes	desert
accurate	beautiful	coincidence	desirable
ache	beggar	colonel	dessert
achievement	beginning	column	deteriorate
acquaintance	behavior	commercial	dining
adequate	believe	commission	disappointed
admittance	benefit	commitment	disastrous
advertisement	bicycle	committee	discipline
aerial	biscuit	competitor	dissatisfied
affect	bookkeeper	concede	distinguish
aggravate	bought	condemn	effect
aggressive	boulevard	congratulate	eighth
agreeable	brief	connoisseur	eligible
aisle	brilliant	conscience	embarrass
all right	bruise	conscientious	enthusiastic
allowance	bulletin	conscious	entrepreneur
aluminum	buoyant	contemporary	envelope
amateur	bureau	continuous	environment
analysis	bury	controversy	equipped
analyze	buses	convenience	equivalent
ancient	business	coolly	especially
anecdote	cafeteria	cooperate	exaggerate
anniversary	calendar	cordially	exceed
anonymous	campaign	correspondence	excellent
answer	canceled	counterfeit	exercise
anticipate	candidate	courageous	exhibition
anxiety	capacity	courteous	existence
apologize	capital	courtesy	experience
appall	capitol	criticism	explanation
appearance	captain	criticize	extension
appreciate	career	curiosity	extraordinary
appropriate	carriage	curious	familiar
architecture	cashier	cylinder	fascinating
argument	catastrophe	deceive	February
associate	category	decision	fiery
athletic	ceiling	deductible	financial
attendance	cemetery	defendant	fluorescent

foreign	minuscule	proceed	_____
fourth	miscellaneous	prominent	
fragile	mischievous	pronunciation	
gauge	misspell	psychology	
generally	mortgage	publicly	
genius	naturally	pursue	_____
genuine	necessary	questionnaire	
government	neighbor	realize	
grammar	neutral	really	
grievance	nickel	recede	
guarantee	niece	receipt	_____
guard	ninety	receive	
guidance	noticeable	recognize	
handkerchief	nuisance	recommend	
harass	obstacle	reference	_____
height	occasion	referred	
humorous	occasionally	rehearse	
hygiene	occur	relevant	
ignorant	occurred	reminiscence	
immediately	occurrence	renowned	_____
immigrant	omitted	repetition	
independence	opinion	restaurant	
independent	opportunity	rhythm	
indispensable	optimistic	ridiculous	
individual	outrageous	sandwich	_____
inflammable	pamphlet	satellite	
intelligence	parallel	schedule	
interfere	paralyze	scissors	
irrelevant	parentheses	secretary	_____
irritable	particularly	siege	
jewelry	patience	solely	
judgment	permanent	sponsor	
knowledge	permissible	subtle	
lawyer	perseverance	subtlety	_____
legible	persistent	superintendent	
legislature	personally	supersede	
leisure	perspiration	surveillance	
liable	persuade	susceptible	
library	phenomenal	tariff	_____
license	phenomenon	temperamental	
lieutenant	physician	theater	
lightning	pleasant	threshold	
likable	pneumonia	truly	_____
liquefy	possess	unmanageable	
literature	possession	unwieldy	
loneliness	possibility	usage	
magnificent	prairie	usually	
maintenance	precede	valuable	_____
marriage	preferable	various	
mathematics	prejudice	vegetable	
maximum	preparation	voluntary	
meanness	previous	weight	
mediocre	primitive	weird	_____
mileage	privilege	whale	
millionaire	probably	wield	
minimum	procedure	yield	

(Acknowledgments continued from page ii)

Penguin Books Ltd., London
From *History of the Peloponnesian War: Pericles' Funeral Oration,* by Thucydides from History of the Peloponnesian Wars, translated by Rex Warner (Penguin Classics, 1954). Translation copyright © Rex Warner, 1954. Reproduced by permission. From *The Rig Veda:* "Creation Hymn" and "Night," from *The Rig Veda,* An Anthology translated by Wendy Doniger O'Flaherty (Penguin Classics, 1981). Copyright © Wendy Doniger O'Flaherty, 1981. From *The Decameron: Federigo's Falcon,* (originally titled "Ninth Story") by Giovanni Boccaccio from The Decameron, translated by G.H. McWilliam (Penguin Classics, 1972 Second Edition, 1995). Copyright © G.H. McWilliam, 1972, 1995. "The Death of Enkidu," (originally titled "from The Death of Enkidu"), from *The Epic of Gilgamesh,* translated by N.K. Sandars (Penguin Classics 1960, Third Edition 1972). Copyright © N.K. Sanders, 1960, 1964, 1972.

Random House, Inc.
From *The Aeneid:* from Book II: How They Took the City, by Virgil from The Aenid, translated by Robert Fitzgerald, copyright © 1980, 1982, 1983 by Robert Fitzgerald. Used by permission of Random House, Inc.

Rupert Crew Limited on behalf of Steve and Megumi Biddle
From "The Origins of Origami" by Steve and Megumi Biddle from *Origami: Inspired by Japanese Prints.* Copyright © 1998 by The Metropolitan Museum of Art. Introduction, instructions, diagrams and models © 1998 by Steve and Megumi Biddle. All rights reserved. Reprinted by permission.

Elyse Sommer
"CurtainUp Review: A Doll's House," copyright April 1997, Elyse Sommer, *CurtainUp. CurtainUp.com* is a 7-year-old online theater magazine: www.curtainup.com. Reproduced by permission of Elyse Sommer.

David Spencer
"A Doll's House by Henrik Ibsen, a new version by Frank McGuinness," reviewed by David Spencer from *www.aislesay.com.* Reprinted by permission of the author, David Spencer.

Minh Ta
"Interview with Shane L. Amaya: Writer of the comic Roland Days of Wrath" by *Minh Ta.* Interview originally appeared in ComicFan website. Reproduced by permisison of the writer.

Tufts University, Perseus Project, Classics Department
From The Perseus Digital Library (http://www.perseus.tufts.edu/Olympics/), reproduced from Tufts University, Perseus Project.

The University of Chicago Press
From *The Panchatantra: Numskull and the Rabbit,* from *The Panchatantra,* translated by Arthur W. Ryder. Copyright © 1925 by The University of Chicago. Copyright renewed 1953 by Mary E. Ryder and Winifred Ryder. All rights reserved. Reprinted by permission of The University of Chicago Press.

Viking Penguin, a division of Penguin Group (USA) Inc.
"On the Bottom," from *If This is a Man* (Survival in Auschwitz)," by Primo Levi, translated by Stuart Woolf, copyright © 1959 by Orion Press, Inc., © 1958 by Giulio Einaudi editore, s.p.a. from *Don Quixote,* (originally titled "from The Ingenious Gentleman Don Quixote de la Mancha, Part 1, Chapter 1") from *Don Quixote* by Miguel de Cervantes Saavedra, translated by Samuel Putnam, copyright © 1949 by The Viking Press, Inc.

W. W. Norton & Company, Inc.
From *The Inferno: Cantos I: The Dark Wood of Error,* from *The Divine Comedy* by Dante Alighieri, translated by John Ciardi. Copyright © 1954, 1957, 1959, 1960, 1965, 1967, 1970 by the Ciardi Family Publishing Trust. This selection may not be reproduced, stored in a retrieval system or transmitted in any form or by any means without prior written permission of the publisher.

The Arthur Waley Estate
From *The Analects of Confucius,* translated by Arthur Waley, George Allen & Unwin, Ltd. London. All rights reserved. Reprinted by permission of the Arthur Waley Estate.

Washington Post Writers Group
"A Lot of Baggage for Nora to Carry: After a History of Misinterpretation, Ibsen's Leave-Taking Heroine Finally Gets Her Due," by Lloyd Rose from *The Washington Post,* April 20, 1997. Copyright © 1997, The Washington Post.

Note: Every effort has been made to locate the copyright owner of material reprinted in this book. Omissions brought to our attention will be corrected in subsequent editions.

PHOTO AND ART CREDITS